Presented To:

_____

From:

_____

Date:

_____

Keys To Passing Your
SPIRITUAL
TESTS

Keys To Passing Your

SPIRITUAL

TESTS

Unlocking the Secrets to Your Spiritual Promotion

ABRAHAM JOHN

DESTINY IMAGE® PUBLISHERS, INC.

P.O. Box 310, Shippensburg, PA 17257-0310

"Promoting Inspired Lives."

This book and all other Destiny Image, Revival Press, MercyPlace, Fresh Bread, Destiny Image Fiction, and Treasure House books are available at Christian bookstores and distributors worldwide.

For a U.S. bookstore nearest you, call 1-800-722-6774.

For more information on foreign distributors, call 717-532-3040.

Reach us on the Internet: www.destinyimage.com.

ISBN 13 TP: 978-0-7684-0288-9
ISBN 13 Ebook: 978-0-7684-8801-2

For Worldwide Distribution, Printed in the U.S.A.

1 2 3 4 5 6 7 8 / 16 15 14 13 12

DEDICATION

To the millions of saints who have been through the water and fire but did not understand the purpose of it all. And to those who have been in preparation to have the fullness of God.

ACKNOWLEDGMENTS

This work would not have been completed if not for the valuable input from a few people whom God brought into my life.

My wife, Tahnya, for her dedication to see this work completed and published. She spent hours proofreading and offering valuable thoughts. Our three children: Rachel, Joshua, and Renee—God is using each of you to teach me the love of my heavenly Father in a deeper way, and to know what it means to be His son. You are truly a blessing from God.

Thanks to all partners of Maximum Impact Ministries. You are truly modern-day heroes of faith. Your faithfulness to the Lord and commitment to His works are an inspiration to me.

Nathaniel Bliss, who offered his valuable time and professional skills to edit this book. You are truly a gift from God. You are always on time. May the Lord reward you abundantly.

Lisa Ott from Destiny Image, who was instrumental in getting this work published. You have been an inspiration from the first time we talked. Your servant heart and passion for the Kingdom of God touched my life.

ENDORSEMENTS

Everyone who is born again would tell you they have times of testing. Some are little, some are middle size, and some are big, but everyone is tested. The blessing of testing is the result that can come because of it. I highly endorse *Keys to Passing Your Spiritual Tests: Unlocking the Secrets to Your Spiritual Promotion* because this is where the rubber meets the road. We all are tested but some of us fall through the cracks. There is no need to fall through the cracks, but use them as opportunities to go to a higher level. God bless you as you read and meditate on this book and as you allow the Holy Spirit to speak to your heart.

Dr. Marilyn Hickey
President/Founder of Marilyn Hickey Ministries

Every believer goes through tests and trials; they are a normal part of our spiritual walk with the Lord. Frankly, most Christians I know are not happy when tests and trials are crossing their path. Although the Lord is using tests and trials to mature us, we are not too pleased when we are in the midst of them.

What we need is a biblical understanding about the purpose of tests and trials; we need to know that the Lord is using them to bring *His* good work into our lives.

We also need to see the example of those who walked with the Lord long before us. Their reaction to trials, and their failures as well as their victories, are such an encouraging testimony to us.

In his new book, *Keys to Passing Your Spiritual Tests*, my friend Abraham John is pointing to these great and helpful areas, giving an overview of the purposes of tests and trials, as well as showing us how the great cloud of witnesses handled tests and trials.

Reading this book will surely help you to understand spiritual tests, and give you down-to-earth, biblical advice on how to stand victoriously during times of tests and trials.

Ivano Lai, Leading Pastor
Swiss Pentecostal Assembly
Bern, Switzerland

CONTENTS

Part IV
KEYS TO VICTORY

INTRODUCTION

A GLOBAL TEST

We are headed for a global test. Life on this earth began with a test in the Garden and will end with a test. God is going to test the human race to see whether we will trust in Him as our Creator and God or in our own strength and the material blessings He has given us. As the time of our final testing draws near, I believe there is a strong chance the majority of the human race will fail unless they are prepared.

But we are reminded in Revelation 3:10: *"Because you have kept My command to persevere, I also will keep you from the hour of **trial** which shall come upon the **whole world**, to **test** those who dwell on the earth."*

There is going to be a remnant made up of those who will stay true to Him and love Him with all their heart, no matter the cost. This book is intended for that small group of people from around the globe. God is telling us these things so we can be ready when the unthinkable happens in our lives, our nation(s), and in our churches. God wants to prepare the bride for His Son. As He said, He will have a bride that is without spot or wrinkle (see Eph. 5:27).

This global test will affect us in three major areas: politically, spiritually, and financially. It will affect us politically because the governments of the world have no regard for justice or righteousness. It will affect us spiritually because people no longer acknowledge God as their Creator or trust in Him—the religious system today hangs on the spirit of mammon and not on the power of God. This leads to the third area of testing, which is financial, because mankind places its trust in wealth and money. God will judge the spirit of mammon that controls the monetary system.

PAYING THE PRICE FOR THE NEXT LEVEL

Wherever I go, I see believers who are hungry to go to the next level in their spiritual and financial lives but do not know where to begin or how to get there. Recently, I was watching a baptism service in a church where each believer baptized stated what he or she believed God for, as a prayer request. Most desired a deeper walk with God. As I sat there, I thought, "I hope they really know what they are asking for!"

You may have picked up this book because you are hungry for more of God and want to go to the next level in your walk with Him. You have chosen the right book, but let me tell you frankly that it is going to *cost* you something. You should only read this book if you are really serious about God and want to know Him more. Otherwise, you are wasting your time and should put this book down and go read something else.

When you desire a deeper walk with God, or when you ask Him to change your heart, or to teach you to walk in His ways, or when you tell Him to do in your life whatever pleases Him, watch out! You are praying dangerous prayers. They are dangerous in the sense that He will begin to do a work in your life that will make your flesh uncomfortable!

When you asked God to change your heart, did you know that change is not easy? Some people would rather die than change the way they think or act. When God begins to do His work in our heart and it causes pain, we often find ourselves resisting the answers to our own prayers or asking Him to rescue us from the very situation He is using in order to change us.

Most people are not willing to pay the price to go to the next level. In fact, most do not even know the price and, if they did, few would pay it. It is like a tree saying it wants to grow and become strong enough to withstand all storms, but not wanting to face any rain or wind. Or it says, "I wish I was a fine piece of furniture but don't want to go through any change." Or like a piece of gold that says it wants to be a beautiful piece of jewelry but does not want to go through the fire. That is impossible!

Each new level we want to achieve in our spirit, character, or finances requires us to pass some tests. You may be going through a spiritual test right now. You may be getting ready to enter one, or maybe you are just coming out of one, but how you respond to your tests will determine your next promotion in the Spirit.

If you want to go higher in life, you need to go deeper in God. If you want to go deeper in God, then you need to let God go deeper into your heart. If you want to let God go deeper into your heart, you need to die some more to your flesh. Every *inch* of God will cost you an inch of your heart and flesh.

Our heart is only the size of a fist, and that is what God, who is immense, unlimited, and almighty, has been fighting for centuries to possess. He wants to have our whole heart. I have seen people who come to church, get saved, and sit on a pew for 40 or 50 years and only give a *tip* to God as the offering plate goes by or dedicate only part of their lives to Kingdom work every now and then, but nothing changes in their life. They are not effective for God or His Kingdom.

THE GOSPEL MESSAGE

Change causes pain and discomfort in many ways. The *churchianity* that we have today is not effective because we have not allowed

God to change our heart. Early believers were called "Christians" because of their passion for Christ. A believer without a passion for Christ is a *churchian* and not a Christian. It is a relationship with God that is only skin-deep. Percentagewise, more Christians live on this planet today than in any other century, but there are also more unreached people than in any previous generation.

We have neglected the core of the gospel message: the conviction of sin that leads to repentance, which results in a changed heart. Instead, we give more importance to the outward change and acquisition of material things. A believer whose heart is not changed is no better than a heathen who worships an idol. Only a changed person can bring change to a family, a community, and a nation.

The reason we do not change is because many have taken the *cross* out of their *gospel* message. A cross-less gospel is a powerless gospel because the preaching of the cross is the power of God unto salvation (see 1 Cor. 1:18,23). How many messages about the cross have you heard in the past year compared to messages about financial blessings and personal success? Paul said, *"We preach Christ crucified"* (1 Cor. 1:23).

Another reason we do not change is because we have neglected God's ways and invented our own ways to opt out of being the agents of change He appointed on this earth. As soon as a person is offended at one church, he will hop to the next one on the other side of the street. He will remain there only as long as he is being celebrated and entertained, and then on to the next one. When something goes wrong in a marriage, instead of yielding to change, many couples separate and choose someone else. The same thing happens in the workplace. We waste the majority of our lives trying to avoid situations that cause change and, as a result, we do not grow.

The third reason we do not change is because people these days do not come to Christ because they are convicted about their sins;

they often convert either to escape the troubles they are in or for the material benefits they believe they will receive. There are two signs the true gospel is being preached: there is the conviction of sin and it is followed by repentance. Jesus tells us to carry our cross *daily*, not just when it is convenient for us (see Luke 9:23). The reason God allows us to go through trials and tests is to change our hearts. Sometimes our hearts will not change unless we go through pain. Just as necessity is the mother of invention, pain is the mother of change.

PURPOSE OF TESTING

There is a growing dissatisfaction among believers because their lives don't show evidence of the fruit (the stuff) that preachers promised would appear when they came to Christ. Neither do they see the genuine power of God manifest in their lives. They are tired of not knowing why only a few are enjoying the wealth and glory many preachers are promising them.

Most unbelievers see today's Christianity as despicable and want nothing to do with it. They would rather become a Muslim or a Hindu instead of a *Churchian*, which is a person who goes to church regularly or occasionally but the true message of the gospel has no affect on how he or she lives. Something has to happen soon. Otherwise, the price we pay will be similar to the one the early century believers paid when they were forcibly converted to other religions.

That is the reason God takes us through spiritual tests. Life on this earth is a series of tests and trials. God has orchestrated our life on this earth in such a way that His training and tests become part of our daily routine. People get promoted naturally and spiritually because they pass a test. God's principles and methods of operation remain the same throughout the ages. Our God is a God of excellence and quality. Before He puts out a product that represents Him, He will make sure it is of the quality and excellence that truly represents His character, and not a counterfeit.

I grew up in India. In Indian markets you can find duplicates of almost anything you can imagine. These duplicates look exactly like the original products. They will have the same name and logo, they smell the same, they are the same size, etc. The only way to find the difference is to *test* these duplicates against the original; duplicates will not withstand the test. Though they may look and smell the same, they are made of inferior substance.

Before any quality manufacturing company puts a product on the market, they will send it to be tested. Before you buy a car, you might take a *test drive* to find out exactly what you are buying. Companies test their candidates to see if they are really qualified for the position before hiring them.

Anyone God chooses to use is led through a series of tests before He places His anointing and blessing on their life. As any loving parent wants to know whether his children are able to handle a responsibility before he entrusts them with it, God, as our loving Father, will let us go through some circumstances to subdue our flesh and train us to live in the spirit by faith.

PETER'S DIVINE TESTING: SEVEN TESTS

When Jesus called Peter, the calling came with some tests. We see in the Gospels that there were seven different tests Peter endured. The first one came when he was washing his net after a long, fruitless night spent trying to catch fish. After not catching anything, along comes a Stranger who asks him to move his boat a little further into the sea so He could teach the people (see Luke 5:2-3).

It was a test. How many of us know it is not easy to help and be kind to others when we are tired, hungry, and disappointed? Have you been there before? Peter obeyed Jesus's request and passed that test. What Peter did not know was that he had just passed the primary interview to be hired by the Creator of the universe to be one of the founders of the largest enterprise He ever had on this earth.

Peter could have come up with all kinds of excuses. He had toiled all night and had no fish to show for it. He likely was hungry and irritated. He was washing his net to go home and eat some food, if there was any, and go to bed. His wife and children might be going hungry for the day. But he had the right *heart* and that was the only thing the Master was looking for.

You might ask what it means to have a right heart. The right heart is one that is willing to help others in the middle of its own pain and inconvenience. The right heart is willing to try something new when all hope is lost. The right heart is one that is willing to learn from others and ready to admit weaknesses and failures. The right heart is one that focuses on people more than it focuses on temporal material achievements. It is willing to share the blessing with others. It is one that is willing to walk away from instant gratification for an eternal destiny. The right heart is teachable and willing to receive instruction from others; it is humble and willing to admit when it is wrong.

Peter might have been an uneducated fisherman from Galilee, but he possessed a heart of gold along with each one of those qualifications that I mentioned above. According to the world's standards, he was not a likely candidate for leading a worldwide organization that would span more than two millennia. The One who made the hearts knows what is in a heart! He chose Peter to be one of His close associates to build His Kingdom on this earth.

The next test came to Peter when Jesus finished preaching and asked him to let his net down for a catch. He was asking these experienced fishermen to do something inconvenient in order to gain something that was unlikely. Peter once again obeyed the request of this Stranger, though he expressed his hesitancy. It is OK to express your hesitancy to God and others. That shows you are not a weakling and will not put up with just anything.

That is what Peter did when he said, *"Master, we have toiled all night and caught nothing; nevertheless at Your word I will let down the net"* (Luke 5:5). Peter did not know that the Person who was asking him to put down the net was the One who created land and sea. Peter obeyed and passed the second test.

The third test came not when he was throwing the net into the water, but with what he felt in his heart when he caught all those fish. He felt something strange which most men are hesitant to feel. He allowed his heart to go places he thought he would never go. With each test, God was going a little deeper into Peter's heart and bringing out things he did not even realize existed.

Peter hauled in the largest catch of his life, but something happened in his heart. His heart began to change, beginning with that event. With this change of heart came a change of focus; he was no longer dwelling on the big catch and how much money it would make, but his focus turned to the One who helped him with the catch. Who, he must have wondered, might this Person be?

Peter had to call his partners to help him with the fish. They all filled their boats and were astonished by the catch he just made. While they were all applauding Peter for his accomplishment, I doubt he shared their excitement.

Peter's heart began to ache with something new. I think he felt convicted and ashamed of who he was and what he had done in his life. Here was a person everyone else considered a tough guy and a successful businessman, who suddenly felt broken, unworthy, and naked. He did not know he was standing in the presence of the Messiah.

His entire life may have flashed before his eyes in a split second. He felt insecure and needed help from Someone bigger. He was totally honest about it and did not try to hide his feelings behind his masculinity. The only thing that came out of his mouth was, *"Depart from me, for I am a sinful man, O Lord!"* (Luke 5:8b). Peter discovered one of the keys of the Kingdom of God that day—conviction of sin that precedes repentance.

The fourth test came when he had to make a quick choice between the fish and the One who made the fish; between his career and the cross; between his business partners and being a partner with God; between things that are temporary and things that are eternal. He passed that test too. Peter forsook everything and followed Jesus from that day onward. His partners also made the same decision. Your decision to follow or not to follow Christ will always have an influence on others around you. This is one of the purposes of spiritual tests—that you follow and trust Him no matter the cost. You can see in the above tests that the intensity increased with each one. As the price of obedience increased with each test, so did the blessing.

"So when they had brought their boats to land, they forsook all and followed Him" (Luke 5:11). Peter began the journey of his life by deciding that he would lay his ambitions down for the One who helped him with the catch. He discovered his spiritual destiny that day. What a transformation! Do you want to go deeper with God? Do you want Him to work in your heart? It will cost you something. Maybe even everything.

Most believers envision going with God (or allowing God to work in their heart) as far as it takes for them to get a big catch, a big house, a big business, or whatever material blessing they can possess. The majority of their prayers and efforts are geared toward it. Then they park their life around that blessing. Today's prosperity teaching only goes this far, but that is only the beginning of a new journey with Christ on this earth, not the end. Sometimes God will bless you materially to see the intention of your heart after you have it. Most do not realize that the wealth they have is a test from God (see 1 Tim. 6:17-19).

That is the reason we have many materially wealthy people in the Kingdom today, but very few that are walking in the power of

God. We should be willing to walk away from anything on this earth at any time if God asks us to do so. The goal of Christian life now in this age is not to be materially wealthy, but to know Him and to make Him known (see Phil. 3:8-11).

Jesus said that if we want to be His disciples, we must forsake all and follow Him. It is not a command to a few but to all that choose to be His disciples. There is a reason why there are only a few today, though Jesus told us to go and make disciples (not just converts) of all the nations.

Jesus said, *"So likewise, **whoever** of you does not **forsake all that he has** cannot be My disciple"* (Luke 14:33). From then on, it was a three-and-a-half year series of tests and trials. The disciples were enrolled in the world's most intense school. They had to finish their course in 42 months, while some in the Old Testament took 15-25, or even 80 years to finish a minor degree.

It was so intense that many days they did not even get time to sleep, let alone eat food. When they started, they had no idea what they were signing up for. With the school came tests. Though they passed the enrollment tests, they failed some midterms—which they had to take again—and, at the end, they passed the final.

What changed an ordinary fisherman into one of the greatest apostles was the training, including the tests he endured during those three and a half years. When we read the Gospels, we see that many failed their enrollment test. One rich young ruler came and asked Jesus what he should do to inherit eternal life. When Jesus told him to keep the commandments, he replied that he had been keeping them since his youth (see Matt. 19:16-22).

Jesus said he still lacked one thing, challenging him to sell everything he had and give it to the poor. The young man went away sorrowful because he was a rich man. He did not allow Jesus to go deeper into his heart like Peter did. His trust was in material wealth rather than the Person who helped him obtain that wealth. He failed the test. If he had given up his material wealth to follow

Jesus, it would have only been a matter of time before he received back a hundredfold what he had given up.

Another time, a man told Jesus he wanted to follow Him but asked first to go and bury his father (see Luke 9:59-60). He failed the test. Jesus cannot be secondary. He does not want to be treated as a side business. He wants to be your only Lord and King. Do you want to be the greatest apostle of your time? Do you want to be a successful Christian businessman? Do you want to be the best mother or father to your children?

The higher you want to go in life, the deeper you need to let God go into your heart. You may have no idea what is in your heart, but His test of fire will reveal all of those hidden agendas and attitudes that you are not even aware of right now. It is not worth coming out of God's fire a second earlier than you should. I am not saying it is easy to stay in fire. Whenever I have cried out to the Lord to rescue me from the fire, I later regretted it and wished I had stayed in it as long as He wanted!

The more you want to know Him, the more it will require you to change. The more you want to do His will, the more you need to die to your own will. If you want to have more of heaven on this earth, then you need to have less attachment to the things of this world.

The fifth test came for Peter when Jesus taught His followers about eating His body and drinking His blood and *most* left Him (see John 6:66). Jesus turned and asked the disciples if they wanted to also leave. Peter's reply expressed the exact words God wanted to hear from the Israelites when they were tested—and from each of us who decides to follow Him when we are tested. He said, *"Lord, to whom shall we go? You have the words of eternal life"* (John 6:68). In other words, Peter was saying that man shall not live by bread alone, but by every word that proceeds from the mouth of God (see Deut. 8:3; Luke 4:4). Peter passed that test with excellence.

In another instance Jesus asked, *"But who do you say that I am?"* (Matt. 16:15). The spirit of revelation came upon Peter and he spoke the words that surprised the other disciples. In response, Jesus spoke to him and said that it was the Father who revealed that to him and He would build His Church upon that revelation. Peter was exalted to a new spiritual height.

However, that did not last for long. Jesus began to reveal to His disciples His upcoming journey to Jerusalem and the cruel death he was going to face. Peter took Him aside and rebuked Him for saying such things. The sixth test came for Peter when Jesus rebuked him in front of the others and called him "Satan" (see Matt. 16:13-23).

Can you imagine the humiliation he must have felt? This is the guy who claimed to be the most spiritual among the disciples and the most loyal friend of Jesus. I can imagine the other disciples' faces when Jesus called Peter "Satan." That may have been what they were hoping or expecting to happen to him because they were a little jealous. They might have turned their faces to conceal their laughter, or they might simply have been in shock. Peter, however, humbled himself and did not react negatively. He understood the power of Jesus's words and yielded to his spirit. What was the result? He passed the test.

The seventh test came to Peter when Jesus was about to be captured by the soldiers, and Peter bluffed again saying he would not leave Him and was ready to die for Him. In a matter of a few hours, everything changed. Jesus was captured and Peter lost all of his courage. He denied his Master three times (see Matt. 26:69-74).

Peter failed that test, but he did not quit. He wept bitterly, repented, and came back to Jesus. After His resurrection, Jesus restored Peter and loved him until the end. He never stopped loving him. He asked Peter three times whether he loved Him for the three times he denied Him. With each test we pass, we will receive a new revelation from God that will take us to the next spiritual season of life.

A BOOK OF BLESSING

I believe this book will be a blessing to you wherever you are in your Christian walk. As I look around in churches and in the Christian world, I see many people wounded and hurt. They did not have a mentor to guide them or they did not have the heart to ask for help when they made decisions at major turning points in life.

They try to hide their pain behind the clothes they wear and cover the disappointment on their face with expensive cosmetics. All that is required for them to be healed and set free is to be totally honest with themselves and at least one other person on this earth, like Peter did when he felt convicted.

They've lost their sensitivity to the Holy Spirit and His Word and are living as Sunday Christians. They were once on fire for God and had a genuine heart toward Him. They started out desiring to live wholeheartedly for God, but somewhere on their wilderness journey they went through some testing and did not know what to do or how to respond. They were not trained or correctly informed about how to overcome those tests.

As a result, their hearts began to grow cold and harder toward the things of God. They began to lose interest in spiritual things and their sensitivity to His Spirit. This did not happen intentionally or in a day or two, but was a long, slow process. They still come to church on Sunday but there is no life in their eyes. They simply *act* spiritual and cover their pain with Christian or church mannerisms.

There is no longer a fire in their heart for God or for people. They still hope that someday their life will get better, that someday their situation is going to improve, and that someday they will wake up in a land that flows with milk and honey. That is the outcome of being a *Sunday Christian;* it will make you a *Someday Christian.*

Dear friend, if that is you or anyone you know, this is the day. How do I know that? The reason you have this book in your hand is because God has answered your prayers, the cry of your heart. He wants to prepare you to inherit His every promise, but He cannot change His ways. He cannot change His Word. He cannot make a shortcut just for you. He has to be faithful and just to everyone who lived before us and who will live after us.

This book will train you to finish your wilderness journey and enter your promise land, which is your destiny. Stop waiting year after year for people and circumstances to change. *The only thing that has any possibility for change or should change is you!*

God has not forsaken you. He loves you and cares for you. This book will prepare you for what lies ahead. This book is the missing link between you and your promise land. Whatever seasons and opportunities you missed in the past, this book will help you regain them and get back on track again.

The revelation contained in this book is not exhaustive to this subject. Our God has no limit. My prayer is that when you read this book the Holy Spirit will open up realms of fresh revelation in your spirit. I know in my spirit that it will happen. When it happens, please write it down in a journal because that is God speaking to you about your life. Contained in this book are spiritual seeds which have unlimited potential to reproduce their own kind.

May the Lord help us to be found faithful when He returns. I pray this book will be a blessing to you on your Christian journey. *"Now to the King eternal, immortal, invisible, to God who alone is wise, be honor and glory forever and ever. Amen"* (1 Tim. 1:17).

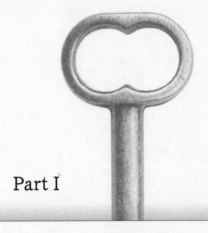

Part I

SPIRITUAL TESTS

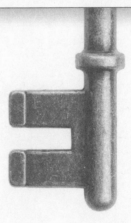

Chapter 1

WHAT ARE SPIRITUAL TESTS?

GOING THROUGH A TEST

Have you been wondering *why* you are going through *what* you are going through? Have you been bombarded with situations that are threatening to sink you? Perhaps you just feel out of place in the crowd; you have no more strength to continue; you feel spiritually and physically weak. Do you need a breakthrough? Have you been praying and fasting and doing the best you can, but still life seems so dry?

Maybe you cannot hear God as clearly as you used to or want to and have lost the joy of your salvation. You feel a heaviness, or a weight in your chest that does not seem to go away. You want to be used by God but do not know where to start or what to do. You want to go to the next level in your walk with God but do not know what will get you there. And you might be feeling frustrated and angry with yourself and others, but are afraid to express it.

You might feel like the psalmist who said, *"I wish I had wings like a dove. Then I would fly away and rest. I would wander far away and stay in the desert"* (Ps. 55:6-7 NCV).

Your supply and resources are at the bare minimum and you are surviving with just enough to move from one challenge to the next, one paycheck to the next. When you overcome one obstacle another pops up in front of you. You do not have a vision for your future and are not sure now whether God has even called you.

You feel like your vision is dead and all that you have gone through so far in life was in vain, and that nothing good is ever going to happen to you. You feel lonely in your walk with the Lord. You want to love God and do everything that pleases Him. Your heart's desire is to walk in God's ways and love Him with all your heart, but a voice is whispering in your ear that you will not make it, and when you think of all the battles you lost, you just want to give up and run away.

You want to be faithful in everything and want to be a person that God can use, but it seems that you are missing something and feel unqualified every time an opportunity to be used presents itself. You are therefore not able to be 100 percent faithful. You want to be anointed, and you know that you are anointed, but the anointing is not manifesting in your life. There are times it seems the anointing manifests when you are in the shower but not when you minister or pray for someone. You have waited for what seems like an eternity for your spiritual or financial promotion but it has not yet manifested.

If you are feeling any of the emotions I mentioned above, it is because you are either going through, or have repeatedly failed, a spiritual test in your life. When you fail a spiritual test, you will not have the confidence or the anointing to face the new season in your life with boldness and maturity.

When you fail in one spiritual test in your life, life will go forward (we cannot go backward in time), but you are not prepared to face or fulfill the assignment God has for you. In God's school you do not sit in the same class again but continue with life and will face two or more tests simultaneously in the next season.

GOD IS THE ONE WHO TESTS

Once you are born again, everything that happens in your life is either ordained by God or permitted by Him. He is well aware of all your circumstances, even those situations you are in because of your own mistakes. This book is not about mistakes, but about tests that you and I daily go through in our walk with the Lord.

I want you to know one thing for sure before you read any further: it is the Lord who tests you and not the devil. He may use the devil as He tests you, but when you are tested, Satan usually comes to tempt you to do evil and disobey God. The devil knows you are emotionally and spiritually vulnerable and most likely to fall for his temptation when you are in the middle of being tested (remember the example of Jesus while He was fasting in the wilderness).

> *The **Lord tests** the righteous, but the wicked and the one who loves violence His soul hates* (Psalm 11:5).

> *But, O Lord of hosts, You who **test** the righteous, and see the mind and heart...* (Jeremiah 20:12).

> *I will bring the one-third through the fire, will refine them as silver is refined, and **test** them as gold is tested. They will call on My name, and I will answer them. I will say, "This is My people"; and each one will say, "The Lord is my God"* (Zechariah 13:9).

TESTING IS PREPARATION

I wish I had this book when I began my spiritual journey. I had to go through these tests in my own life and God allowed me to write this so that it can bless you and prepare you to face every circumstance with boldness and courage. This book will help you to walk in spiritual and natural victory from this day forward. It does not matter how many tests you have passed or failed. The reason you are alive today is because God loves you and He has a plan for your life. He has not given up on you, for God is longsuffering and His mercies are new every morning.

Like the prophet Elijah, I have been in that pit of despair where the only way out seemed to be asking God to take my life.

I wanted everything God had for me, but I reached a place in my life where I felt I could not endure one more test. God, in His mercy, kept me alive so that I could be a blessing to your life. As long as you will not give up on Him and your dreams, He will use your life to be a blessing to others. That is the purpose of the Christian life.

Human life is at the peak of its prosperity. During His earthly ministry, Jesus repeatedly reminded us through His parables that He is entrusting this planet to us and one day He will come back to receive His harvest. He is returning to receive the fruit of His vineyard and we will have to give an answer for our stewardship. What we have been through in the last ten years has been preparation for the test that is coming.

THE COMING TESTS

During a 2010 New Year's Eve church service, God began to speak to me about what is coming to our lives and our churches in this decade. God has shown me that there are three groups of people in the body of Christ.

The Battle for Your Soul

The first group is coming out of the battle for their soul; coming out of Egypt and from being under the bondage of slavery. Egypt represents sin or the world and Pharaoh represents Satan. This group is entering the wilderness to be tested before they inherit their promise land.

In Egypt, you do not own anything. Everything you have is owned by the devil. You are not able to exercise true liberty or pursue your dreams. In Egypt, you struggle and labor but do not earn anything because you are under a taskmaster. He decides what you can have, how much you can have, and when you can have it. Pharaoh represents Satan and the taskmaster represents the particular principality that rules in the area you live.

Though Pharaoh is long dead and gone, there is a spirit that represents that same name, which keeps the people of God in bondage and hinders them from receiving the blessings God has for them. *Pharaoh* was not the name of one person but was a generic name for the ruler of Egypt. The spirit that works behind that name is called the spirit of bondage or slavery.

The Bible says we have not received the *"spirit of bondage again to fear"* (Rom. 8:15). The main object of the spirit of bondage is to make us slaves to the elementary things of this world. He will use habits, familiar sins, emotional dispositions, traditions, and strongholds to keep us in bondage. He holds back our spiritual freedom so we will not prosper or fulfill our purpose. This spirit will give us just enough to survive through life and will keep us miserable. Egypt is a place of just enough.

While Egypt is a place of just enough, the wilderness is a place of abundance. That might be a surprise to many because everyone thinks the wilderness is a place of lack. You need to know that when you come out of Egypt you come with all its wealth. When you are saved, you are not just redeemed from sin, but everything you lost because of sin is redeemed. All the resources and wealth you could ever dream of is available to you, but you lack the proper revelation to utilize that wealth.

The wilderness is a place where you have the wealth of Egypt with you but are not able to utilize it to your benefit. It is a place where you know everything you need is available to you but you cannot enjoy it. You know in your spirit that you should not be poor but you are not able to receive the blessings. You have resources but you are not staying in one place long enough to invest in anything. The wilderness is a place of testing and transition.

The purpose of the wilderness test is to teach us that we shall not live by bread (material things) alone, but by every word that comes out of the mouth of God. The purpose of the wilderness is to teach us that we should trust God no matter the circumstances.

Our trust should not be in the wealth or opportunities we may have. We must love God and others regardless of how we feel. We are commanded to walk by faith and not by sight; we are commanded to love by faith and not by feeling.

The Battle for Your Inheritance

The second group in the body of Christ is comprised of those who have spent a significant amount of time in the wilderness. They have been tested in various ways, especially in the last ten years, and God is moving them into a new season in their lives. They are entering a new battle: the battle to possess their Promise Land. This is a different kind of battle than you faced in Egypt. In Egypt it was the battle for your soul, but this is a battle for your inheritance.

The battle you now enter is not fought with flesh and spirit, but one fought by faith and obedience. For those of you who are currently in this battle, whatever the Lord says to do, do it immediately. When you obey the voice of the Holy Spirit by faith, He will dispossess the forces of darkness and you will possess your inheritance. Sometimes it will require radical obedience that seems contrary to reason. This group will have faith in their heart even when there are challenges in the natural.

The Battle to Pass Your Tests

The third group consists of those who have been in the wilderness but did not pass their tests. They will go through some intense testing beginning this year. It has already begun! A few have lost their spiritual sensitivity because of their repeated failures in the tests God has given them.

I believe God is saying that you will see sudden changes and shifts in the spiritual, political, and business world. Many will be removed from their positions. Secret sins will be brought to light. Many who are in the mainstream of these spheres will be removed and the world, and the Church, will feel a leadership vacuum.

36

From what the world would consider chaos, God will raise up an army who will truly represent His Kingdom. The Church will have an increased revelation and experience of the Kingdom of God. You and I are part of that end-time army. This book is dedicated to those whom God has been preparing, but do not understand the purpose of all that is going on in their lives.

That is why Daniel 11:35 says, *"And some of those of understanding shall fall, to refine them, purify them, and make them white, until the time of the end; because it is still for the appointed time."*

DEFINING SPIRITUAL TESTS

Spiritual tests are part of the process God allows us to go through in order to conform us into the image and likeness of His Son, Jesus Christ (see Heb. 12:10-11).

Spiritual tests are tests of our character that God lets us go through in life, where we face unusual circumstances in order to promote us, both spiritually and materially (see Deut. 8:16).

Spiritual testing is the process God uses to transform us from the carnal nature to the nature of our inner man through the things we experience in life (see Job 23:10).

Spiritual tests are the trials and challenges we face in life in order to learn spiritual warfare (see Judg. 3:1; 1 Cor. 16:9).

Spiritual tests are a series of incidents God allows in our lives to teach us His principles and statutes (see Ps. 119:71).

Spiritual tests come in the form of mishaps, delays, and sometimes disappointments that occur in the natural in order to crucify our flesh and train us to walk in the spirit (see Jon. 2:1-2).

Spiritual tests are opportunities in the spirit for us to draw closer to God and to understand how He operates (see Ps. 34:18).

Spiritual tests are events that are orchestrated by God to teach us His ways (see Ps. 25:12-13).

Spiritual tests are milestones in our Christian walk where we learn, gaining wisdom and understanding about life on this earth (see Job 7:17-18).

Spiritual tests can appear as hindrances and obstacles God places in our way, to direct our path according to His will (see Num. 22:23-25).

Spiritual tests are chastisements God the Father gives to His children in whom He loves and delights (see Ps. 94:12-13; Heb. 12:5-6).

Spiritual tests are part of the process in which God develops our spiritual maturity (see Col. 1:28).

Spiritual tests are difficulties and delays that we face in order to increase our emotional and spiritual capacity (see Ps. 119:32).

Spiritual tests are spiritual exercises God uses to develop our spiritual faith muscles (see John 6:5-6).

Spiritual tests are adverse circumstances God allows to train us to trust in Him and His Word at all times (see Ps. 105:17-19).

Spiritual tests are sufferings God allows to teach us obedience (see Heb. 5:7-8).

Spiritual tests are disciplines God uses to train us as a father disciplines his son (see Heb. 12:6-7).

Spiritual tests are various trials we go through when God tests our faith to produce patience and endurance (see James 1:2-3; Rev. 2:10).

Spiritual tests are incidents that God allows us to go through in order to see all that is in our heart (2 Chron. 32:31; 1 Chron. 29:17a).

Spiritual tests are ways God tests the heart and mind to reward us according to our works (see Jer. 17:10).

Spiritual tests are a part of God's pruning process to position us to bear more fruit (see John 15:2).

Spiritual tests are incidents that God allows to remind us what we are really made of. It is when we are tested that the real stuff that is in us comes out. Things we thought we dealt with will suddenly manifest once again. After we go through a mountaintop experience with God, we may immediately go through experiences where we wonder if we are really saved or not. That is a test.

Spiritual tests are God's way of training us to see whether or not we will believe and obey His word regardless of our circumstances (see Deut. 8:3).

Spiritual tests are the wilderness experiences we go through, between our salvation and the time we enter into our destiny, that teach us to walk by faith and not by sight (see Deut. 1:30-33).

Spiritual tests are places God takes us to develop intimacy with Him (see Gal. 1:17).

TIMES AND SEASONS OF TESTING

Life on this earth is progressive. Progress comes by the things we learn and the tests we pass as we experience life. Our time on earth is a lifelong learning experience and is a preparation for eternity. Progress and promotion come in times and in seasons. God has ordained these in the spirit and in the natural. Everything on this earth is governed by, and subject to, times and seasons. Whatever season you are going through right now is only temporary.

In each season, God prepares us and lets us go through some tests that, if passed, will allow us to move to the next level. Before God entrusts us with anything, He tests us to see whether or not we are faithful. Many times when we *think* we are ready for a spiritual promotion, unfortunately God does not think the same way. Instead, He might be thinking to send us a test. He prepares us before the tests come, but He never tells us when they are going to come. He doesn't grade on a curve or give partiality. He uses the same standard for every person and every culture.

Before God entrusts us with our own money, He will test us with someone else's money. Before God trusts us with true riches (spiritual power and revelation), He will test us with natural riches. He tests us in our natural life before He entrusts us with spiritual treasures.

I believe life's tests begin when we are teenagers. The teenage years are when we lay the foundation for the rest of our life. This is also a time of great temptation when we are tempted to lose focus and waste time doing stupid things. Later in life, many regret what they did when they were teenagers.

If a person does not decide what he wants to do with his life and does not focus on it between the ages of 18 and 25, there is a possibility he will not achieve much with his life. When you get married, you will be tested again in your commitment to your partner. Many fail in that test and wreck their marriage and life.

The Bible says we are God's workmanship created in Christ Jesus for good works, which God foreordained before the foundation of the earth (see Eph. 2:10). Though God foreordained our purpose and the works we are supposed to be doing before we were born, He does not reveal them to us before He tests us.

THE WAY GOD TESTS

In the natural, our mind, maturity, and stability develop in stages. It is the same way in the spirit. Maturity comes in stages through learning from experiences. Whom God calls, He separates; and whom He separates, He tests; and whom He tests, He promotes. These stages cannot be skipped and we cannot move from one to the next until we satisfy His criteria. Many receive the call and jump into ministry before God separates and prepares them. They have the passion but no roots to withstand the trials and storms that come with life and ministry. So they fall and walk away from God's call and become another casualty in the Kingdom.

There is a difference between tests taken in the natural and the way God tests us. In the natural, when companies hire for a position they select the strongest, the smartest, and the most knowledgeable person in that particular field. In the spirit, when God tests, He is not looking for the strongest, smartest, or the most knowledgeable. He is looking for the most empty, most surrendered, and sometimes the weakest so that He can show Himself strong through that person. God seldom calls the qualified, but He qualifies those who are called.

God does not delight in the strength of man or in his might or talent. The reason He tests us is to empty us of all our selfish ambitions and desires so that He can fill those places with His dreams, grace, and glory.

The psalmist said, *"The speed of a horse is nothing to Him. How puny in His sight is the strength of a man. But His joy is in those who reverence Him, those who expect Him to be loving and kind"* (Ps. 147:10-11 TLB).

The apostle Paul said that when he was weak, God's power and grace most strongly manifested in his life. He delighted in his weakness because then the power of God could rest on him (see 2 Cor. 12:9-10). The more God tests you and you come out victorious, the weaker you will feel in the natural or in your flesh.

Your insecurities will terrify you and you will feel like running away. You will have nothing in the flesh to hold on to or trust, but will be able to trust in God alone. Although it is one of the most vulnerable places to be, it is the best place spiritually because when anything good happens, God gets all the glory. You will know it is not your strength that accomplished it but God did it through you and for you. No flesh shall glory in His presence.

PROMOTED TOO EARLY

It is dangerous to be promoted in the Kingdom before your time comes. It is dangerous to have gifts and anointing before you are tested and tried. It is dangerous to get into ministry before God commissions you.

Paul was powerfully and dramatically called on his way to Damascus (see Acts 9). Within three days He was filled with the Holy Spirit and entered into ministry. He began preaching immediately (see Acts 9:20). He did not even wait a day. As soon as he had strength to stand up on his feet, he began preaching. He was as zealous as he used to be before he was saved. He might have thought, "I can't believe all of these people are perishing without Jesus. It is my job to preach and save them from hell. So let's go. Jesus is coming back soon. There's no time to lose. I have to do it. If I don't do it, no one else will." Have you been there? I was there.

Paul began to teach and preach and tried to prove to the Jews that he was called to preach to them and that Jesus was the Messiah. He was zealous and full of himself, and he confounded the Jews with his preaching. But there was no fruit. No churches were established or sinners saved because of his preaching. What was the result? He almost got killed twice and he barely escaped Damascus with his life.

But then Saul increased in strength: *"But Saul increased all the more in strength, and confounded the Jews who dwelt in Damascus, proving that this Jesus is the Christ"* (Acts 9:22). He had not become Paul yet, because he had not yet been through God's school to prepare him for his calling. He was still the old Saul trying to do the ministry of the Lord Jesus Christ in his own strength. But that did not last long. When he came out of that school, his testimony had changed. Then he said, *"I have been crucified with Christ; it is no longer I who live, but Christ lives in me…"* (Gal. 2:20), and, *"Therefore I take pleasure in infirmities….For when I am weak, then I am strong"* (2 Cor. 12:10). What a change!

What happened to Saul to change him so dramatically? God had to empty Saul of everything he thought was his strength. It took more than 14 years to accomplish that process. The old Saul that he knew was dead and now he was no longer living for himself but for Christ who gave His life for him. Neither was he living, but Christ was living in him and through him.

In the beginning, Paul did not know that he had entered a new Kingdom and that the rules of the game had changed. In this Kingdom, battles are not won because you have the strongest army on earth, your promotion does not depend on the best performance your ability can muster, and you and God are stronger than the majority. The old tricks and talents won't work now.

At Paul's conversion, Jesus did not tell him to go out and start preaching. The last order from the Boss was to go to the city and wait. But he did not wait for the next order from God—he was too excited about his experience. He disputed with everyone (see Acts 9:29). That shows he was a little bit arrogant and wanted to show everyone how much he knew. He increased in strength, but not in the strength of God.[1]

Jesus called him but did not commission him to enter into his calling. He told Ananias a little bit about his call, but Jesus said, "*I will show him*" (Acts 9:15). It was not Ananias's job to show Paul his call. It was Jesus's job. He is the One who called him.

If God has called you into the ministry, do not make a move before He tells you. Do not try to do anything He has not specifically commissioned you for. Do not twist His arm for gifts or anointing. He might give it to you if you force Him, but it won't benefit you in the end. If He has called you, He knows exactly for what purpose and when to release you into what He has planned. Our job is to wait and prepare.

Many precious saints get into trouble or step out to do things they have not been called to do. They assume things God did not say exactly, and they misinterpret signs and symbols. They add to what God said. They construct a sentence out of a word He has spoken and create a vision out of a daydream.

For example, I know a couple of brothers who worked with me in India and assumed they were called to specific areas of ministry to which God did not call them. One of these brothers told me his wife had a vision that he was participating in giving communion service. They interpreted it as a call to pastor a church. You do not have to be the senior pastor of a church to serve communion. I believe God will be more specific if He wants someone to be in pastoral ministry because a pastorate is a very serious call.

The second brother told me that, while in prayer, God spoke to him from the book of Ezekiel about being a watchman on the wall. He interpreted it as a "call" to apostolic ministry. I had to bring him into the right understanding that the call to be a watchman on the wall is a call to the ministry of prayer and intercession. He received that from me but the first one did not because he was not *dead* yet.

Paul had a similar experience here. He knew he was called by God to preach the gospel, but he did not wait for God's timing and training. We see that the Jews in Damascus plotted to kill him and he escaped by night in a basket (see Acts 9:23-25). Then later, the Hellenists attempted to kill him and Paul finally went back to Tarsus, his hometown (see Acts 9:29-30). That is what happens to us when we fail a test, we will be back where we started.

DEVELOPING MATURITY AND SUBMISSION

Later on, Paul *"spoke boldly in the name of the Lord Jesus and **disputed** against the Hellenists, but they attempted to kill him. When the brethren found out, they brought him down to Caesarea and sent him out to Tarsus"* (Acts 9:29-30).

This same Paul, when he was later writing epistles to train his protégés, repeatedly told them not to enter into disputes. Where did he get that maturity? It came from personal experience (see Rom. 14:1; 1 Tim. 1:4; 6:4; Titus 3:9).

He might have thought that all he needed was a call from God and everything would work out for him. That was not the case then and it still is not the case today. When you know you have a call from God (and if you are smart), please go and work with a man or woman of God who will allow you to serve them in ministry. There is nothing greater you could do to prepare yourself for what God has called you to do than serving another ministry in any capacity. I wish someone had told me this earlier in my life.

If you are called to any field in life, find a person who is doing what you would like to do and try to get as close as you can to that person and serve that person in any capacity. If that person is not physically accessible, then try to learn as much as you can from books and other materials that are available.

Many wait around for the opening of a senior pastor or associate pastor's position to begin their ministry. I would say get involved in anything—ushering, picking up mail, children's ministry, etc. Before he was commissioned, Paul was delivering messages and donations between the churches at Jerusalem and Antioch (see Acts 11:30).

Paul had to wait a long time before he was sent out to fulfill his call—he had to follow some protocol before he was sent out to fulfill the mission. It was over 14 years after he was called that he was commissioned to do what he was called to do. Those 14 years were years of preparation and testing.

I know from personal experience that it is difficult for people who have a dramatic call like Paul to submit to other ministers. When they receive the call, they feel they are special and that everyone else should submit to them. But the truth is far from any such thought.

Paul may have thought that if the apostles in Jerusalem could hear his great testimony, surely they would accept him and appoint him as their new bishop. If only someone would introduce him to them, everything else would be wonderful. So his friend Barnabas came and took him and brought him to the apostles in Jerusalem.

Paul might have reasoned, "All I need is a connection with one of the big shots in Jerusalem." What happened there was also disappointing. What he did in Jerusalem was *coming in and going out*" (Acts 9:28). Barnabas recommended Paul and he shared with the leaders the wonderful experience he had in Damascus.

The Bible says Barnabas *declared* to them about Paul. He did not just share or tell them about Paul, but really *declared* (see Acts 9:27). That did not get Paul where he wanted to be in ministry. The "big shots" in Jerusalem were not willing to include this outsider, or the "new kid on the block," into their circle of influence. They were not that impressed because after hearing his testimony they knew he had not yet been tested. This is the process each of us will go through whether we are called to full-time ministry or a secular career.

Paul eventually had to have hands laid on him by unknown ministers of a local church and be sent out by other apostles and believers to fulfill his ministry. He tried to do the ministry on his own and failed. If you want to *have* spiritual authority, you need to be *under* authority. It is a spiritual truth in the Kingdom, and no one is exempt.

Do you know what Paul did after his life was threatened a few times? He began to serve other ministers and churches, waiting patiently for the next assignment from God. Perhaps it was during this time that he learned the trade of tent making as a means of supporting himself.

STEPPING OUT OF GOD'S TIMING

Many people I know got sick and died before it was God's time for them to be commissioned. They had stepped out of God's timing and tried to do what God called them to do in their own strength. There is nothing more dangerous than doing the right thing at the wrong time, and then, when your time finally does come, you are not around to do it or you do not want to do it anymore!

Moses knew he was called to deliver his people but was not commissioned until he was 80 years old. There is nothing more repugnant to God than when we attempt to accomplish spiritual things with our own strength and ideas. The Bible says a wise man's heart discerns both time and procedure:

> *Whoever obeys his command will come to no harm, and the wise heart will know the proper time and procedure. For there is a proper time and procedure for every matter, though a man's misery weighs heavily upon him* (Ecclesiastes 8:5-6 NIV).

When you are called, you need to discern the time, then you need to discern the process of how to fulfill the call. God reveals to you the time and the process but you need to put together the plan and execute the process. That comes by learning from personal study, other people, and life experience.[2]

Many fail because they do not understand the purpose of tests and trials when they go through them. They think all trials come from the devil. They think that if they are doing the will of God, they should not face any challenges. This is not so. We see in the Bible, in both the Old and New Testaments, that people who were in the will of God went through various trials and tests before, during, and after they accomplished what God had called them to do.

God does not test us with evil (see James 1:13). Evil comes from the enemy. God will not give you sickness, cause accidents, or send any other form of evil to test you. We do not see that in the Bible. God will not violate His own Word. If we live in deliberate disobedience, then we will reap the result of the law of sowing and reaping. If we sow into the flesh we shall reap death and destruction (see Gal. 6:8).

In the following pages, we are going to look in detail at the purpose of testing and ways God tests us so that we can be ready the next time our season of promotion comes. Whenever something goes wrong, most believers default to blaming the devil and fighting with him. We are going to see that this is not the way Christian life works all the time.

ENDNOTES

1. The Greek word for *strength* here also means "bold" or "headstrong."

2. To find out more about this subject, please read my book *Recognizing God's Timing For Your Life* available at www.maximpact.org.

Chapter 2

THE PURPOSE OF SPIRITUAL TESTS: PART I

MAN: A THREE-PART BEING

God created man as a three-part being: comprised of spirit, soul, and body. Man is a spirit being who has a soul and dwells in a body. We have a physical body because we live in a physical world. We have a soul that serves as the connection between our spirit and body. God is Spirit and He created man in His own image and likeness. He created man to represent Him and His Kingdom, to be a dwelling place for God, and to exercise dominion on the earth. God's intention was for man to be led by his spirit.

God intended that man would subdue the physical world by his spirit. The physical world is subject to the spiritual world. Before the fall and the introduction of sin, man's body and soul were working in union with, and were subject to, his spirit. Man possessed incredible power and ability, and was capable of overcoming any obstacle or challenge that came his way. But, mankind was given free will and the opportunity to either obey or disobey God.

When God created man in His image and likeness, He gave man His nature, which made him second only to God in power and authority. When he disobeyed God, sin entered the earth and man lost God's nature. His nature was corrupted and, instead of God's nature, he inherited a subordinate sinful nature that subjects him to the forces of the flesh, feelings, and emotions.

His thinking process was no longer in line with God's order, but always led him away from God. His soul became defiled and rebellious toward his spirit. Sin affected man's spirit, soul, and body equally and the spirit was no longer in control of his three-part being. He became a being led by his feelings and emotions rather than by truth. Sin brought self-consciousness and man lost God-consciousness. Feelings are of the body, emotions are of the soul, and truth is of the spirit. When we are led by our feelings, we become carnal. When we are guided by our emotions, we become soulish. But, if we are led by the truth of God's Word, we become spiritual.

The corrupted nature man now has is called the flesh or sinful nature. Those who live according to their carnal nature can never please God. The carnal nature is comprised of three major forces: the lust of the flesh, the lust of the eyes, and the pride of life (see 1 John 2:16).

Man became his own worst enemy. These three forces began to work against him. No matter how hard he tried to do the right thing, man could not overcome them through his own strength, discipline, or religious practices. God had to set us free from them. He made a way for us through Jesus Christ.

Man began to do things he did not want to do, and the good things he wanted to do, he was not able to perform. His own nature began to fight against him and man became a slave to his own sinful nature. His capacity to overcome the forces on the earth was also greatly diminished.

OVERCOMING INTERNAL AND EXTERNAL FORCES

When we pass spiritual tests we will overcome those three forces. When we are born again, the Spirit of God comes to dwell in us. He leads us into all truth and begins to show us the things that are not right in our life. Then, God fills us with His Spirit to empower us to overcome those forces. We call this being Spirit-filled.

The Holy Spirit works in three levels in a believer's life. The first is when we are born again through the work of the Holy Spirit. The second is when we are filled with the Spirit to overcome our flesh. And the third is baptism in the Holy Spirit, where God anoints an individual to accomplish a specific task or mission in the body of Christ.

When Jesus was filled with the Spirit, the Bible says the Holy Spirit *led* Him into the wilderness to be tempted by the devil (see Luke 4:1-2). He did not lead Him to do the work of the ministry. He was in the wilderness for 40 days overcoming His own battles. Before we can help others to overcome their battles, we need to win our own.

When the 40 days of temptation were finished, the Bible says He came out of the wilderness in the power of the Holy Spirit and power began to flow out of Him (see Luke 4:14). God fills us with His Spirit to overcome our internal battles, and then He baptizes us with His power to overcome external battles.

To be led by the Spirit means to be led by God's Word. To be led by our flesh is to live according to what we feel and see. Through spiritual tests, God is bringing us back to our original way of thinking and acting, which is according to the Word of God. Before the fall, our *operating system* was the spoken Word of God. We used to think and act just like God. As a result of the fall, the flesh became our *operating system*.

The process of going from being led by the flesh to being led by the Spirit (Word) is called *dying to self*, or, as the Bible calls it, walking in the Spirit. Being led by your spirit means you are *dead* to selfish ambitions and ready to do anything God asks of you in order to glorify Him.

Thanks be to God for His redemption through Jesus Christ. When we believe in Jesus Christ and accept His work on the cross, our spirit is born again and we receive a new nature, but our soul and body remain the same and do not show any immediate change.

BORN-AGAIN EXPERIENCE

Through the born-again experience, our spirit received once again the capacity to overcome every force on this earth, but we do not see that manifest right away because our soul and body deliberately contradict our spirit.

Transformation does not occur in a day or two. Through a series of trials and testing, our soul and body will give in to our spirit and we will begin to enjoy our new life led by the Spirit of God. What God desires to accomplish through spiritual tests is to bring us back to where we are led by our spirit so we can partner with Him and fulfill the purpose He has for us and for the earth.

Our born-again spirit is a new creature that never before existed. The challenge is to train our soul and body to be subject to that spirit and work in unison with each other. Our soul and body will not accept this naturally, so they need to be brought under subjection through faith and by receiving understanding of the revelation of God's Word.

Our sinful nature is like a wild horse and it will not admit defeat. It has to be brought under subjection to our spirit and it will fight back as long as we live in this body. The Bible calls this the good fight of faith. It requires discipline to live according to what the Word says about our born-again nature. All of the good qualities that we would like to exhibit already exist in our spirit.

RENEWED KNOWLEDGE

Many times, we do not know or believe that because we do not feel it. God takes the initiative in teaching us what changes need to be made in our soul and body by taking us through a series of *spiritual tests* that bring forth what is in our spirit. In the natural, a test is given to show how much we really know and to promote a person to the next level. Spiritual tests are given to let us know what is really in us so we can make progress in our spiritual life.

This is what happens when we go through spiritual tests: knowledge and pre-conditioned mindsets will be removed and new knowledge and the understanding that is needed will be added to our soul. The Bible calls this the renewing of our mind (see Rom. 12:1-2). Since our mind is made up of images and information, the reason we function the way we do is based on the knowledge and information that has been programmed in our mind. If we are to function in a different way, we need to get rid of the old knowledge and acquire some new knowledge.

This is why Paul writes in Colossians 3:10: *"And have put on the new self, which is being renewed in knowledge in the image of its Creator"* (NIV). Another translation says it this way: *"You are living a brand new kind of life that is continually learning more and more of what is right, and trying constantly to be more and more like Christ who created this new life within you"* (TLB).

Our soul needs to receive knowledge in order to renew itself. We renew our mind with the knowledge of God so that it can be trained to fall in line with those things deposited in our spirit through the born-again experience. The sooner we feed our mind with this new knowledge, the faster it will be renewed.

Since we know all things work together for good to those who love God and are called according to His purpose (see Rom. 8:28), the Bible tells us to rejoice when we are tested, knowing that we will be in a better place than before (see James 1:2-3). All the good qualities and habits that we wish to have in our life are already in our spirit. The fruit of the spirit—love, joy, peace, longsuffering, etc.—are already in our spirit but they need to be activated and the soul needs to recognize them. We need to go through some difficulties in order to know what we are really capable of overcoming.

Transitioning from a soulish and carnal life to a spiritual life is not that easy. The flesh and soul are two rebellious characters. They always think and act contrary to our spirit. Unfortunately, many in the Church never transition from being a carnal person to a spiritual person. To be *spiritual* means to be led by our spirit, or as the Bible calls it, walking in the spirit. It is not keeping a bunch of rules and rituals or a particular dress code. In other words, many are saved but not benefiting from their salvation experience.

Once we are born again and are in Christ, we are more than conquerors and God always leads us to victory. There is nothing on this earth that we cannot overcome or endure with God. It does not matter what happened to you or what you are going through; if you are born again, you have the ultimate victory, which God has already provided through the cross. You are no longer a slave to sin, but a servant of righteousness (see Rom. 6:18).

Spiritual tests help us awaken to our true nature that was restored when God gave us a new birth. Spiritual tests help us to build our character and become strong in our spirit. Again, when I say *spiritual tests* I do not mean sickness, death, accidents, or any type of calamity. The devil is the source of all that is evil.

REASONS FOR SPIRITUAL TESTS

We read in the book of Job about the reasons and the results of going through tests.

> *Behold, happy is the man whom God corrects; therefore do not despise the chastening of the Almighty. For He bruises, but He binds up; He wounds, but His hands make whole. He shall deliver you in six troubles, yes, in seven no evil shall touch you* (Job 5:17-19).

Job's experience was allowed by God but not imputed by God. The devil was envious of Job and his blessings and wanted to afflict him, hoping that Job would curse God. Job did not know what had happened behind the scenes in the spirit realm. He did not know about the conversations Satan had with God. He thought that God had afflicted him with what he was going through. That is the case with many believers today. They point to God as the cause for all the evil they face.

That is the way the devil works. He will bring evil things upon us and make us believe those things were from God. The book of Job is one of the best books to read to know about the goodness of God toward human beings. He wants to bless and prosper us, but the enemy wants to steal, kill, and destroy everything we receive from God.

We do not know why God allowed Satan to afflict Job. Perhaps he opened the door to him through fear. I also believe there are some people like Job whom God allows the enemy to afflict to show man's faithfulness to God regardless of their circumstances.

The apostle Paul was another individual whom God allowed Satan to buffet. The Scripture says God will test us seven times and after the seventh time no evil will touch us anymore. We will be spiritually mature to overcome the troubles or calamities the devil tries to bring to our lives. That means there is spiritual maturity that takes place, or should take place, each time we go through a test. After we pass these seven tests we will reach a new level of maturity in the spirit and will be ready to move into the blessings that God promises us in the following verses. I have seen that God will test us in one area more than once until He knows without a doubt that we are capable of overcoming it without being shaken.

If you search your life, you may find there are seven major tests you have been through. Depending on where you are in your Christian walk, you may not be through all of them. Some will say they have been through at least 20. No. They may have failed in some and repeated the same tests in different seasons of their life. I do not believe God will test a person more than seven times and you will learn about those in the following chapters. That does not mean we will never face any more challenges or trials in our lives.

It simply means we will spiritually be in a place where we will be able to discern the works of the enemy and the works of God, walking in victory all the time (see Heb. 5:14).

THE BLESSINGS OF PASSING TESTS

Job 5:19-27 talks about the 13 blessings of those who pass the 7 tests. I want you to read the scripture below and then I will list out the 13 blessings that this passage talks about:

He shall deliver you in six troubles, yes, in seven no evil shall touch you. In famine He shall redeem you from death, and in war from the power of the sword. You shall be hidden from the scourge of the tongue, and you shall not be afraid of destruction when it comes. You shall laugh at destruction and famine, and you shall not be afraid of the beasts of the earth. For you shall have a covenant with the stones of the field, and the beasts of the field shall be at peace with you. You shall know that your tent is in peace; you shall visit your dwelling and find nothing amiss. You shall also know that your descendants shall be many, and your offspring like the grass of the earth. You shall come to the grave at a full age, as a sheaf of grain ripens in its season. Behold, this we have searched out; it is true. Hear it, and know for yourself.

The blessings mentioned in the above verses are:

1. In famine He shall redeem you from death—God promises us constant provision of substance and food.

2. In war from the power of the sword—we will have protection in spiritual battle.

3. You shall be hidden from the scourge of the tongue— we will have protection from evil words, curses, and people who hate us.

4. You shall not be afraid of destruction when it comes—this speaks of protection from the forces of nature.

5. You shall laugh at destruction and famine—God will give you joy and peace in the midst of trouble.

6. You shall not be afraid of the beasts of the earth—protection from the wild and poisonous beasts (demons) of the earth.

7. You shall have a covenant with the stones of the field—blessings in the areas of agriculture and precious stones.

8. The beasts of the field shall be at peace with you—cooperation from the animal kingdom.

9. You shall know that your tent is in peace—peaceful and prosperous home and family life.

10. You shall visit your dwelling and find nothing amiss—protection from thieves and accidents.

11. You shall also know that your descendants shall be many—no barrenness and plenty of children.

12. Your offspring shall be like the grass of the earth—generational blessings.

13. You shall come to the grave in full age as a sheaf of grain ripens in its season—long and healthy life.

Wow! I do not think there is anyone who would not like to have those blessings. Yes, they are for us, but we need to pass some spiritual tests in order to enjoy them. If we study the life of Job carefully, we see that he went through seven tests in his life before he inherited all the above blessings (see Job 42:10-17). Though the time of testing he went through was not initiated by God, at the end God turned it around for a blessing in his life.

SEVEN AREAS JOB WAS TESTED

We are now going to look at the seven areas in which Job was tested.

1. The Sabeans came and took the oxen and the asses and killed the servants (see Job 1:15). The destruction and loss of assets and work force: the oxen were in the field plowing when they were destroyed. In those days the main business was agriculture and livestock.

2. The fire of God fell from heaven and burned the sheep and the servants (see Job 1:16). In the Bible, sheep represent provision and investments. In the Old Testament, sheep were used for meat, milk, and wool for clothing.

3. The Chaldeans came and took the camels and killed the servants (see Job 1:17). Camels represent trade and transportation. In those days they used camels to ride and to carry heavy loads on long trips through the wilderness.

4. The wind came and destroyed the house and killed his children (see Job 1:19). Loss of family members and real estate.

5. Satan smote Job with boils from the sole of his foot to the crown of his head (see Job 2:7). Personal health was affected (sickness and disease).

6. His wife told him to deny his integrity, curse God and die (see Job 2:9). Betrayal and rejection by loved ones.

7. His three friends came and accused him of unrighteous deeds for the cause of the calamities that fell on him (see Job 4:7–5:16). This was difficult social

relationships and attacks on his character and reputation—his friends misunderstood Job.

GOD TESTS ACCORDING TO CALL AND PURPOSE

I believe God tests each individual according to their call and purpose. We all come into this earth with certain defects. While we all benefit from generational blessings, we also have generational toxic waste that was dumped on us at birth. God knows in what areas we need growth, change, or improvement, and He will allow us to go through particular situations that will address each of those defects.

There are things that need to be cleaned, removed, pruned, and replaced, and some new things need to be put in us before we become useful to God. The principles remain the same for everyone. One of Job's weaknesses was fear. He lived in fear that one day he was going to lose all of his possessions and family. So he constantly offered sacrifices to the Lord on behalf of his children.

So it was, when the days of feasting had run their course, that Job would send and sanctify them, and he would rise early in the morning and offer burnt offerings according to the number of them all. For Job said, "It may be that my sons have sinned and cursed God in their hearts." Thus Job did regularly (Job 1:5).

For the thing I greatly feared has come upon me, and what I dreaded has happened to me (Job 3:25).

You may not have thought you would go through any of these tests to receive the above blessings in your life. The problem is that when we go through a test, we do not think about the blessings as we are often consumed by the discomfort it causes in our flesh. It is for our benefit that God allows us to go through some testing. The problem is that testing comes unexpectedly, and when we are tested we may feel like we are being punished for doing something wrong. Beware of this!

The Bible says Jesus endured the cross by foreseeing the joy that was set before Him. The cross was a test for Jesus that He endured for us. Hebrews 12:2 says: *"Looking unto Jesus, the author and finisher of our faith, who for the joy that was set before Him endured the cross, despising the shame, and has sat down at the right hand of the throne of God."*

God blessed Job at the end with more than he had in the beginning. Everything was restored to him and multiplied: *"Now the Lord blessed the latter days of Job more than his beginning"* (Job 42:12).

When we study the life of Joseph we see that he experienced seven tests before he became the prime minister of Egypt. Joseph was the son of Jacob, who loved him more than any of his other children. Jacob made a coat of many colors and gave it to him. Joseph's brothers envied him and would not talk peaceably with him. That was the first test he went through.

1. His brothers hated him because of his coat (see Gen. 37:4).

2. His brothers hated him *more* after he shared with them the first dream (see Gen. 37:5).

3. His brothers envied him for his second dream (see Gen. 37:11).

4. His brothers wanted to kill him but later took him and cast him into a pit (see Gen. 37:24).

5. His brothers sold Joseph to the merchants for twenty pieces of silver (see Gen. 37:28).

6. Potiphar's wife tried to seduce him to sleep with her (see Gen. 39:7-12).

7. He was falsely accused and unjustly cast into the prison where the king's prisoners were bound (see Gen. 39:20).

And, in reference to Joseph's testing, the psalmist spoke: *"He sent a man before them—Joseph—who was sold as a slave. They hurt his feet with fetters, he was laid in irons. Until the time that his word came to pass, the **word of the Lord tested** him"* (Ps. 105:17-19).

God uses His Word to test us. Joseph went through the trials to be tested by the Word of the Lord. The Word of the Lord is tested and tried seven times and it is pure (see Ps. 12:6). When God gives us His Word or promise, we will be tested seven times so that our whole being can come into agreement with that Word.

This is why Jesus told the parable of the seed:

> *But he who received the seed on stony places, this is he who hears the word and immediately receives it with joy; yet he has no root in himself, but endures only for a while. For when tribulation or persecution arises because of the word, immediately he stumbles* (Matthew 13:20-21).

There are others throughout the Bible who were tested seven times. We will look into the lives of the Israelites in the wilderness, and at the life of David later in this book. This will give us greater insight into what to expect when we are being tested. Everything we need to know while we are being tested is written in the Word of God.

Chapter 3

THE PURPOSE OF SPIRITUAL TESTS: PART II

HOW TO KNOW YOU'RE BEING TESTED

Tests come unexpectedly and without any warning. But there is a way to know when you are going through a test: you will feel like your life is coming to an end. If your marriage is going through a test, you will feel that your relationship is hopelessly ruined. If you are tested in the area of finances, you will feel like the only way out is bankruptcy. Do not trust those feelings. Nothing is irreparable or over until God says it is over. Each time you are tested you may feel like it is the end of something, and in the natural realm it is, but it is just the beginning of something new in the Spirit.

When the Israelites were in the wilderness, they faced shortages of water and food. Each time they had a shortage, they thought they were going to die. What they did not know was the fact that they were being tested. So they murmured and complained against Moses and God and wanted to go back to Egypt. That is what people do when they fail a test: either they rebel against God or they return to their old ways and do something crazy. One of these is likely to happen each time we fail a test.

When God tested Abraham and asked him to sacrifice his only son, he obeyed God without doubting, believing God was

63

able to raise a son for him from the ashes. That is the attitude of a person who passes a test (see Heb. 11:17).

When God gives you a promise, you will go through circumstances that appear contrary to that promise. During these times, instead of looking at the circumstances, we need to look at the Word and hold onto its promises because that is what God is looking for from us. That is the way we mature in our walk with the Lord.

Tests are designed to teach us to listen to the Holy Spirit and walk in the spirit. When we fail to listen to the Holy Spirit's direction, we cannot pass the test. God sends opportunities our way to see whether we will listen to His Spirit or follow our own fleshly feelings and emotions.

BLESSED WITH EVERY SPIRITUAL BLESSING

He who did not spare His own Son, but delivered Him up for us all, how shall He not with Him also freely give us all things? (Romans 8:32).

God gave us the Holy Spirit so that we can know the things He has freely given to us. He has blessed us with all spiritual blessings. Everything you need has been deposited by God into your spirit. There is nothing left that God has not given you, and there are no blessings left in heaven that He has not blessed you with already (see Eph. 1:3). But, they have to move from the spirit world into the natural. Our soul and body are at war with our spirit and need to succumb to our spirit in order for those blessings to manifest.

The only way our soul and body will give way to our spirit is if they are dead to their own desires and ambitions. They do not die naturally; we need to put them to death. Unfortunately, no one will put them to death without going through some hard times. We need to learn to discern and differentiate between the nature and work of our flesh with its pitfalls and the nature and work of our spirit with its benefits.

God enables us to put the nature and works of the flesh to death through the tests we endure. Each time we are tested, it is an opportunity to say "No" to the desires of the flesh and say "Yes" to the mind of the spirit.

It is the believer's responsibility to know what God has made available to us through Jesus Christ. He did not save us to have an ordinary life or to sit idly by waiting to be taken to heaven. The following are a few examples of what He has given us.

The power that is available to us is exceedingly great: *"The exceeding greatness of His power toward us who believe, according to the working of His mighty power"* (Eph. 1:19).

The gifts that are available to us are indescribable: *"And by their prayer for you, who long for you because of the exceeding grace of God in you. Thanks be to God for His indescribable gift!"* (2 Cor. 9:14-15).

The joy that is available to us is unspeakable and full of glory: *"Though now you do not see Him, yet believing, you rejoice with joy inexpressible and full of glory"* (1 Pet. 1:8).

What God wants to do for us is exceedingly abundantly above all that we ask or think: *"Now to Him who is able to do exceedingly abundantly above all that we ask or think, according to the power that works in us"* (Eph. 3:20).

The riches of His grace toward us are exceeding: *"That in the ages to come He might show the exceeding riches of His grace in His kindness toward us in Christ Jesus"* (Eph. 2:7).

The peace that is available to us passes all human understanding: *"And the peace of God, which surpasses all understanding, will guard your hearts and minds through Christ Jesus"* (Phil. 4:7).

The love God has for us is unfathomable: That we *"may be able to comprehend with all the saints what is the width and length and depth and height—to know the love of Christ which passes knowledge; that you may be filled with all the fullness of God"* (Eph. 3:18-19).

And First John 4:9 says, *"In this the love of God was manifested toward us, that God has sent His only begotten Son into the world, that we might live through Him."* Later on, John tells us, *"Behold what manner of love the Father has bestowed on us, that we should be called children of God!"* (1 John 3:1).

God has blessed us with all blessings in heaven: *"Blessed be the God and Father of our Lord Jesus Christ, who has blessed us with every spiritual blessing in the heavenly places in Christ"* (Eph. 1:3).

If God has made all of this available to us, where are all these precious treasures? Why are most of us unable to tap into them? All these gifts are available to every believer and they are already present within our spirit. If you are born again, these treasures are in you. Man is a triune being made of spirit, soul, and body. We usually live by what we feel in our soul and body. Because of the fall, our born-again spirit is, in a manner of speaking, imprisoned in our soul and body. Man became a soulish being instead of a spiritual being. He has more self-awareness than God-awareness.

GOD BRINGS FORTH LIFE THROUGH TESTS

If these qualities are to manifest in our life, they will have to break through the shells of our soul and body. When you plant a seed, if it remains by itself, it will not grow and become a plant. The seed has to break through its shell and then the life that is in the seed will manifest. God has orchestrated a way to bring forth the life that is in our spirit and that way is through spiritual tests. The outcome of all spiritual tests is to train us to be led by our spirit and not by our emotions or feelings. Emotions are from the soul and feelings are of the body.

Through testing, the power of our soul and body will be broken and the life of the spirit will begin to manifest. Our body and soul are like the shell that covers a seed. There are two layers in every seed. There is an outer layer, which is the seed coat, and an inner layer that protects. The outer layer is our body and the inner layer is our soul. The innermost part of the seed is our spirit.

The seed has to be placed in unusual circumstances and buried in the ground for the life inside to come out. When it is buried in the ground, the pressure and moisture cause the seed inside to change its shape and grow. Eventually, the shell breaks open and the life that was in the seed comes out. It is impossible to grow without change.

The body and soul both need to give way to the spirit. This occurs when we die to our self as we deal with the things we go through in our life, often through painful experiences—or what the Bible calls fires—or dying to self. In order for the life to come out of it, the seed must endure some pain as its shell breaks.

Jesus said, *"Most assuredly, I say to you, unless a grain of wheat falls into the ground and dies, it remains alone; but if it dies, it produces much grain"* (John 12:24).

Oh, I wish I could tell you more about this death. It is impossible to describe in words. When you ask God to use you or to change you, He will take you through experiences that are severe, that the shell (power) of our soul and body might die so the life of the spirit may manifest in us.

DYING DAILY

Many Christians live their entire lives without ever tapping into the life within their spirit. As soon as their flesh gets uncomfortable, many quit or retaliate. There is unlimited potential and creativity in your spirit, but only a few have ever tapped into even the minutest part of it. The more you want the anointing of God in your life, the more your self needs to die.

When I say death or dying, I am not talking about ceasing to exist from this earth, but dying to your own selfish desires, taking up the cross and following Jesus. It is choosing to do His will instead of following your emotions and desires. It is much easier to talk about this than to actually live it.

There are many layers and levels of these shells to our body and soul. Every experience has formed a layer in our soul. Everything we learned and experienced as children has formed a layer in our memory and soul and caused us to develop particular expectations that determine our mindset and thought processes. God has to undo these layers and form new ones, new ways of thinking according to His Word. Each test is designed to deal with one layer at a time.

The deeper you want to go with God, the more intense and severe the dying process, and the more painful the test. It does not get easier. Satan tempted Jesus at the beginning of His ministry, but that was nothing compared to what He endured at the Garden of Gethsemane. It was deeper, more intense, and more painful. There are no adequate words to explain that experience.

The focus of all testing is to promote us in the spirit. Each time Joseph went through a test he was promoted. It was not a material promotion, but he was getting closer to his destiny than he was before. The testing that God allows in our life is meant to develop our inner man more than any temporary material promotion.

Every trial and obstacle you face during your Christian walk can be turned around to your advantage. James says, *"My brethren, count it all joy when you fall into various trials, knowing that the testing of your faith produces patience. But let patience have its perfect work, that you may be perfect and complete, lacking nothing"* (James 1:2-4).

Four divine purposes of testing mentioned in the above passage are: 1. To develop our patience, 2. That we may be perfect, 3. That we may be complete, and 4. That we may lack nothing.

Another purpose of tests is to build our patience. The above verse says when we are patient we are perfect and will reach a place where we lack nothing. God already knows if we are capable of doing what He called us to do but, too often, people do not believe it or they are overly confident in themselves rather than placing their confidence in Him. He wants us to trust in Him and in His power with all our heart.

PURPOSE, PROCESS, AND RESULTS OF SPIRITUAL TESTS

I want to take a moment to talk about the purpose, process, and results of spiritual tests. There is no other scripture in the Bible that addresses more clearly the nature of spiritual tests and their process than this verse:

> *For You, O God,* **tested us**; *You refined us like silver. You brought us into prison and laid burdens on our backs. You let men ride over our heads; we went through fire and water, but You brought us to a place of abundance* (Psalm 66:10-12 NIV).

There are seven ways God tests us, and we are going to study them in detail below.

1. God has tested us (see Ps. 66:10).

God will test us whether we like it or not. It is one of the ways He prepares us for His glory. The Bible sometimes uses the word *chastisement*. We will chastise our children with the intention that they will grow and mature into better people, not with the intention of destroying them. In the same way, God will test us because He loves us and wants us to grow spiritually.

The author of Proverbs stated: *"My son, do not despise the chastening of the Lord, nor detest His correction; for whom the Lord loves He corrects, just as a father the son in whom he delights"* (Prov. 3:11-12).

Another translation says, *"My son, do not make your heart hard against the Lord's teaching; do not be made angry by His training: For to those who are dear to him the Lord says sharp words, and makes the son in whom He delights undergo pain"* (BBE).

2. He will refine us like silver (see Ps. 66:10).

The second way God tests us is by refining us like silver is refined. It is interesting that the Bible compares the refining of the precious metal silver to the process of change that we go through with God. In David's time, silver was purified seven times before it was considered pure enough for use.

The first purifying fire was used to burn away the combustibles in the silver-bearing rock. Then, the ore container was sealed from the air, first having some material added, such as charcoal, which would chemically remove the oxygen from the silver oxide. This would result in silver metal flowing to the bottom of the container with the molten rock above it. This process was repeated a few times to separate the silver from the original ore.

The second step was to separate other impurities and metals, like copper (spiritually, think of this as being representative of sin), arsenic (wrong attitudes), etc. from the silver. Because they have different melting temperatures, they had to be carefully removed in fires of different temperatures. This process would be repeated seven times before the pure silver was extracted. If the wrong process was used, the resultant metal could be copper instead of silver.

Why are we compared to silver and not to any other metal? In the old days, one of the methods by which the quality of silver was determined was by how well it reflected an image. Fausset's Bible Dictionary says, "The Lord, with perfect wisdom and love, leaves His people in affliction till, their dross being purified, He sees them reflecting His holy image; just as a 'refiner of silver' sits watching the melting silver until he sees his own image reflected, then he knows the silver has been long enough in the furnace and withdraws it."[1]

The Lord will allow us to go through circumstances that seem dire. Each of these experiences is focused toward drawing out the impurities that hinder His love from flowing to us and from us. Silver contains certain qualities that other metals do not possess. It is used for some specific purposes that can be compared to our nature in God. Below are some of the common uses of silver.

Batteries: Many batteries, both rechargeable and disposable, are manufactured with silver alloys as the cathode. (A cathode is an electrode through which an electric current flows out of a polarized electrical device.) The silver battery provides the higher voltage and long life required for quartz watches, cameras, and other electronic devices. Batteries are used to store portable power. God chose us to store His power and to bring His power where it is needed.

Bearings: Some of the heaviest and largest pieces of machinery use silver bearings to support their weight. Steel bearings electro-plated with high purity silver have greater fatigue strength and load-carrying capacity than any other type of bearing. Once a person has been through the fire of God, he receives an unusual capacity to carry burdens and go through extraordinary challenges. Not just our own, we are also made capable of helping others who are going through trials.

Soldering: Silver facilitates the joining of materials and pro-duces naturally smooth, leak-tight and corrosion-resistant joints. Soldering is joining two cables or wires to complete a circuit. God uses us to connect with people and work together as a team. He has given us the ministry of reconciliation to restore relationships that are broken. He uses us to help others be connected with Him.

Catalysts: Silver is used widely as a catalyst to increase the productivity of chemical reactions without getting involved in the reaction. It is amazing how God uses us to encourage others and motivate them to do extraordinary things without becoming directly involved in their personal life.

Electrical: Silver is the best electrical conductor of all metals; hence, it is used in many electrical applications. When a person comes out of the refining fire of God, He will fill that person with His power and utilize him or her as a conductor that will channel that power to others in need. And after we have gone through all of the tests, the power of God will freely flow through us without any hindrance.

Jewelry and Silverware: Silver possesses working qualities similar to gold but enjoys greater reflectivity and can achieve the most brilliant polish of any metal. God created us in His image and likeness to reflect His glory and nature. When we come out of the fire, we will reflect God's image and likeness (love and compassion) better than ever before.

Photography: When Joseph Nicephore Niepce tested the first photographic image obtained through a camera-like device in 1813, it was silver nitrate that made it possible. We have the ability to store and produce images in our heart. God puts a picture of our purpose or future in our heart, which we call a vision. Like a photograph, we have the ability to reproduce what we see in the natural and in the spirit.

Depending on our purpose, God will refine us like silver and use us for whatever purpose He has created us for. He will let us go through fires with different temperatures, each time drawing new dross or impurities out of our lives. He is the master Silversmith and He knows what kind of fire is needed to cleanse us from flaws that are hindering us from being used by Him. In this case, the fire represents circumstances and trials that we will face in our lives. God decides the furnace (circumstances) and the temperature, and we decide how long we want to stay in it. The end result is always clear. He wants to bring us to a wealthy place, a place of abundance.

God asks through Isaiah: "Do you see what I've done? I've refined you, but not without fire. I've tested you like silver in the furnace of affliction" (Isaiah 48:10 MSG).

3. Bring us into the prison or net (see Ps. 66:11a).

God will lead us into circumstances in which we will feel inextricably trapped. *Net* means a circumstance or situation that you are in and do not see any way out. You feel "stuck" in place, but it was God that led you there. He restricts our mobility and keeps us in one place until we pass that test.

Joseph was such a person; he was not planning to be in prison or in the pit. He wasn't even going through such things because he did something wrong. God brought those circumstances into his life to prepare him for the future. I could write about more than one incident where I heard the voice of God telling me to do something and, once I did it, I felt like I was in a trap and did not know how to get out of it!

During those times, the Lord taught me valuable lessons and principles that changed my life forever. When you are in a pit or in a net, it is difficult to believe that the Lord led you into it or that you have any hope beyond it. You have to make sure you heard the voice of God and it is not your disobedience or rebellion that got you into the net.

For Joseph, God used the pit; for Peter, He used the boat; for Jonah, a fish; and for Elijah, a brook. For David, He used King Saul. He will use whatever best fits our life and purpose to test us.

4. Laid burdens on our backs (see Ps. 66:11).

You will go through seasons where you feel like the burden of your life is unbearable and you cannot move forward in life because of the weight in your heart. Sometimes you can feel in you the weight of the burden. You will try to shake it off and cast it to the Lord, but it will not go away for a time because there is a reason behind it.

5. Let men ride over our heads (see Ps. 66:12).

God will let us go through times in life where we feel like other people are taking advantage of us. You will be ill-treated and betrayed by others in ways that are unjust and will feel as if no one cares about you. David was anointed by God, but Saul became jealous of him and tried to kill him for no other reason. All David did was help and serve Saul. What he received in return was total rejection and cruelty.

6. He will let us go through water (see Ps. 66:12).

Water represents the problems and natural circumstances that we go through in life. Sometimes God puts obstacles in our way to see how we respond to Him. We need to master our circumstances and move forward.

7. He will let us go through fire (see Ps. 66:12).

Fire represents the refining process that we go through internally in our spirit, heart, and soul.

CHARACTER DEVELOPMENT AND THE TIMING OF TESTS

One of the purposes of a test is character development.[2] To God, our character is more important than talent. He looks at the heart to discern the intents of our innermost being and determine our promotion. Psalm 17:3 says, *"You have tested my heart; You have visited me in the night; You have tried me and have found nothing; I have purposed that my mouth shall not transgress."* And Deuteronomy 8:16 says it was God *"who fed you in the wilderness with manna, which your fathers did not know, that He might humble you and that He might test you, to do you good in the end."*

Though it is impossible to know the exact time God will test us, there is a pattern that we see in the Bible that helps us to recognize the season. If we study the lives of the people in the Bible, we see they were tested just before and after they had a breakthrough or mountaintop experience in their life.

Abraham was tested after he had Isaac, the long-awaited blessing. Joseph was tested right after he received the coat of many colors from his father as well as the dream from God. Elijah brought fire from heaven and saw one of the biggest breakthroughs in history, then went through a test immediately afterward and ran away, fearing for his life.

When the people of Israel came out of Egypt with mighty miracles and wonders, they headed for a test at the Red Sea. Right after Jesus fed the 5,000, He asked the disciples to get into the boat and cross over to the other side. While they were on their way a great storm arose. It was a test that God allowed in their lives.

Moses went up to the mountain to receive God's law. He was there with God for forty days and forty nights. When he came down from the mountain with the two tablets in his hands and saw the people worshiping the golden calf, he reacted in the flesh and threw the tablets to the ground and broke them. It was a test for him.

Jesus waited 30 years before ministering. When the time came, He was baptized in water and the Holy Spirit came upon Him like a dove. The Father spoke from heaven and it was the best commissioning ceremony ever. Right after that, the Bible says the Holy Spirit led Him to the wilderness to be tested.

Immediately after the transfiguration experience with Jesus, the disciples faced a test involving the healing of a boy who was oppressed by the devil. His father brought him to the disciples but they could not heal him (see Matt. 17:14-21). It is interesting that in the three synoptic Gospels (Matthew, Mark, and Luke), the transfiguration is mentioned right before this test. We will face our spiritual tests either before or after a mountaintop experience.

God will seldom test us when we are enjoying a mountaintop experience. The Bible says, *"Yea, though I walk through the valley of the shadow of death, I will fear no evil; for You are with me...*" (Ps. 23:4). Spiritually, a valley is a place of testing; there is no shadow of death on the mountaintop.

The next time you have an anointed meeting or a breakthrough, watch out: you are headed for a test. Sometimes people consider this an attack from the enemy, but it is a test from God. If you pass the test, you will go from glory to glory. That is the way God designed our lives. Often we go from glory to darkness and from strength to weakness because we receive a miracle from God and then, instead of paying attention, we relax and fail the test that immediately follows.

ENDNOTES

1. Definition of "Silver," *Fausset's Bible Dictionary*, www.bible-history.com/faussets/S/Silver/, accessed on May 1, 2012.

2. From the above two chapters we learned that the purpose and reasons God tests us are the following: 1. To develop our character, 2. To develop our endurance, 3. To enlarge our heart, 4. To increase our trust in Him, 5. To bring stability in our walk with Him, 6. To be an example to other people, 7. To promote us, 8. To bless us, 9. To bring new revelation of the Word and of Himself, 10. To enable us to know Him more, 11. To increase our dependency on Him, 12. To prove to the enemy our commitment to Him, 13. To make us overcomers, 14. To develop our faith, 15. To see what is in our heart, 16. To show us who we are, and what we are made of, 17. To see if we still love Him, 18. To enable us to comfort others, 19. To develop our patience and longsuffering, and 20. To transform us into His image.

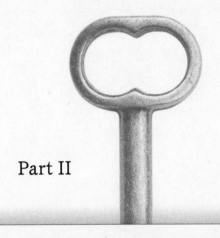

Part II

SPIRITUAL TESTS IN OUR PERSONAL LIVES

Chapter 4

SICKNESS: A SPIRITUAL TEST?

MANY WHO ARE SICK

As I previously mentioned, God does not test us with sickness. But there are many people in the body of Christ who are physically sick and believe God is testing them. Why is that? If Jesus not only died for our sin but for our sickness and poverty, then why do so many believers remain sick in the Church?

It is not God's will that we should suffer in any area for which Jesus paid the price:

- He became sin for us so the human race no longer needs to be a slave to sin (see 2 Cor. 5:21; Rom. 6:18).

- He became poor for us that we may be made rich (see 2 Cor. 8:9).

- He became a curse for us so we do not need to be under any curse (see Gal. 3:13).

- He became sick for us that we will be made whole (see Isa. 53:5).

- He delivered us from the power of darkness and conveyed us into the Kingdom of God (see Col. 1:13).

Jesus suffered on this earth, but that does not mean we are immune to suffering. Jesus carried the cross, but that does not mean we will never be asked to bear our own cross. He overcame this world, but that does not mean we do not need to also be over-comers in this world. Instead, He commanded us to suffer for His name, to carry our cross, and to overcome this world.

JESUS: REVEALING THE FATHER

Within the body of Christ there are numerous belief systems which vary widely concerning sickness and healing. My intention here is not to attack any particular stream of faith, denomination, or personal belief. My intention, by the guidance of the Holy Spirit, is to bring to light some truth that has largely been ignored by the body of Christ.

Most of the Christian belief systems concerning sickness and healing are based on Old Testament theology and, sometimes, Old Testament saints. It is good to know before we go any further that God does not deal with you and me based on the Old Covenant (Mosaic Code). He has made a New Covenant with us. As believers in Christ, our belief system should be based solely on what He accomplished for us on the cross.

Jesus came to reveal the will of God to humanity. He came to reveal the Father and the heart of God. If we want to know God's will concerning our lives, we need to look at Jesus and what He did and said in the Gospels. What Jesus did not do to a person, God will not do to anyone. What Jesus did to anyone, He will do for everyone.

Jesus said that He and His Father are one. Those who have seen Him have seen the Father. He came to reveal the name of His Father. He does the works of His Father and speaks His words. Jesus possessed the same character and essence as the Father, but was present in human form and He is the only way to the Father.

The Gospel accounts do not record Jesus cursing anyone with sickness as a punishment, or as a trial or test to increase their faith, or even to make them more holy. Jesus did not turn away any sick person saying, "No, I can't heal you right now, what you have is given to you by My Father for a reason." No. He never did that and He never will.

At the same time, not all of the sick people that were in Israel were healed during Jesus's time. The people who were healed were people who came to Him in faith, or were brought by someone who had faith in Him. Jesus himself said:

> *Assuredly, I say to you, no prophet is accepted in his own country. But I tell you truly, many widows were in Israel in the days of Elijah, when the heaven was shut up three years and six months, and there was a great famine throughout all the land; but to none of them was Elijah sent except to Zarephath, in the region of Sidon, to a woman who was a widow. And many lepers were in Israel in the time of Elisha the prophet, and none of them was cleansed except Naaman the Syrian* (Luke 4:24-27).

In the Gospels, we read that Jesus healed *all* the sick people who came to Him (see Matt. 8:16). Likewise, in the early Church there was no one sick among them. Everyone who believed in Jesus was healed (see Acts 5:16). To those who profess Old Testament theology for the New Testament believer in Christ, I want to say that when the people of Israel came out of Egypt there was no sick or weak person among them (see Ps. 105:37).

They were all healed by the power of God as they partook of the Passover meal, which is a type of the sacrament of communion and also represented Christ's death on the cross. Not only that, He made a covenant that He would not put the sicknesses and diseases upon them that were on the Egyptians (see Ex. 15:26). The provision for healing and deliverance was made available to the whole world through the work on the cross. Now it is up to each person to decide how much of that provision they are willing to accept.

GOD GIVES SICKNESS?

Many who say that God gives or allows sickness to come upon people use two major examples from the Bible, which we will closely examine. The first example cited is the life of Job and his suffering. Job was a contemporary of Abraham, at a time when it was not yet revealed to man that God is a Healer. Though Abraham prayed for Abimelech and his people for their healing, it was not known to the common people that God is a healing God. He did not make a covenant with Israel regarding healing until they came out of Egypt (see Ex. 15:25-26).

Job's Example

There was no precedent for Job to hold onto that he could believe for his healing. He was an individual through whom God chose to reveal His wisdom to the devil and his kingdom. Job's ordeal should not be considered a template that all humanity must follow. It is a tendency of fallen minds to choose negative experiences and appropriate them to our lives. While there are so many positive events recorded in the Old Testament that we do not appropriate to our lives, many people tend to blindly accept the negatives because our fallen nature is conditioned to do so.

Job was the richest man in the entire region in which he lived. Historians say his suffering lasted only about a month. After he suffered, God restored to him seven times more than he had. My suggestion to those who think their suffering and sickness is from God, is to have a life like Job before or when they come out of their suffering. And remember, Job did not die in his sickness.

Paul's Thorn in the Flesh

The second theory is based on Paul's thorn in the flesh, and many believers use that as an excuse to remain sick in their bodies.

Many think his expression "thorn in the flesh" was a sickness, though the Bible does not call it a sickness. Biblically, a thorn in the flesh never portrays sickness nor does a "messenger of Satan" portray a disease. If Paul's thorn in the flesh is not sickness and the messenger of Satan is not a disease, then what were they?

The Bible says no scripture is for private interpretation (see 2 Pet. 1:20). We should not take one isolated scripture and make a doctrine out of it, nor should a person interpret a verse as he feels. Instead of assuming personal interpretations, let us read what Paul said about them. He himself explained in the scriptures his thorn in the flesh and the messenger of Satan.

Not Knowing the Scriptures

The reason many do not understand the Scriptures is because they do not read enough for themselves, but rather believe what someone else has said about a particular verse. They will take one scripture and try to interpret the entire Bible based on a preconceived idea. That is not the way it works.

Jesus told the Pharisees that they erred because they did not know the scriptures or the power of God: *"Are you not therefore mistaken, because you do not know the Scriptures nor the power of God?"* (Mark 12:24).

How could Jesus tell people who memorized half of the Bible that they did not know the Scriptures? It is very possible. I grew up in church and inherited some of the most erroneous teachings and belief systems imaginable—some of which I am still working to rid myself of. Most of my challenges came because of those horrendous belief systems. There was a time I thought, like the Pharisees, that what I believed from the Bible was the ultimate truth, until the light went on and I saw my error.

Here is a basic rule of interpreting the Scriptures. When you read a word in the Bible, you need to look at that word in the light of the entire verse that is mentioned. When you try to interpret a verse, you need to look at that verse in the light of the whole paragraph. When you try to understand a paragraph in the Bible, you need to look at it in the light of the whole chapter. If you want to understand a chapter of the Bible, you need to look at it in the light of the whole book. If you want to understand a book of the Bible, you need to study it in the light of the entire Bible. Then you can arrive at a conclusion regarding a subject because you have actually tested it against the Scriptures, not because your grandpa told you something was true. You need to establish the truth and revelation of the Bible precept upon precept and line upon line.

Every scripture in the Bible has a "mate" that exactly fits it somewhere else in the Bible. Isaiah 34:16 says, *"Search from the book of the Lord, and read: Not one of these shall fail; not one shall lack her mate. For My mouth has commanded it, and His Spirit has gathered them."*

When you study a subject, thing, word, place, event, or a person, do not read one verse and come to a conclusion. You need to search out every other scripture that addresses that particular subject, thing, word, place, event, or person and then make a sound judgment.

In other words, interpreting the Bible is like putting together a puzzle with the pieces scattered all throughout. We need to find the ones that exactly match and put them together, and then it will make sense. If something is mentioned only once, then we cannot make a doctrine out of it. So you cannot base an interpretation concerning any subject on any single scripture.

Another major rule of establishing doctrine is this: we cannot take one person's experience from the Bible and establish a doctrine for everyone. Just because a subject is mentioned once does not make that experience normative for all. If something is to be doctrinally applicable for the New Testament believer, it must be mentioned at least two or more times specifically to everyone. The

Bible says by the mouth of two or three witnesses all matters are established (see 2 Cor. 13:1).

All scriptures are written *for* us but not *to* us. What God said to a particular person may not apply to the entire human race. We do not take incidents and experiences from the Old Testament and make doctrines for the New Testament Church. If what you and I practice is not a doctrine in the New Testament, then you do not need to keep it. If you try to keep the Old Testament and its doctrines, you are not under grace but under the law (see Gal. 5:4).

Back to Paul's Thorn

Now keep in mind what you just read and let us go back to Paul's thorn in the flesh to find out what he was talking about.

> *And lest I should be exalted above measure by the abundance of the revelations, a thorn in the flesh was given to me, a messenger of Satan to buffet me, lest I be exalted above measure. Concerning this thing I pleaded with the Lord three times that it might depart from me. And He said to me, "My grace is sufficient for you, for My strength is made perfect in weakness." Therefore most gladly I will rather boast in my infirmities, that the power of Christ may rest upon me.* **Therefore I take pleasure in infirmities, in reproaches, in needs, in persecutions, in distresses,** *for Christ's sake. For when I am weak, then I am strong* (2 Corinthians 12:7-10).

First of all, we need to understand why this thorn in the flesh was given to Paul. The reason is mentioned in verse 7, *"Lest I should be exalted above measure by the abundance of the revelations."* God chose Paul to reveal the mystery of the Church, which he does in the Epistles he wrote:

> *If indeed you have heard of the dispensation of the grace of God which was given to me for you, how that by revelation*

He made known to me the mystery as I have briefly written already (Ephesians 3:2-3).

Of which I became a minister according to the stewardship from God which was given to me for you, to fulfill the word of God, the mystery which has been hidden from ages and from generations, but now has been revealed to His saints (Colossians 1:25-26).

So, this thorn in the flesh was exclusively given to Paul for a particular reason and purpose: because of the abundance of revelations he received; and the purpose was that he would not boast about it above measure. No one else can have this thorn in the flesh because it was a personal experience of one individual given for a particular reason.

No one else can have the revelation of the Church that Paul had because whatever God had to reveal about His Church has already been revealed through him. What we now receive is the *interpretation* of that revelation, not a *new* revelation. In other words, if God had given Paul three legs to keep him humble because of all the revelation he was given, that does not mean anyone else in the body of Christ should have three legs. That is ridiculous!

In verse 10 of Second Corinthians 12 he explains what the thorn and messenger of Satan were: they were *infirmities, reproaches, needs, persecutions,* and *distresses.* Wherever Paul went to establish a new work, he faced tremendous opposition from the devil through people. He speaks about this throughout Second Corinthians:

*We give no offense in anything, that our ministry may not be blamed. But in all things we commend ourselves as ministers of God: in much patience, in **tribulations**, in **needs**, in **distresses**, in **stripes**, in **imprisonments**, in **tumults**, in **labors**, in **sleeplessness**, in **fastings**...* (2 Corinthians 6:3-5).

*Three times I was **beaten** with rods; once I was **stoned**; three times I was **shipwrecked**; a night and a day I have been in*

86

the deep; in journeys often, in perils of waters, in perils of robbers, in perils of my own countrymen, in perils of the Gentiles, in perils in the city, in perils in the wilderness, in perils in the sea, in perils among false brethren; in weariness and toil, in sleeplessness often, in hunger and thirst, in fastings often, in cold and nakedness—besides the other things, what comes upon me daily: my deep concern for all the churches. Who is weak, and I am not weak? Who is made to stumble, and I do not burn with indignation? If I must boast, I will boast in the things which concern my infirmity (2 Corinthians 11:25-30).

We do not see any reference to sickness in the above verses. There is no other person besides Jesus Christ who suffered for the Kingdom of God as Paul suffered. That was part of His calling. Jesus said in Acts 9:16, *"For I will show him how many things he must suffer for My name's sake."* He was chosen specifically to suffer (see Col. 1:24).

Infirmities

The word *infirmity* does not always mean sickness. It can mean sickness or weakness caused by an evil spirit or human frailty. In Luke 13:11, John 5:5, and First Timothy 5:23, we read about three other people who had infirmities. Two of them were physically deformed and could not function as normal human beings and the third had a digestive problem.

One was a woman who was bent and could not walk upright. The other was a man who had been sick for 38 years and was bedridden. If Paul's infirmity was physical sickness, we do not find in the Bible that he was bedridden or not fit physically to do the work God called Him to do. He faithfully finished his course.

The Greek word used for *infirmity* is *astheneia*. When it is used to express something of the human body, it means lack of strength, its native weakness and frailty (see 1 Cor. 15:43), feebleness of health or sickness. When it is used of the soul, it means lack of strength to understand a thing (see Rom. 6:19), lack of human wisdom to do things great and glorious and to bear trials and troubles (see Rom. 8:26).[1]

Though an evil spirit caused Paul's thorn in the flesh, it was not a physical sickness. Nowhere does the Bible state that he was deformed or dysfunctional. Another assumption people adopt comes from something Paul wrote in the book of Galatians, applauding believers who were willing to pluck out their eyes and give them to him. Many people say Paul wrote his letter to them with big letters because he could not see with his eyes properly (see Gal. 6:11), which is completely out of context.

Neither in the above scriptures or anywhere else in his writings does Paul say that he suffered any sickness or disease. Paul did not die because of sickness. There is no evidence that he stayed at home or in the hospital because he was sick. He finished his race and fulfilled his purpose. He also knew when and how he was going to die (see 2 Tim. 4:6-8).

People who say they have sickness because Paul had it, do so because of their ignorance of the Word of God. The enemy has deceived them in order to keep them sick and to destroy their lives before God's time. Let me tell you, when the enemy comes to you, he comes with a portion of the Word, taken out of context, intended to keep you in bondage. If this is you, by the mercy of God I command you to be free and healed in Jesus's name.

The thorn in the flesh for Paul was an evil spirit that was assigned to persecute him, both physically and verbally, and to bring false accusations to discredit his ministry. Paul had to endure those things to finish his course faithfully.

Second Timothy 4:17 says, *"But the Lord stood with me and strengthened me, so that the message might be preached fully through me, and that all the Gentiles might hear. Also I was delivered out of the mouth of the lion."*

The Bible also says every good and perfect gift comes from the Father above (see James 1:17). As I mentioned earlier, though God made provision for redemption, not all are redeemed. Likewise, though God made provision for healing, not all are healed. Why not? It is because there must be a personal appropriation of the truth of the Word of God.

ENDNOTE

1. These definitions were adapted from *Thayer's Greek Lexicon*.

Chapter 5

THE TEST OF SUFFERING

DECEIVING AND DEFEATING

There is another word used in the Bible for *testing*. Though the words are different, the objects of both are the same. In the following chapters, we are going to learn about one of the most exciting but ignored doctrines of Christian faith—suffering.

We do not hear much teaching about suffering these days. Most people do not like to hear that word because, when they do, they always connect it to the devil. The blessings and prosperity we have experienced have blinded us from some basic teachings in the Bible. Because of this, the Church has lost the power of the gospel and is in danger of becoming ineffective and lukewarm. You may ask yourself, "How can suffering be exciting?" It is not exciting to the flesh but, in the spirit and in heaven, there is a great reward.

Did you know the devil cannot defeat you? He could never defeat a born-again believer, even if he tried for a million years. He did not even defeat Adam and Eve in the Garden. He *deceived* them and they defeated themselves; he stole from them what was rightfully theirs. That is what he does to you and me in this age of grace. He deceives us and we defeat ourselves. The Bible says, *"He who is in you is greater than he who is in the world"* (1 John 4:4)

If the devil cannot *deceive* us, he cannot *defeat* us. The Bible does not use the word *defeat* in relation to a believer and the enemy.

It most commonly uses the words *deception*, *ignorance*, and *captive*. Though Christians use the word *defeat* often in their conversations, the words *defeat* or *defeated* are not mentioned in the New Testament at all concerning a believer. The only place that meaning appears is in the book of Revelation. It says the devil and his army will be defeated by the saints (see Rev. 19:17-21).

DECEPTION THROUGH IGNORANCE

Believe it or not, we defeat ourselves by our own ignorance. The devil is the master of deception and he uses our ignorance to deceive us. The Church fell into the deception of the enemy in the past centuries and defeated herself. Toward the end of his ministry, the apostle Paul warned against heresies and heretical teachers who would creep into the Church to deceive many (see Acts 20:29-30; 1 Tim. 4:1).

And that is exactly what happened. The Church went through a series of changes, transitions, alterations, wars, and fights. There is nothing you can imagine that the Church did not go through. But Jesus said He would build His Church and the gates of hell would not prevail against it (see Matt. 16:18). The Church survived every onslaught of the enemy and carnal people, and has reached a turning point in this century.

We are living in a historic era and the responsibility has come upon us to decide what type of legacy we are going to leave for the next generation. The present Church is the product of what our fathers did in the last century. What we do today will determine the future of the Church.

The Church has suffered under so many erroneous teachers and doctrines that many people do not know what to believe and what not to believe. They are confused about what is biblical and what is heretical. How much of the Old Testament should a believer in Christ obey? What are the New Testament doctrines of the Church? Are we under grace or are we under the law? What is the difference between grace and the law?

I believe God gave me this book mainly because of the teaching of "cheap grace" and the "millionaire syndrome" that is going around in the body of Christ. I want you to know I strongly believe salvation is by grace through faith and there is nothing I could do to be saved or loved by God. Any work or performance I do to be forgiven, accepted, or loved by God is self-righteousness and it is called *religion*. Anything I do to remain saved or to live a holy life based on my performance or behavior is called *legalism*.

Motivation of Goodness

There is a difference between doing good to be good rather than doing good because God made you good. Every Christian must perform good works because God made us righteous in Christ Jesus. The Bible says we are created to do good works (see Eph. 2:10). I also strongly believe that God blesses His children. He wants us to prosper in what we do, but that is not the purpose of our life on this earth.

The eternal punishment for Adamic sin was borne on the cross. Now that we are redeemed, whatever we do, whether good or evil, we will be judged or rewarded for both here on earth and in the age to come.

Paul wrote concerning this:

> *For we must all appear before the judgment seat of Christ, that each one may receive the things done in the body, according to what he has done, whether good or bad. Knowing, therefore, the terror of the Lord, we persuade men; but we are well known to God, and I also trust are well known in your consciences* (2 Corinthians 5:10-11).

And Revelation 2:23 says:

> *And all the churches shall know that I am He who searches the minds and hearts. And I will give to each one of you according to your works.*

Suffering Hardship

Another teaching that is going around in some circles is that a believer in Christ does not need to suffer any hardship on this earth because Jesus suffered for us all, and we are called only to be blessed and monetarily prosper. If that were true, most of the saints who lived in Bible times would not make it to heaven because they were not *millionaires*; they were *martyrs* for Christ.

Instead, the Bible says in 1 Peter 2:21, *"For to this you were called, because Christ also suffered for us, leaving us an example, that you should follow His steps."* Christ suffered for us and left us an example. Nowhere in the Bible do we learn that because He suffered for us we do not need to suffer. Rather, we are commanded to follow in His footsteps.

Paul exhorted the believers by saying, *"That no one should be shaken by these afflictions; for you yourselves know that we are appointed to this"* (1 Thess. 3:3).

According to this teaching, Elijah and John the Baptist would never see heaven because all John wore was camel's hair and a leather belt and he ate locusts. Yet Jesus said there was no one greater that was born of woman than John the Baptist (see Matt. 11:11). When Jesus evaluates the strength or success of a person, He does it based on how strong that person is in the spirit, not according to his personal wealth.

Prosperity and the Coming Kingdom

According to this theology, the apostles were really ignorant people because they did not enjoy the blessings God had prepared for them on this earth. Is that what really happened? Or did they know something we have not yet discovered (or purposely ignored)? Couldn't they have used some of their spiritual power or faith to obtain some material wealth on this earth?

They could have utilized their power to acquire material wealth, but they determined in their heart that it was not the time for it.

They denied the pleasures this world could offer and invested in a better life in eternity. Did you know you can only upgrade your life after death now, while still present on the earth? If you want a better position in the coming Kingdom, you need to invest in it now. You cannot do anything to improve your eternal life after you die.

The more you hoard here; the less you will have in eternity. The more you give away and invest into the Kingdom of God; the better life will be then. Things you leave here on this earth and for others will not be deposited into your account in heaven. Only what you willingly invest now into the Kingdom will go into that account.

I also strongly believe in the prosperity and blessings God gives to His children, but to be materially wealthy or to be a millionaire is not the goal of the Christian life. The Kingdom needs men like David and Joseph of Arimathea (both who were wealthy), and Elijah and John the Baptist (who were not so wealthy).

POSSESSING THE POWER

How many of you are ready to have everything God has prepared for you? The world has yet to see the Church God intended. Though we are the *body* of Christ, the world has yet to see the true manifestation of Christ through us. When Jesus was raised from the dead, all the authority in heaven and on earth was given to Him. In turn, He gave all that power and authority to the Church, which is His body (see Eph. 1:22-23). A person's strength is in his body.

Unfortunately, we do not use that power and each individual tries to do his own thing. Jesus did not give the power to an individual, but to a body, and a body is made up of more than one member. What if one part of our body tries to do what all of the body parts are supposed to do together? Not much work will get done that way. That is what is happening in the church world today. One member tries to do everything from the pulpit every Sunday and the rest of the body sits and watches for two hours.

Jesus said that if two of us agree on earth touching anything and ask in His name, then He will do it. Again, He said wherever two or three are gathered in His name He will be there (see Matt. 18:19-20). In the Old Testament, God gave power to individuals. It takes a minimum of two people to accomplish a mission for God in the New Testament.

TRUE LIFE

The future of a nation depends on the part of the Church residing in that nation, not the government. We put the responsibility on the government because we do not understand our spiritual significance and authority. We fail to recognize that the spirit world rules over the natural and the Kingdom of God rules over the kingdoms of men (Daniel 4:17). The problems we face today on earth in different nations are not political problems; they are spiritual problems. The solutions to the problems the nations face are not in the capitol buildings of those nations; they are in the house of God.

A Chinese preacher told me that it took 156 days for Hudson Taylor to reach China. In many churches today, people complain if the service is longer than an hour. They complain about the lights, chairs, sound, and the air conditioning because they are not comfortable enough. We might say the times have changed, but the truth has not.

The Church is trying to become what God has already made us. Jesus did not just forgive our sins; He made us one with Him (see 1 Cor. 6:17). Something changed in the Western Church over the last 50 years. People come to church, not to know Christ and Him crucified, but with the expectation of having a better life on this earth.

They come to church because they like the principles of Christ and the Word of God that work for their personal benefit and make them financially rich. In other parts of the world, people come to Christ to die for Him.

As a result, we have people with abundant *stuff* but no life of God manifesting through them. Jesus promised us abundant *life*, not abundant *stuff*. We misunderstand what He says. Having *life* is different from having a lot of material things. Life is different from stuff, just like joy is different from happiness and milk is different from water. Jesus said, *"I am the way, the truth, and the **life**..."* (John 14:6).

We can have abundant life without having a lot of stuff, just like we can have joy when our circumstances are contrary. The abundance of stuff around you does not determine the quality of life inside you. Rather, the quality of life inside you will determine your environment. Life in Christ is not comprised solely of the abundance of material wealth we possess (see Luke 12:15). Paul had abundant life, and even joy in the Philippian jail, and encouraged others to rejoice when every material thing was stripped off of him. That is the true abundant life.

THE COST

It costs something to be a Christian. I am not talking about paying a tithe or a membership fee here. We have nearly 7 billion people on this earth today and, out of that, 2 billion profess to know Jesus, including all forms of Christianity. That means 5 billion remain unreached, but it is not because we do not have enough Christians to spread the gospel!

In the first century, 12 ordinary men evangelized the whole known world. Their problem was that there were not enough places for them to go and preach. They accomplished something that 2 billion Christians are struggling to do with the help of all imaginable modern technology!

One hundred years ago, people came to Jesus to know Him and to make Him known. In the last 50 years, we have put ourselves first instead of the gospel or Christ. We became self-focused and self-absorbed. We say, "Let me take care of myself and make my future financially and materially secure first and then I will bless the Kingdom or do what God wants me to do." We are like the "would-be disciple" who came to Jesus and said, "I will follow you, but first let me go and bury my father" (see Luke 9:59-60). Needless to say, he could not be Jesus's disciple.

MADE FREE FROM SIN

As a result, we lost the power of the gospel. It costs only 10 percent of the money we make to be a Christian in most churches, and we indulge ourselves with the 90 percent and call it prosperity. If you are a true Christian, your life does not belong to you. God bought us with a price (see 1 Cor. 6:19-20). That means we were slaves of sin, dead in trespasses and transgressions, and people without God. Jesus paid the price and made us His own. No true Christian can say their life belongs to them.

We have been made free from sin but we have become slaves to Christ and righteousness. We do not live for ourselves, but for the One who bought us. This is what Paul was saying to the Romans:

But God be thanked that though you were slaves of sin, yet you obeyed from the heart that form of doctrine to which you were delivered. And having been set free from sin, you became slaves of righteousness.

For when you were slaves of sin, you were free in regard to righteousness....But now having been set free from sin, and having become slaves of God, you have your fruit to holiness, and the end, everlasting life (Romans 6:17-18,20,22).

When we come to Christ, to the cross, there is a crucifixion that takes place and we die to ourselves. If we are dead, we do not live for ourselves, but we live for someone else. If we want the life of the resurrection to manifest in our life, there has to be death. If there is no death, there is no resurrection. If there is no resurrection, there is no power. Paul said, *"I die daily"* (1 Cor. 15:31). We need to die to our own will and take up our cross. Accepting God's will over our will is the cross that we need to carry daily, not just on Sunday morning.

When Paul encountered Jesus, there was a death that took place. He died to all of his personal ambitions and dreams. This did not happen overnight, but was a process of many years. He reached a place in his spirit where he could say, "I have been crucified with Christ and it is no longer I that live but Christ lives in me..." (see Gal. 2:20). Again, he says, *"But God forbid that I should boast except in the cross of our Lord Jesus Christ..."* (Gal. 6:14).

THE GOAL OF THE CHRISTIAN LIFE

The goal of Christian life is not to be wealthy and famous. It is to know Christ, the power of His resurrection and the fellowship of His suffering. It is to do the will of God who saved you, bought you, and called you with a holy calling. If it is His will for you to be materially wealthy, He gave that wealth to you to use in building His Kingdom on this earth.

You and I came empty-handed to this earth and we will leave empty-handed. What is done according to the will of God will remain forever. When we come to the cross, we come to a crossroad. From there on it is either our will or God's will. We either surrender to Him or continue doing our own will and being miserable.

Whatever we try to do without Him will not produce much fruit. Whatever we pursue other than knowing Him will not satisfy us. Wherever we find pleasure and joy other than being in His presence is an idol in itself. Welcome to the journey God has prepared for you before the foundation of the world. If you keep your life for yourself, you will lose it. But if you lose your life for the sake of the gospel, you will gain it.

We live in a time when people want the prize without paying the price. They want to be promoted without passing the test. Some schools have almost eliminated tests. Tests are not something we usually enjoy, but they are necessary for growth. God has not eliminated tests from His school. He is the same yesterday, today, and forever. If you want to be promoted in the Kingdom, you need to pass some tests and go through some fires.

With the help and guidance of the Holy Spirit, this book is my humble attempt to help you prepare for the tests that are going to come into your life. You might have heard the age-old saying, "Without the cross there is no crown." I would like to add to it by saying that without passing the tests, there is no promotion. Without passing the tests, there is no spiritual growth. Without suffering, there is no glory (see Rom. 8:17).

WHAT IS SUFFERING?

By this time you might be asking, "Then what is suffering?" *Suffering* is an inconvenience, challenge, crisis, loss, or pain (both physical and emotional) you endure for the sake of your faith in God and for your love for Jesus Christ and others.

In the beginning, God created the heavens and the earth. God created the spiritual world and the natural world. He is the Author and Creator of everything we see on this earth. And everything God created was good. You do not have to leave the physical to become spiritual. When Jesus said to deny ourselves and follow Him, He did not mean to leave the physical world and follow Him. He meant to deny our selfish ambitions, prideful attitudes, and our ungodly attachments to the world, and follow His will.

God created man to be a dwelling place for Himself. Man partnered with God in the physical world and was given dominion and authority to rule over the earth. There was no suffering and sickness on this earth. Everything was perfect and peaceful.

When man committed treason against God, he lost the spiritual glory and blessings, and physical suffering entered into life on this earth. There are certain kinds of suffering that we need to go through on this earth that were established by God and no one is exempt. In the Western world, we do not hear much teaching about Christian suffering.

We tend to forget the scripture that says, *"Yes, and **all** who desire to live godly in Christ Jesus will suffer persecution"* (2 Tim. 3:12). And Philippians 1:29, which says, *"For to you it has been granted on behalf of Christ, not only to believe in Him, but also to suffer for His sake."*

The whole world is running after prosperity teaching. Then, when something goes wrong, they think they are out of the will of God or the devil is attacking them. The Bible uses different words to express different kinds of suffering, but, for now, we will use the word *suffering* until we take a more detailed look.

Suffering is not something that we purposely bring upon ourselves to become spiritual, to please God, or to gain a better place in heaven. That is not biblical teaching; those are merely afflictions imposed upon people by the religious spirit and the religious system. There are people who physically and emotionally afflict themselves for the penance of their sins and the sins of others and call it suffering for God. These are nothing but demonically inspired, self-imposed afflictions.

SPIRITUAL AND NATURAL WORLDS

The spirit world has power over the natural world. God always works in partnership with the physical world. To abstain from the physical world and from things God gave us to use is not a teaching from the Bible, it is a teaching invading the Christian world from Eastern religions. It is a form of mysticism.

Some people hear the word *suffering* and think of sickness, poverty, being maimed for your faith, or becoming a martyr for Christ. Since they do not like that word, there is a lack of teaching on the subject in the body of Christ today. Suffering for Christ is not being sick or poor. In fact, it is just the opposite. We do not need to be a slave to anything that Christ died to set us free from, and sickness and poverty are in that category.

You can be healthy and rich but you are still called to suffer for Christ.

- You do not need to suffer because of sin; Jesus became sin for us (see 2 Cor. 5:21).

- You do not need to suffer by being poor; Jesus became poor for us (see 2 Cor. 8:9).

- You do not need to suffer because of any curse; Jesus redeemed us from the curse of the law (see Gal. 3:13).

- You do not need to suffer any sickness; Jesus carried our pain and sickness on the cross (see 1 Pet. 2:24).

People today are suffering with those things for which Jesus suffered on our behalf and are trying to escape from those areas God has ordained for us to suffer. What does that mean? I have seen believers who are struggling with sin, sickness, curses, and poverty. Some have willingly accepted these as part of their spirituality and are running around looking for a miraculous escape from the things God has placed in their life to overcome.

Paul told Timothy to fight the good fight of faith and endure hardship and affliction as an evangelist (see 1 Tim. 6:12; 2 Tim. 4:5). He did not tell him to fast or to get hands laid on him so that he could be free from his afflictions. Dear child of God, there are certain struggles in your life that will not go away—they are there for you to overcome. The reward is for those who overcome (see Rev. 2:7,11,17,26; 3:5,12,21).

OVERCOMING SUFFERING

In Second Corinthians 11:23-28 Paul writes about the things he suffered and overcame. Jesus had to overcome rejection from His own brothers. Why didn't they fast and find escape from those things? Because they left an example for us. Do not wait until all your problems are over before you begin to live for God and step into what He has called you to do. It will never happen. The time to take action is now!

Jesus carried His cross and overcame this world. Likewise, we need to carry our cross and overcome this world rather than becoming a slave to this world and its system. In the process of overcoming this world and our self, we will face challenges and trials. This is called suffering.

In order to be His disciple, one must take up their cross and follow Him. The cross means suffering, pain, and shame. This is why Jesus reminds us, *"And he who does not take up his cross and follow after Me is not worthy of Me. He who finds his life will lose it, and he who loses his life for My sake will find it"* (Matt. 10:38-39).

THREE CONCEPTS OF SUFFERING

There are three concepts of suffering in the body of Christ today. The first concept says that if you are a Christian, the only thing you will have on this earth is suffering; all the blessings and good things have been stored up for us in heaven.

The second concept says that if you are truly a child of God, you will never have to go through any suffering because Christ suffered for us and now all suffering is of the devil.

I do not believe in either of the above concepts because they are both biblical truths that have been taken to an extreme. We fall into error whenever we take one truth of the Bible to an extreme.

But there is another concept that is mentioned in the Bible: as long as we live on this earth, blessing and suffering are part of our life and, through God, we have victory over suffering and challenges.

The Father loves you with the same love He has for Jesus. His love did not spare Jesus from suffering on this earth. Instead, *"He learned obedience by the things which He suffered"* (Heb. 5:8).

SIX SOURCES OF SUFFERING

The suffering we go through in our Christian life is not sickness or poverty. These are from the devil or due to our ignorance; we need to resist and fight against them. The suffering we go through in the Christian life are the afflictions we face from the following six sources:

1. The Enemy/Adversary

If you are a child of God, then you have an enemy who constantly looks for opportunities to attack and destroy you. He has three objectives: to steal, kill, and destroy (see John 10:10). But the Bible reminds us:

> Be sober, be vigilant; because your adversary the devil walks about like a roaring lion, seeking whom he may devour. Resist him, steadfast in the faith, knowing that the same sufferings are experienced by your brotherhood in the world (1 Peter 5:8-9).

There are certain kinds of suffering that come from the devil. Anything that is evil or causes pain or wounds, either emotionally or physically, is of the enemy. The devil is called a serpent and a scorpion in the Gospels—venomous creatures that inflict pain—but we have authority to trample on them (see Luke 10:19).

Paul's thorn in the flesh was one of these demons, afflicting him with physical pain through persecution wherever he went to preach. And John reminds us to be to be faithful until death in the midst of persecution, and Jesus will give us the crown of life (see Rev. 2:9-10).

The enemy uses people, demons, and the world system to afflict us, but we have authority and power over his tactics through Jesus Christ. We should not be ignorant of his devices (see 2 Cor. 2:11).

2. People

The most common form of suffering we face comes from people. People from our own family, workplace, church, or from the world will come against us in one way or another. They will hate and reject us for our faith in Christ and the blessings we receive from God. Both Christians and non-Christians will persecute us for our faith in Christ. Our relatives, and even people that we know, may become jealous of us and reject us.

But Jesus promised us: "Blessed are you when they revile and persecute you, and say all kinds of evil against you falsely for My sake. Rejoice and *be exceedingly glad, for great is your reward in heaven, for so they persecuted the prophets who were before you*" (Matt. 5:11-12).

When Jesus sent His disciples to preach, He warned them of persecution and rejection. He did not say He would spare them from it, but He told them to expect it. We would be like sheep in the midst of wolves, and *"brother will deliver up brother to death, and a father his child; and children will rise up against parents and cause them to be put to death. And you will be hated by all for My name's sake. But he who endures to the end will be saved"* (Matt. 10:21-22; see Matt. 10:16-22).

Even our own family members may become our enemies:

> Do not think that I came to bring peace on earth. I did not come to bring peace but a sword. For I have come to "set a man against his father, a daughter against her mother, and a daughter-in-law against her mother-in-law"; and "a man's enemies will be those of his own household" (Matthew 10:34-36).

> For son dishonors father, daughter rises against her mother, daughter-in-law against her mother-in-law; a man's enemies are the men of his own household (Micah 7:6).

3. The World

Though we live in this world, we are not of this world. What does this mean? It means we live in this world but we do not function and behave like the people in the world. We have a different "operating system" than others. The world and its lusts will pass away, but he who does the will of God will remain forever. Jesus said, *"In the world you will have tribulation"* (John 16:33), and, *"If the world hates you, you know that it hated Me before it hated you"* (John 15:18).

The world and its system will fight against a believer, but we are commanded to go into the world and overcome it by faith. We are warned by God not to become entangled with the things of the world:

> *Adulterers and adulteresses! Do you not know that friendship with the world is enmity with God? Whoever therefore wants to be a friend of the world makes himself an enemy of God* (James 4:4).

Why does God not want us to be connected to this world? We need to know what it means when the Bible uses the word *world*.

God's plan is that men dwell in His Kingdom on this earth. When God created Adam, He put him in the Garden of Eden, a visible form of the Kingdom of God operating on this earth. Man had everything he needed in the Garden and never had to become sick or poor. It was a place of plenty, peace, and joy. God's presence was dwelling in the Garden. He came down to commune with man every evening.

We are created to live in communion with God. As a result of disobedience and sin, man was removed from the Kingdom and began to live on his own. The devil wanted to rule this earth. He was jealous of man's relationship with God and the position he had as a result of that relationship, so he approached man with a temptation. Man gave in and the devil took over the earth and its resources.

The enemy used that opportunity and, with the cooperation of man, created a counterfeit of the Kingdom of God on this earth.

This is called the world system or the kingdom of darkness. In the last 6,000 years or so, man has been trying to re-create a substitute for what he lost in the Garden of Eden.

Every luxury and comfort that exists through this world system is an alternative to what God had originally given us. It is comprised of seven different segments: Culture, Religion, Economy, Education, Entertainment, Science and Technology, and Government. That is why Satan is known as the god of this world.

Satan uses the world system to rule over nations, regions, and people: *"For we are not fighting against flesh-and-blood enemies, but against evil rulers and authorities of the unseen world, against mighty powers in this dark world, and against evil spirits in the heavenly places"* (Eph. 6:12 NLT).

There is a difference between the earth and the world. The earth is the physical planet; the world is the system by which the earth and everything on it functions. The world and the Kingdom of God operate according to principles that are contrary to each other. They are like water and oil; it doesn't matter how much we try, they will not mix.

The world system operates against the Kingdom of God and its principles. That is why it is so difficult for us to receive the benefits of the Kingdom of God. From childhood we are programmed by the world and its system, which explains why it is difficult to reprogram our minds according to Kingdom principles. Actually, that process is called repentance, or renewing the mind.

> *Do not love the world or the things in the world. If anyone loves the world, the love of the Father is not in him. For all that is in the world—the lust of the flesh, the lust of the eyes, and the pride of life—is not of the Father but is of the world. And the world is passing away, and the lust of it; but he who does the will of God abides forever* (1 John 2:15-17).

Do not marvel, my brethren, if the world hates you (1 John 3:13).

I have given them Your word; and the world has hated them because they are not of the world, just as I am not of the world. I do not pray that You should take them out of the world, but that You should keep them from the evil one. They are not of the world, just as I am not of the world. Sanctify them by Your truth. Your word is truth. As You sent Me into the world, I also have sent them into the world (John 17:14-18).

Through Christ, we have victory over the world. We overcome the world not through living an ascetic lifestyle in a cave—the only thing that helps us overcome the world is our faith.

John writes and tells us, *"For whatever is born of God overcomes the world. And this is the victory that has overcome the world—our faith. Who is he who overcomes the world, but he who believes that Jesus is the Son of God?"* (1 John 5:4-5).

4. God

God does not afflict us with suffering. He is our loving Father, and fathers discipline their children. Just like a father chastens his children, God will chasten us—and it will not be pleasant. God prunes us so we will bear more fruit. No pruning process is enjoyable when it is happening, it is extremely painful and, at the same time, extremely necessary. Some of these things I do not need to explain. The scriptures are self-explanatory:

And you have forgotten the exhortation which speaks to you as to sons: "My son, do not despise the chastening of the Lord, nor be discouraged when you are rebuked by Him; for whom the Lord loves He chastens, and scourges every son whom He receives." If you endure chastening, God deals with you as with sons; for what son is there whom a father does not chasten? But if you are without chastening, of which all have become partakers, then you are illegitimate and not sons. Furthermore, we have had human fathers who corrected us, and we paid them respect. Shall we not much more readily be in subjection to the Father of spirits and live? For they indeed for a few days chastened us as seemed best to them, but He for our profit, that we may be partakers of His holiness. Now no chastening seems to be joyful for the present, but painful; nevertheless, afterward it yields the peaceable fruit of righteousness to those who have been trained by it (Hebrews 12:5-11).

Behold, happy is the man whom God corrects; therefore do not despise the chastening of the Almighty. For He bruises, but He binds up; He wounds, but His hands make whole (Job 5:17-18).

Paul says in Romans 8:35:

Can anything ever separate us from Christ's love? Does it mean He no longer loves us if we have trouble or calamity, or are persecuted, or hungry, or destitute, or in danger, or threatened with death? (NLT).

Moreover He called for a famine in the land; He destroyed all the provision of bread. He sent a man before them— Joseph—who was sold as a slave. They hurt his feet with fetters, he was laid in irons. Until the time that his word came to pass, the word of the Lord tested him (Psalm 105:16-19).

In this scripture we read some of the things that God did. He called for a famine to come. He destroyed all the provision of food. He sent Joseph to Egypt as a slave. It was not the enemy. God did those things to bring His purpose to pass.

In another scripture we read that He caused the Egyptians to hate the people of Israel (see Ps. 105:25). When God wants to deal with an area of our life, He will send a person to reveal that area either through a conflict, through friendship, or through His

Word. Or He will allow a circumstance to expose the area that needs to be dealt with in the light of the Scriptures. God's purpose is to expose the deception of the enemy by which we are blinded to certain truths from the Word of God.

In the New Testament, we see that when a person continually disobeyed God and walked in rebellion or habitual sin, God would hand over such a person to the enemy for the destruction of the flesh and for the salvation of his soul. At the end, this person will face a premature death, either by sickness, a sudden accident, or other means (see 1 Cor. 5:5).

5. Our Sinful Nature

Human life on this earth is a battle between good and evil. Spiritual life for us is a battle between our spirit and flesh. In our mind there is a constant battle going on between the voice of our spirit and the voice of our flesh.

Though we are saved from sin, the sinful nature we inherited from Adam still abides in our body and soul. It wars against our spirit and our mind. Romans 7:23 says, *"But I see another law in my members, warring against the law of my mind, and bringing me into captivity to the law of sin which is in my members."*

The sinful nature manifesting through the members of our body is called the flesh. There will be times when the flesh will lust against our spirit and influence us to do things we should not do.

Paul wrote to the Galatians: *"For the flesh lusts against the Spirit, and the Spirit against the flesh; and these are contrary to one another, so that you do not do the things that you wish"* (Gal. 5:17).

The solution to the suffering that we face through our sinful nature is to walk in the Spirit: *"I say then: Walk in the Spirit, and you shall not fulfill the lust of the flesh"* (Gal. 5:16).

To walk in the Spirit means to obey the promptings of your spirit and live your life according to the Word of God. Galatians 5:24-25 says, *"And those who are Christ's have crucified the flesh with its passions and desires. If we live in the Spirit, let us also walk in the Spirit."*

6. Harvest of Our Own Actions

There are things we suffer on this earth as consequences of our own decisions and actions. Life is a total sum of the decisions we make. Every decision carries repercussions. We are spiritual beings with willpower and are able to make choices based on our judgment. Some suffering comes because we did not make wise choices in life.

When you buy a house and you do not know what is involved with signing a loan agreement, you will face some challenges down the road. God is not to be blamed for that. It was your responsibility to study the details. If you venture out to do something new and do not account for what it is going to cost and how long it is going to take, you are asking for trouble. Jesus said to count the cost before you go out to battle against an enemy (see Luke 14:31).

The Bible says we will reap whatever we sow (see Gal. 6:7). Abraham made a poor choice while he was waiting for the fulfillment of God's promise. He listened to his wife's counsel and had a baby by her maid. The whole family suffered for it; the whole world is still suffering as part of the consequence of his action.

We cannot blame God, the devil, or others for the consequences of our actions. We need to take responsibility. That is why, before we make a major decision or commitment, we need to collect all of the information so we can avoid unnecessary trouble.

FOUR REASONS FOR SUFFERING

1. For Righteousness' Sake

Jesus said, *"Blessed are those who are persecuted for righteousness' sake, for theirs is the kingdom of heaven"* (Matt. 5:10).

Anyone who did the will of God on this earth went through great trials and suffering. Suffering is a doctrine of the Bible and is applicable to every New Testament believer. We cannot just ignore it by saying we are the people of faith. One of the reasons faith was given to us is to overcome the world. Hebrews 11 is the "hall of fame" of the people of faith and tells us the circumstances people overcame by their faith. The purpose of faith is not only to receive from God, but also to overcome the circumstances of this world.

It is unfortunate that when we hear about someone being imprisoned or beaten for preaching the gospel, we think they must be going through those things because of their lack of faith, or because they "missed" God on something, or were disobedient. That would mean Paul was totally out of the will of God most of the time. First-century Christians believed it was a privilege to suffer for Jesus (see Acts 5:41). We need to get free from our self-preservation and security and serve the One to whom we belong with all of our heart.

Why do we believe in Jesus? Is it to benefit ourselves and fatten our pockets while we are on this earth? Will an unbeliever come to Christ by observing our conduct and seeing Christ in us? Or do we have to scare them with hell and damnation or lure them with our *new* blessings to get them to receive Christ?

This world is not going to come to Jesus by seeing our prosperity. But they will come if we live a selfless life, help them sacrificially, and show them the love of Jesus through our actions. Peter writes:

> *For what credit is it if, when you are beaten for your faults, you take it patiently? But when you do good and suffer, if you take it patiently, this is commendable before God. For to this you were called, because Christ also suffered for us, leaving us an example, that you should follow His steps: "Who committed no sin, nor was deceit found in His mouth"* (1 Peter 2:20-22).*
>
> *But even if you should suffer for righteousness' sake, you are blessed. "And do not be afraid of their threats, nor be*

troubled." But sanctify the Lord God in your hearts, and always be ready to give a defense to everyone who asks you a reason for the hope that is in you, with meekness and fear; having a good conscience, that when they defame you as evildoers, those who revile your good conduct in Christ may be ashamed. For it is better, if it is the will of God, to suffer for doing good than for doing evil (1 Peter 3:14-17).

When we read the testimony of Paul the apostle, we see the things he endured in order to fulfill his call:

We give no offense in anything, that our ministry may not be blamed. But in all things we commend ourselves as min-isters of God: in much patience, in tribulations, in needs, in distresses, in stripes, in imprisonments, in tumults, in labors, in sleeplessness, in fastings; by purity, by knowledge, by longsuffering, by kindness, by the Holy Spirit, by sincere love, by the word of truth, by the power of God, by the armor of righteousness on the right hand and on the left, by honor and dishonor, by evil report and good report; as deceivers, and yet true; as unknown, and yet well known; as dying, and behold we live; as chastened, and yet not killed; as sor-rowful, yet always rejoicing; as poor, yet making many rich; as having nothing, and yet possessing all things (2 Corin-thians 6:3-10).

"Well," you might say, "Paul's call was different from mine and he was called to suffer." Let us see what he says to other believers who became Christians through his ministry.

And when they had preached the gospel to that city and made many disciples, they returned to Lystra, Iconium, and Antioch, strengthening the souls of the disciples, exhort-ing them to continue in the faith, and saying, "We must through many tribulations enter the kingdom of God" (Acts 14:21-22).

And in Second Thessalonians 1:3-4, he says:

We are bound to thank God always for you, brethren, as it is fitting, because your faith grows exceedingly, and the love of every one of you all abounds toward each other, so that we ourselves boast of you among the churches of God for your patience and faith in all your persecutions and tribulations that you endure.

According to this scripture, our faith and love grow in the midst of persecution and tribulation. Suffering is a call for every generation; not just the first century believers. *"For to you it has been granted on behalf of Christ, not only to believe in Him, but also to suffer for His sake"* (Phil. 1:29).

2. Punishment for Doing Evil

The Bible also talks about suffering because we are being punished for our rebellion against God's authority or governmental authority; or reaping the consequences of our own bad habits.

For what credit is it if, when you are beaten for your faults, you take it patiently? But when you do good and suffer, if you take it patiently, this is commendable before God (1 Peter 2:20).

Therefore whoever resists the authority resists the ordinance of God, and those who resist will bring judgment on themselves. For rulers are not a terror to good works, but to evil. Do you want to be unafraid of the authority? Do what is good, and you will have praise from the same. For he is God's minister to you for good. But if you do evil, be afraid; for he does not bear the sword in vain; for he is God's minister, an avenger to execute wrath on him who practices evil (Romans 13:2-4).

3. The Trial of Our Faith

That the genuineness of your faith, being much more precious than gold that perishes, though it is tested by fire, may be found to praise, honor, and glory at the revelation of Jesus Christ (1 Peter 1:7).

The third reason we go through trials and suffering is because God tests our faith. The reason He tests our faith is to make us healthy in that area. There is healthy faith and there is weak faith. Weak faith cannot withstand the storms of life. When the disciples were in the boat with Jesus, they were afraid of the wind and storm. But after Jesus calmed the sea and storm, He pointed out the disciples' lack of faith (see Luke 8:24-25).

What does this mean? It means their faith had sufficient power to overcome that storm but it did not benefit them because their perception of faith was weak at the time. The faith God gave us is enough to sustain us through any problems we face. Paul told Titus to rebuke the Cretans so they would become healthy in their faith (see Titus 1:13).

How do we know if our faith is healthy or not? Listen to what you say while you are going through your trials. The disciples in the boat were afraid and cried out for help. They could not overcome the storm; instead of overcoming the storm, the storm overcame them. God will let us go through trials until we learn to stay in faith and speak *to* our storms, instead of speaking *about* the storms. A healthy faith will speak positively in accordance with God's Word regardless of the circumstances or feelings.

This is why James writes: *"My brethren, count it all joy when you fall into various trials, knowing that the testing of your faith produces patience"* (James 1:2-3).

4. It Is the Will of God for Us to Suffer

The scriptures below make it very clear that God has appointed blessings and suffering as part of a Christian's life on this earth.

*Therefore let those who **suffer according to the will of God** commit their souls to Him in doing good, as to a faithful Creator* (1 Peter 4:19).

For it is better, if it is the will of God, to suffer for doing good than for doing evil (1 Peter 3:17).

For you have been given not only the privilege of trusting in Christ but also the privilege of suffering for Him (Philippians 1:29 NLT).

In Acts 14:21-22, Paul *"returned to Lystra, Iconium, and Antioch, strengthening the souls of the disciples, exhorting them to continue in the faith, and saying, 'We must through many tribulations enter the kingdom of God.'"*

The disciples asked Jesus what their reward would be for following Him and leaving everything they had.

Then Peter began to say to Him, "See, we have left all and followed You."

So Jesus answered and said, "Assuredly, I say to you, there is no one who has left house or brothers or sisters or father or mother or wife or children or lands, for My sake and the gospel's, **who shall not receive a hundredfold now in this time—houses and brothers and sisters and mothers and children and lands, with persecutions—and in the age to come, eternal life** (Mark 10:28-30).

HOW LONG DO WE NEED TO SUFFER?

The Bible says we are to suffer for a little while.

In this you greatly rejoice, though now for a little while, if need be, you have been grieved by various trials (1 Peter 1:6).

Be sober, be vigilant; because your adversary the devil walks about like a roaring lion, seeking whom he may devour. Resist him, steadfast in the faith, knowing that the same sufferings are experienced by your brotherhood in the world. But may the God of all grace, who called us to His eternal glory by Christ Jesus, after you have suffered a while, perfect, establish, strengthen, and settle you. To Him be the glory and the dominion forever and ever. Amen (1 Peter 5:8-11).

*For our **light affliction**, which is but for **a moment**, is working for us a far more exceeding and eternal weight of glory, while we do not look at the things which are seen, but at the things which are not seen. For the things which are seen are temporary, but the things which are not seen are eternal* (2 Corinthians 4:17-18).

THE PURPOSES OF SUFFERING

1. To Make Us Perfect

Hebrews 2:10 says, *"For it was fitting for Him, for whom are all things and by whom are all things, in bringing many sons to glory, to make the captain of their salvation perfect through sufferings."*

When the Bible talks about perfection, it is not talking about a behavioral or physical perfection, or a point in life when you will never think or do anything wrong or negative. Only certain areas of our life will be perfected while we are on this earth. For instance, our spirit man is perfect in Him:

> *But may the God of all grace, who called us to His eternal glory by Christ Jesus, after you have suffered a while, **perfect**, **establish**, **strengthen**, and **settle** you. To Him be the glory and the dominion forever and ever. Amen* (1 Peter 5:10-11).

The above scripture talks about the four benefits of suffering: to perfect, establish, strengthen, and settle us. Jesus said, *"Be perfect as your Father in heaven is perfect"* (Matt. 5:48). God lets us go through things in life to perfect our character. For Him to make us perfect in our character, we need to first be perfected in patience and longsuffering.

When we hear the word *perfect*, we usually think about our behavior and not doing anything wrong. I do not think we can achieve that kind of perfection in this life. God will not ask us to do or be something we are not able to do or be. I believe that when the Word says be perfect as our heavenly Father is perfect, it is not talking about our behavior but about our attitude when we go through trials. God is not moved by anything that happens on this earth; He is unshakable. He does not panic or get stressed out about anything.

I believe we can achieve that kind of perfection on this earth. Paul was such a man—what happened to him did not shake his revelation of who he was in Christ. He was immovable; trials and persecutions did not change his attitude. Though he knew beforehand what would happen to him, he went straight ahead to face them (see Acts 20).

Paul wrote in First Corinthians 15:58 to *"be steadfast, immovable."* Such strength comes through unshakable trust in God. In order to trust God like that, we need to know Him and His character. That is why the Bible says to taste and see that the Lord is good (see Ps. 34:8). Only those who have tasted the Lord can really say that He is good all the time.

2. To Teach Us Obedience

Hebrews 5:8 says, *"Though He was a Son, yet He learned obedience by the things which He suffered."*

Sometimes we will not obey God until we go through something. The more obedience requires the death of our flesh, the more we will resist obeying God. The more it requires us to trust God to obey Him, the more likely we are to delay in our obedience.

Jonah was asked to go to Nineveh to deliver an oracle against the city. He disobeyed God and went to Tarshish instead. He disobeyed God because he knew God wanted to show His mercy to the people in that city. The people of Ninevah were wicked and they did not like the Israelites. Jonah did not like the idea of showing mercy to them. He did not know God well enough. He doubted that God was able to protect him from the people while he obeyed His voice. The main reason we do not obey God is because we do not trust Him. The reason we do not trust Him is because we do not know Him enough.

Even though Jesus was the Son of God, He needed to learn obedience through the things He suffered. If the Son of God had to suffer to learn obedience, we better get ready to go through some stuff!

3. To Cease From Sin

Therefore, since Christ suffered for us in the flesh, arm your-selves also with the same mind, for he who has suffered in the flesh has ceased from sin, that he no longer should live the rest of his time in the flesh for the lusts of men, but for the will of God (1 Peter 4:1-2).

As we grow and mature in Christ, there are certain sins that no longer influence our lives. We will master them and will no longer be a slave to them. If you still have the same challenges you had when you were first born again, that means you have not spiritually grown much. God expects us to grow and mature to reach the full stature of Christ.

4. To Be Glorified With Him

And if children, then heirs—heirs of God and joint heirs with Christ, if indeed we suffer with Him, that we may also be glorified together.

For I consider that the sufferings of this present time are not worthy to be compared with the glory which shall be revealed in us. For the earnest expectation of the creation eagerly waits for the revealing of the sons of God (Romans 8:17-19).

And Romans 8:30 says, *"Moreover whom He predestined, these He also called; whom He called, these He also justified, and whom He justified, these He also glorified."*

5. To Learn to Comfort Others

Blessed be the God and Father of our Lord Jesus Christ, the Father of mercies and God of all comfort, who comforts us in all our tribulation, that we may be able to comfort those who are in any trouble, with the comfort with which we ourselves are comforted by God. For as the sufferings of Christ abound in us, so our consolation also abounds through Christ. Now if we are afflicted, it is for your consolation and salvation, which is effective for enduring the same sufferings which we also suffer. Or if we are comforted, it is for your consolation and salvation. And our hope for you is steadfast, because we know that as you are partakers of the sufferings, so also you will partake of the consolation (2 Corinthians 1:3-7).

Unless we suffer in a particular area, we will not have compassion for people who are going through that suffering. God allows us to suffer so that we will be effective in ministering to others. Unless we personally experience what others go through, we will not be effective when we minister to them. The Bible says one of the reasons Jesus is able to help us when we are in trouble is because He suffered and was tempted in every area we will ever suffer in or be tempted. Hebrews 4:15-16 says:

For we do not have a High Priest who cannot sympathize with our weaknesses, but was in all points tempted as we are, yet without sin. Let us therefore come boldly to the throne of grace, that we may obtain mercy and find grace to help in time of need.

6. To Partake of His Holiness

Furthermore, we have had human fathers who corrected us, and we paid them respect. Shall we not much more readily be in subjection to the Father of spirits and live? For they indeed for a few days chastened us as seemed best to them, but He for our profit, **that we may be partakers of His holiness.** *Now no chastening seems to be joyful for the present,*

but painful; nevertheless, afterward it yields the peaceable
fruit of righteousness to those who have been trained by it
(Hebrews 12:9-11).

Prior to gaining biblical revelation and perspective, I could not believe the above scripture because I had heard the religious people saying, "God punishes us to make us more holy." I had to change my mind about this particular thought. God does chastise us to partake of His holiness, but He doesn't punish us out of spite or wrathful intention.

God wants us to be holy as He is holy. Holiness does not mean being white or wearing something white. Many in the religious circles think that if they wear something white they will *look* or be holy. The Bible does not teach such heresy. God is holy but not because He wears a white robe. Being holy means that in our thoughts, words, and conduct we are like Jesus.

That does not come naturally. Sin brought an evil nature into our lives and we are prone to think, speak, and act negatively. So God allows us to go through some fire to burn that nature off of our life until all that remains is the Word of God.

7. To Manifest God's Wisdom

There are people, like Job, who God appoints to go through afflictions in order to prove to the enemy man's faithfulness to Him. Most people will not go through such trials and remain faithful to God. Job is an example of a person that God could trust to remain faithful regardless of what he went through.

One of the purposes of the Church is to reveal the manifold wisdom of God to the principalities and powers (see Eph. 3:10). In the Old Testament, God chose Job to manifest His wisdom to Satan and his kingdom. In the New Testament, God chose Paul to reveal His wisdom and patience to principalities and powers. Paul said that the suffering he endured was designed to complete what was lacking in the afflictions of Christ (see Col. 1:24-26).

Chapter 6

TEN KINDS OF SUFFERING

There are specific reasons why God allows us to go through different types of suffering. Each kind of suffering is planned to develop a different area of our character and heart. When we discipline our children, we do it to make their life better when they grow up. No loving parent would ever chastise his child without cause—that would be insanity. That is why the Scripture says that all things work together for our good (see Rom. 8:28).

God does not waste any event in our life. He will use each one to accomplish a divine purpose. We are going to look at each of these ten kinds of suffering to see what specific purpose it accomplishes in our life.

TEMPTATION

Temptation does not come from God—He does not tempt us. Temptation can come when we are drawn by with our own desires of the flesh. When the enemy recognizes that, he brings an opportunity in order to entice us to fulfill those desires and lusts. When we are tempted, we need to endure and not yield to it. When we yield to the temptation, the enemy uses the opportunity to entice us to sin further. God utilizes the temptation as a means of revealing and destroying the enemy's strongholds in our lives. It also shows us what we are really made of.

James writes to the Church:

Blessed is the man who endures temptation; for when he has been approved, he will receive the crown of life which the Lord has promised to those who love Him. Let no one say when he is tempted, "I am tempted by God"; for God cannot be tempted by evil, nor does He Himself tempt anyone. But each one is tempted when he is drawn away by his own desires and enticed. Then, when desire has conceived, it gives birth to sin; and sin, when it is full-grown, brings forth death (James 1:12-15).

Though God does not tempt us and He is not the source of temptation, sometimes He will allow the enemy to tempt us to see whether we are real and ready for the things of God. We see in the Gospels that the Holy Spirit led Jesus into the wilderness to be tempted by the devil. The Holy Spirit did not tempt Jesus; He led Jesus. The devil tempted Him.

Jesus was tempted in every manner, yet without sin. We will be tempted in different areas by the enemy. Temptation is one form of suffering. As long as we live in this fallen world with our mortal body, we will be tempted in different areas of our life. God does not tempt us, but He will *test* us.

When Jesus taught the disciples to pray, He taught them to pray not to be led into temptation (see Matt. 6:13). How do we clarify this? In one place the Bible says the Holy Spirit led Jesus into temptation and a few verses later Jesus is telling us to pray not to be led into temptation.

Two Kinds of Temptation

There are two kinds of temptation: one is led by the Holy Spirit, and the other is enticed by our own fleshly desires and lusts (see James 1:14).

The word *temptation* means to try or test before making a public show. It is the same meaning as when a product is made and the company tests it by putting it through adverse terrain, temperatures, or circumstances to see whether it will withstand them. So, once it reaches the public, the success of the product depends on how much adversity it can handle, or how long it can run without breaking down.

God in His wisdom will do the same with us. Before He puts us out there saying we are His ambassadors and representatives, He will let us go through some testing to see whether we are able to remain faithful when things go wrong or when the world and its lusts tempt us.

If we judge ourselves, then God will not judge us. Paul tells us to test ourselves (see 2 Cor. 13:5), and, if we judge ourselves, we will not be judged by God (1 Cor. 11:31).

God allows the enemy to tempt us to see if there is anything in us that belongs to him. If there is anything in us that belongs to the enemy, we will fall prey to his deceptions. We will be tempted in the same area more than once, until we mature in that area and that particular temptation is no longer a threat to our spiritual well-being. Jesus did not have anything that belonged to the enemy in Him and the enemy was defeated. He said, *"For the ruler of this world is coming, and he has nothing in Me"* (John 14:30).

Any time you feel like operating in any of the works of the flesh (see Gal. 5:19-21), that is a temptation. Anger, lust, wrath, strife, pride, offense, etc., are some of the areas in which we will be tempted by the enemy to yield. When we yield to any one of these temptations, we will bring forth sin and sin eventually will bring forth death.

How do you know the difference between the two temptations? With the temptation that God allows in our life, He always provides a way out. The temptation that comes from our fleshly nature we need to deliberately endure by the grace of God (see James 1:12).

Paul reminds us, *"No temptation has overtaken you except such as is common to man; but God is faithful, who will not allow you to be tempted beyond what you are able, but with the temptation will also make the way of escape, that you may be able to bear it"* (1 Cor. 10:13).

And Peter says, *"The Lord knows how to deliver the godly out of temptations"* (2 Pet. 2:9).

The key to overcoming temptation is through prayer (see Matt. 6:9-13; 26:41).

PERSECUTION

In many parts of the world, Christians are persecuted because of their faith in Christ. In India, when a person comes to Christ from Hindu or other religious backgrounds, sometimes all hell breaks loose. His or her own family and community will often disown and forsake them.

Persecution comes from other people who do not believe what we believe. It can come from an individual or a group of people. Paul told Timothy, *"Yes, and **all** who desire to live godly in Christ Jesus will suffer persecution"* (2 Tim. 3:12).

He did not say some, or a few in certain parts of the world, but *all*. That includes everyone and everywhere, including both you and me.

There are different kinds of persecution, and not all of us will be persecuted the same way. The purpose of persecution is to establish our faith in Christ and make us a stronger witness for Him. In any culture where there was a lot of persecution, the Church and believers grew stronger and became a mighty force. The opposite was also true—where there was no persecution, the Church grew weaker and was swallowed up by the world or became a mere form of religion (see Matt. 13:20-21).

Another opportunity for persecution and tribulation to come is when you receive a Word from God. A vision or a dream from

God can sometimes bring persecution or tribulation. This means other people will come against you because they do not understand you. The best example is Joseph in the Old Testament. God gave him a dream for his future, but when he shared that with his brothers, they persecuted him. Such persecution can come from a community, a family member, or from a particular denomination or religion.

When persecution arises against us because of the Word or our faith, we need to stand strong and follow the example of Christ and others who have gone before us. There are also different types of persecution.

Verbal Persecution

This is when people say all kinds of false things about us and propagate evil reports against us through any type of media. Jesus said:

> *Blessed are you when they revile and persecute you, and say all kinds of evil against you falsely for My sake. Rejoice and be exceedingly glad, for great is your reward in heaven, for so they persecuted the prophets who were before you* (Matthew 5:11-12).

Rejection

Rejection is when people hesitate to associate or fellowship with you. Communities and cultures will reject people because of their faith in Christ. I have a friend who became a Christian from a Hindu background, and the shops near his home would not sell anything to him because he became a Christian.

Physical Persecution

This is when people hurt you physically because of your faith in Christ. Beating, stoning, burning, imprisonment, and any other form of punishment that involves physical pain is also a type of physical persecution.

Paul was persecuted for his faith in almost every place he preached. That was his thorn in the flesh. He asked the Lord to remove it from him, but Jesus said *"My grace is sufficient for you, for My strength is made perfect in weakness."* Paul then said, *"Therefore most gladly I will rather boast in my infirmities, that the power of Christ may rest upon me"* (2 Cor. 12:9).

Death

Stephen was the first martyr in the New Testament. Now, hundreds of people are being killed every day because of their faith in Christ. Jesus told the disciples, *"Then they will deliver you up to tribulation and kill you, and you will be hated by all nations for My name's sake"* (Matt. 24:9).

To remain faithful when you are persecuted, ask God for the grace to endure it. The key to overcoming persecution is praising and rejoicing in the Lord (see Acts 16:25; Phil. 4:4).

TRIBULATION

There are two kinds of tribulation mentioned in the Bible: the tribulation that every believer experiences on this earth and the Great Tribulation, which is mentioned in the book of Revelation. Tribulation occurs when the world systems, governments, and other political organizations come against Christians to persecute them, to stop the growth of the Church and the preaching of the gospel, and to interfere with the everyday life of Christians. The purpose of tribulation is evident in Romans 5:3-5:

> *And not only that, but we also glory in tribulations, knowing that tribulation produces perseverance; and perseverance, character; and character, hope. Now hope does not disappoint, because the love of God has been poured out in our hearts by the Holy Spirit who was given to us.*

There is a difference between patience and perseverance. *Persevere* means "to persist in a state of life, in the pursuit of an end, or especially in an enterprise undertaken in spite of counter influences, opposition, or discouragement."[1] Tribulations produce perseverance, and perseverance produces character. Trials produce patience, and patience produces contentment, a place where you lack nothing.

Jesus promised us in John 16:33, *"These things I have spoken to you, that in Me you may have peace. In the world you will have tribulation; but be of good cheer, I have overcome the world."*

Tribulation is the emotional and mental pressure we feel from the world system and the god of this world when they come against us to oppress our mind and spirit.

We are to be patient in tribulation: *"Rejoicing in hope, patient in tribulation, continuing steadfastly in prayer"* (Rom. 12:12). It is interesting to see this verse written by Paul to those believers who were in Rome, where, at the time, the Roman government was not favorable toward Christians. Tribulation comes from the world in the form of persecution, harassment, rejection, and oppression against Christians. Jesus said the world will hate us for His sake (see Luke 6:22).

First Thessalonians 3:4 says, *"For, in fact, we told you before when we were with you that we would suffer tribulation, just as it happened, and you know."*

The key to overcoming tribulation is to be patient (see Rom. 12:12).

SUFFERING

Suffering comes in various forms. It is a combined word used for all of the other kinds of challenges we go through as Christians. The purpose of suffering is to know Christ and experience what He went through while He was on this earth. When we suffer, we fellowship with *His* suffering (see Phil. 3:10).

Peter writes:

Beloved, do not think it strange concerning the fiery trial which is to try you, as though some strange thing happened to you; but rejoice to the extent that you partake of Christ's sufferings, that when His glory is revealed, you may also be glad with exceeding joy. If you are reproached for the name of Christ, blessed are you, for the Spirit of glory and of God rests upon you. On their part He is blasphemed, but on your part He is glorified (1 Peter 4:12-14).

And Hebrews 10:32-33 says:

But recall the former days in which, after you were illuminated, you endured a great struggle with sufferings: partly while you were made a spectacle both by reproaches and tribulations, and partly while you became companions of those who were so treated.

The key to overcoming suffering is fellowship with Christ on a daily basis (see Phil. 3:10).

CHASTENING OF THE LORD

There is another kind of suffering that the Bible talks about and that we go through as Christians. God is our Father and we are His sons and daughters. Every parent who loves their children disciplines them. The reason we discipline them is to develop them so they will become mature.

Just as with natural parenting, if we say nice things and be nice to our children all the time, they have a tendency to take advantage of it and not do what they are supposed to do or show us respect as they ought. When they get like that and disobey their parents, they need to be corrected and disciplined. It is painful for them at that time but, as parents, we know it is for their good that we discipline them.

The same principle applies in the Spirit. God is our Father and He corrects and disciplines us for our good: *"If you endure chastening, God deals with you as with sons; for what son is there whom a father does not chasten? But if you are without chastening, of which all have become partakers, then you are illegitimate and not sons"* (Heb. 12:7-8).

The key to overcoming chastening is to abide in the Father's love (see Prov. 3:11-12).

TRIALS

James tells us to rejoice when we fall into various trials (see James 1:2-4). Trials come to develop patience in us. They are challenges, obstacles, delays, betrayals, and problems that we face in our day-to-day life. They come to bring out the character of God in us. But temptation is used by God to take out of us what belongs to the enemy.

When we have patience, we will be perfect, complete, and lack nothing. There are only two real needs in our life: wisdom and patience. *Patience* means "the capacity or habit of enduring evil, adversity, or pain with fortitude"; or to have "forbearance under stress, provocation, or indignity."[2]

The key to overcoming each trial is to endure it by faith.

REVELING AND REPROACHES

Reveling comes from other people and is an emotional persecution. It includes mockery, rejection, ridicule, and reproaches; it's things people say about you because of your faith in God, mission in life, or because you are doing something no one in your family or community has ever done. In other words, you are stepping out of the boat. The purpose of reveling is to develop our self-control in the area of our hearing and speaking. The Bible says we are to be quick to hear and slow to speak (see James 1:19).

And Jesus called us blessed: *"Blessed are you when they revile and persecute you, and say all kinds of evil against you falsely for My sake. Rejoice and be exceedingly glad, for great is your reward in heaven, for so they persecuted the prophets who were before you"* (Matt. 5:11-12).

The key to overcoming reveling and reproaches is to keep an eternal perspective.

AFFLICTIONS

Some believe that the Old Testament saints were pilgrims who did not possess any material wealth on this earth. They say this because they misunderstand Hebrews 11:13, which says that when the Old Testament saints died, they confessed they were pilgrims and strangers on this earth. It does not say they lived like pilgrims, but they *confessed* they were pilgrims on their deathbed. Some say this teaches that they were nomads, homeless, and poor. That is far from the truth.

All of the Old Testament saints were wealthy. Some of them were the wealthiest people of their time (Abraham, see Gen. 13:1-2; Isaac, see Gen. 25; Jacob, see Gen. 32; and Job, see Job 1:3). And First Chronicles 22 gives an account of the wealth David collected to build the temple. This is one man's donation to the work of God—he was neither poor nor sick.

But they all went through trials and afflictions:

> Lord, *remember David and all his afflictions; how he swore to the Lord, and vowed to the Mighty One of Jacob: "Surely I will not go into the chamber of my house, or go up to the comfort of my bed; I will not give sleep to my eyes or slumber to my eyelids, until I find a place for the Lord, a dwelling place for the Mighty One of Jacob"* (Psalm 132:1-5).

In the Psalms, we read about how David's enemies afflicted him. He went through depression, discouragement, and betrayal several times in his life.

Moses went through afflictions in his life as well. When the Bible talks about affliction, it is not talking about poverty or sickness. Most of the time, it is talking about problems and challenges that are caused by other people. *Affliction* is anguish or distress we experience in our life and it is mainly an emotional state.

> *Many are the afflictions of the righteous, but the Lord delivers him out of them all* (Psalm 34:19).

> *But you be watchful in all things, endure afflictions, do the work of an evangelist, fulfill your ministry* (2 Timothy 4:5).

> *And though the Lord gives you the bread of adversity and the water of affliction...* (Isaiah 30:20).

> *That no one should be shaken by these afflictions; for you yourselves know that we are appointed to this* (1 Thessalonians 3:3).

The key to overcoming affliction is to endure.

TESTS

This book is entirely about this particular subject and I do not need to expound much here. The key to overcoming each test is to employ the wisdom of God.

ADVERSITIES

Adversity comes in the form of hindrances, obstacles, accusations, and opposition you face in the natural from people when you do the will of God. Adversity could also be demonically influenced or initiated.

Psalm 38:20 says, *"Those also who render evil for good, they are my adversaries, because I follow what is good."* And First Corinthians 16:9 says, *"For a great and effective door has opened to me, and there are many adversaries."*

When you trust in God, He will turn your adversaries and adversities to your advantage: *"For I will give you a mouth and wisdom which all your adversaries will not be able to contradict or resist"* (Luke 21:15).

The key to overcoming adversaries is to trust in the Lord (see 1 Pet. 2:22-23).

ENDNOTES

1. "persevere." *Webster's Third New International Dictionary, Unabridged.* Merriam-Webster, 2002. http://unabridged. merriam-webster.com (30 Apr. 2012).

2. "patience." *Webster's Third New International Dictionary, Unabridged.* Merriam-Webster, 2002. http://unabridged. merriam-webster.com (30 Apr. 2012).

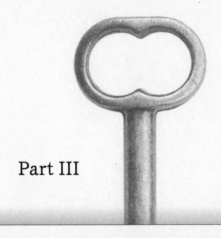

Part III

EXAMPLES OF SPIRITUAL TESTS

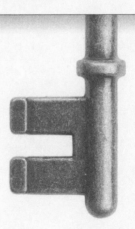

Chapter 7

THE TESTS OF THE ISRAELITES IN THE WILDERNESS

INHERITING THE PROMISES

There is no other example in the Old Testament that has more hidden revelation concerning our life as a Christian and God's ways than the deliverance of the Israelites from Egypt and their subsequent journey to the Promise Land. Everything they went through has a spiritual meaning for our life in Christ Jesus.

If we study and keep those lessons in our heart, we will not stumble as Christians in our daily walk. Their life and experience is a spiritual roadmap to our salvation and our life after salvation. Whatever they experienced in the natural, we will experience in the spirit. Paul is very clear about this when he writes:

Now these things [everything that happened to the people of Israel] *became our examples, to the intent that we should not lust after evil things as they also lusted....Now all these things happened to them as examples, and they were written for our admonition, upon whom the ends of the ages have come* (1 Corinthians 10:6,11).

The Israelites were the "Church in the Wilderness," and God was taking them to a land that flowed with milk and honey. The

Bible says there were 600,000 men, plus women and children. They had to pass some tests on their way to inheriting the promises.

They had a divine destiny, just as you and I do. God tested them in the wilderness to see how many would listen to His voice and walk by faith and not by sight. Only two made it through the wilderness, Joshua and Caleb. It is not much different in the Church today. Most believers are falling short of their Promise Land (destiny) that God has given them in Christ.

THE WILDERNESS

*And you shall remember that the Lord your God led you all the way these forty years in the wilderness, **to humble** you and **test** you, to **know what was in your heart**, whether you would keep His commandments or not* (Deuteronomy 8:2).

The moment you are saved, you are God's property. From that moment He is in control of whatever happens in your life. When the "honeymoon" of the salvation experience is over, God takes each believer to a place called the *wilderness* to be tested.

Deuteronomy 8:2 reveals the way God works. First, He takes us to a place called the *wilderness* to humble and test us. The purpose of the humbling and testing is to know what is in our heart and whether or not we will obey His commandments and believe His Word when things are not going the way we would like them to go. Do you want to know what is really in your heart and whether you believe His Word? Watch what comes into your mind (internal communication) and out of your mouth, and check your attitude toward His Word the next time you are tested or humbled.

Most believers are living in some form of extremism. Some are too "holy" and not good for anything on this earth. Others are too poor and have accepted their poverty as part of their spirituality. Others are too rich and they live like this earth is their final destination. Others are too heavenly-minded and have lost sight of their purpose on this earth. And still others live as if they are married to the world and money is their nearest kin. They have no vision for the Kingdom of God. The only thing we should live to the extreme is our love and faith toward God and our love for others.

These are all people who are stuck in the wilderness and do not know how to get out. The Bible says, *"All Scripture is given by inspiration of God…that the man of God may be complete, thoroughly equipped for every good work"* (2 Tim. 3:16-17). This is God's will for every single believer, that we will be equipped to do every good work. We are created by God for good works (see Eph. 2:10).

A Different Mindset

They did not fully understand that they could not enter the Promise Land with the same mindset and spiritual understanding they had when they were in Egypt. Right after they were delivered from Egypt, God took Israel to a special university called the *wilderness* to train and equip them to enter and inherit the Promise Land. There were valuable lessons and tests they had to learn and pass in order to graduate and enter Canaan. This was a time of intensive training where God taught His people practically about everything concerning their life.

He taught them about warfare (see Ex. 13:17), business, parenting, relationships, worship, finances, civil laws, how to relate to and respect God, social life, personal hygiene, leadership, self-control, dietary rules, the husband and wife relationship, etc. Everything you can imagine about life on this earth, God taught them while they were in this university of the wilderness.

Unfortunately, only two went through the training successfully and passed all the tests. All of the others failed and perished in the wilderness. There were 600,000 men, plus women and children, which would be about 3 million people who went through this training.

We might feel sad when we read their story, but the truth of the matter is that we are in the same school and are going through those same tests daily. After we are saved, we also may have a great dream about our future, but God takes us into a place in the spirit called the *wilderness*. We may even go through times when our basic needs are not being met.

You might have believed in God because you heard that He is good and will provide for your every need. Then, when you believed, all of a sudden your source of income was taken away, or unexpected challenges and crises came into your life. That means you are in the wilderness and are being tested by the Lord.

The good news for us is that God has not changed the curriculum or the tests. He still uses the 4,000-year-old syllabus (we may call Him old school) and tests for everyone He chooses to train. Only the location, environment, and teachers of His university have changed. The syllabus, tests, name, the Founder and President of the university—these are the same as they were when the Israelites were in the University of the Wilderness.

We are more privileged than they because we can learn from their experience and avoid making the same mistakes. So we can get through the training a lot faster than they did. Sadly, however, many Christians are going through their life the same way the Israelites did in the wilderness. Many die without entering the place of their destiny.

Reasons We Fail

> *Therefore, since we are surrounded by such a huge crowd of witnesses to the life of faith, let us strip off every weight that slows us down, especially the sin that so easily trips us up. And let us run with endurance the race God has set before us* (Hebrews 12:1-2 NLT).

Another privilege we have is that these tests always come in the same order as the Israelites went through them. Should we expect God to make things any easier than this?

One of the reasons we feel all mixed up is because we have failed so many of these tests and God gives us another chance. We are trying to pass the new tests while we are retaking the old ones we failed. Once you fail a test, your life will keep moving forward but miss the order because you can fail in one and pass in another one. God will let you keep taking the one you fail until you pass it, or until you die.

You might think it is easy to learn these lessons and pass these tests. Without the help of God, it is almost impossible to go through the wilderness experience. But with God all things are possible.

The number one reason we fail in these tests is because God does not tell us in advance when He is going to test us or what lesson He is going to teach us. We have to use discernment, wisdom, and patience to understand when we are going through something and know why we are going through it.

The second reason is that His training and testing is part of our daily life and we need to be vigilant all the time. His course and tests are all part of our daily life's experience—we do not go to a classroom to sit, learn, and write a test.

God had their trip planned in advance and the routes fixed all the way to the Promise Land:

> *God did not lead them by way of the land of the Philistines, although that was near, for God said, Lest perhaps the people change their minds when they see war, and return to Egypt." So God led the people around by way of the wilderness of the Red Sea. And the children of Israel went up in orderly ranks out of the land of Egypt* (Exodus 13:17-18).

When we study their journey and all of the major places they encamped and what they went through, we will gain a great deal of spiritual wisdom concerning what is going on in our Christian life. According to the grace given to me, we are going to study these and the tests they went through so we can avoid the pitfalls in our own lives.

RAMESES TO BAAL-ZEPHON

They started their journey from Rameses, Egypt (see Ex. 12:37), and reached Succoth. The departure from Egypt represents our salvation from sin and from the bondage of the devil. There is great joy and celebration just after we get saved. Succoth means "tents." From Succoth they went to Etham (see Ex. 13:20), which means "their strength." From Etham they went to Pi-Hahiroth, meaning "mouth" and encamped against Baal-Zephon, which means "lord of the north, hidden, or secret" (see Ex. 14:2). In the Hebrew language, the meaning of a name or a word signifies its very essence and carries tremendous, even prophetic, meaning.

It is interesting to notice the progression of their journey. They were slaves in Egypt and did not have a place of their own. The first place God took them was Succoth (tents). Tents are a temporary shelter. This means that whatever they were experiencing at the time was only temporary and they should not put down any permanent roots. Whatever we experience right after our salvation is just the beginning of what God has for us. Do not get settled in your initial experience. From Succoth they went to Etham (strength), where they were no longer weak slaves.

Once they were redeemed, God became their strength. God had to teach them that their strength was in their mouth and in what they spoke, so He took them to Pi-Hahiroth (mouth). Once you are saved, life and death, blessings and curses, depend on what you believe in your heart and what you say with your mouth. This is the first principle God wanted them to learn.

Speaking Goodness

If you do not speak anything good *over* your life, do not expect anything good to happen *in* your life. If you speak evil, you will reap evil. We can build or destroy our destiny with our mouth.

That is what happened to the Israelites. They fell short of the plan of God, not because He was not powerful enough to perform what He said, but because of the words they spoke when they were tested (see Num. 14:28).

Life and death are in the power of the tongue (see Prov. 18:21). Everything that happens immediately after you get saved has great spiritual meaning, but we do not pay much attention to this because nobody teaches us these things.

Once they knew this much, God took them to teach them one of the first spiritual secrets of defeating the hidden forces of the north, which is our enemy the devil. This was crossing the Red Sea, which represents water baptism to a believer in Christ. This is a type of separation from past mistakes, failures, and the world.

They reached the place of their first test, which was by the Red Sea. They were stuck in a dangerous place, unable to escape in any direction. In front of them was the Red Sea, on both sides were mountains, and behind them Pharaoh and his army were coming to capture them. The people were afraid and cried out to the Lord and complained to Moses.

> *And then when Pharaoh drew near, the children of Israel lifted their eyes, and behold, the Egyptians marched after them. So they were very afraid, and the children of Israel cried out to the Lord. Then they said to Moses, "Because there were no graves in Egypt, have you taken us away to die in the wilderness? Why have you so dealt with us, to bring us up out of Egypt? Is this not the word that we told you in Egypt, saying, 'Let us alone that we may serve the Egyptians'? For it would have been better for us to serve the Egyptians than that we should die in the wilderness"* (Exodus 14:10-12).

This testifies that they had not learned their lesson about how to use their mouths. They spoke according to their emotions, but because their schooling had just begun, God was patient with them and He did not respond to their complaint.

If they had instead said, "Thank God for all He has done so far. Though our circumstances make it look as though it will never happen, He is faithful to fulfill what He has promised. Let us praise and thank Him for His goodness," their situation would have been much different.

The reason God brought them to such a place was to give them another experience of His great deliverance and to establish their faith in His power to help them overcome their circumstances. He will give us similar experiences to establish our faith before He tests us so that our faith will not fail during the trial.

They did not trust God. Instead of crying out to Him in faith, they murmured and doubted God and His appointed leader.

CROSSING THE RED SEA— WATER BAPTISM

Though they complained and murmured against Moses at the Red Sea, God did not respond to their complaining because He was getting them ready for the tests that were ahead. He did the fighting for them and kept their enemy away from them. He parted the Red Sea and the people walked over to the other side. God does not repay us according to our sins; He is merciful and compassionate.

Baptism represents the death, burial, and resurrection of Jesus Christ. When Christ died on the cross, we died with Him, were buried, and were also resurrected with Him. When we are baptized, we are declaring to the world that we died, were buried, and were resurrected with Jesus. Everything we did up to that day— and everything we were—ended, and a new beginning occurred with baptism.

Baptism is a separation from past sins and dead works. It is a separation from the enemy and a declaration that he no longer has power over us. That is why we go under the water, representing the burial process. Once we are buried, all sin and dead works remain in the water (grave), and when we rise from the water, they do not rise with us.

First Corinthians 10:1-2 says, *"Moreover, brethren, I do not want you to be unaware that all our fathers were under the cloud, all passed through the sea, all were baptized into Moses in the cloud and in the sea."*

Once we are baptized, the past has no power over us. That does not mean we do not have to fulfill human obligations. If you owe someone something, you need to pay it back. I am simply talking about spiritual things that had a claim on your life. Once you are baptized, each time the past tries to creep up, you need to constantly remind yourself that you are free from it. You have been made free from Adamic sin and its consequences.

SEVEN WILDERNESS TESTS

There are seven major stops and tests the Israelites went through during their journey in the wilderness after they crossed the Red Sea. The places I mention below are not the only places they stopped on their way. These are mainly based on the book of Exodus. But a more detailed list is found in Numbers 33:5-49. The Israelites failed all of their tests, though they were given repeated opportunities to pass the same test. The Bible says they tested God ten times (see Num. 14:22).

Marah: The Test of Trusting in God

After they crossed the Red Sea, Israel traveled through the wilderness for three days and did not have any water to drink. The place they reached was called Marah, which means "bitter" (see Ex. 15:23). Everyone was thirsty, but the water was bitter and they could not drink it. The Israelites complained against Moses, and the Lord was not pleased. This was the first time God tested

Israel. Exodus 15:25 says, *"There He made a statute and an ordinance for them, and there He tested them."*

Water is one of the basic necessities of life. You cannot survive without it. Similar things will happen in our own life. We may not go through the exact problem that they did, but we will be faced with similar situations where our basic necessities will be withheld from us. Please note that this was God who was leading them through the wilderness; it was not the devil that messed up their provision of water.

As Charismatics, we have been taught to jump on the devil when something is not going the way we want. The celebration and excitement of salvation, unfortunately, does not last long. We live in a fallen world and we will go through incidents that will be bitter and unpleasant. In those times, we should not walk by sight or by what we feel; we must walk by faith.

Many people have no problem believing God for salvation, but they have a problem trusting Him for their daily needs. Most believers need to go through a process of emotional healing for their soul (center of our emotions) after they are saved because only our spirit is healed through salvation.

After baptism, however, God expects us to have some level of maturity to face challenges and not be bothered by them. Each of the tests is designed to take us from one level of maturity to the next, so that we will be able to endure greater challenges, which will move us toward maturity. Once we are baptized, we should not let the guilt and condemnation of our past sins bother us.

The Israelites, rather than changing their attitude, acted with the same response as when they came out of Egypt: *"And the people complained against Moses, saying, 'What shall we drink?'"* (Ex. 15:24).

The Lord showed Moses a tree and he cast the tree into the water. The water became sweet and everyone drank from it. The tree represents the cross of Jesus Christ. After you are baptized, the next thing a believer needs is a revelation of the benefits and the power of the cross of Jesus Christ. Only through the cross can we go through the pain life will bring. Jesus went through every form of shame and pain on the cross for us, both emotional and physical.

Though we are freed from the past, sometimes life on this earth can be cruel. We may be betrayed, ridiculed, accused, misunderstood, abandoned, rejected, beaten, persecuted, or forsaken by people and relatives. The only way we can overcome those circumstances is to bring them to the cross (or bring the cross to the experience), leave them there, and receive healing (see Heb. 12:2-3).

You will be tested in these areas and will go through painful circumstances. All the Christians we expect to be nice to us and love us may not be showing their born-again nature. You need to develop the habit of coming to the cross regularly. There is emotional maturity that needs to take place in every believer's life. Most will get hurt and not seek healing from the cross. They will carry their hurt for the rest of their lives. I used to get upset and offended by little things and it took me many years to develop maturity in this area. Thank God I am not where I used to be.

It is interesting to note that God did not punish Israel for their murmuring and complaining until they reached Mount Sinai. The reason was because the law was not yet given. If there was no law, there was no punishment (see Rom. 5:13).

God wants us to trust Him for our every need. Nothing pleases God more than when all of our natural circumstances look chaotic but we choose to trust Him and praise Him in the midst of them. If you can learn this as early as possible in your life, you will be amazed at the heights God will take you. It may be one of the hardest disciplines to be learned, but without this you will not make it through life victoriously.

Elim: The Place of Rest

After you mature emotionally to deal with the bitterness and disappointments in life, God will take you to the next level, Elim.

Elim means "rams, the strong, and stags." *"Then they came to Elim, where there were twelve wells of water and seventy palm trees; so they camped there by the waters"* (Ex. 15:27).

Elim was like a little picnic or retreat after semester's end. After each test, God will give us a little break before the next one. That is the time we will feel everything is going to be all right; it is as if we are having a mountaintop experience. You and I will have similar experiences in our walk with God. Once in a while God will take us places and comfort us before we enter into the next test.

The number 12 speaks of government in the Bible and the water represents His Spirit. It quenches the thirst of others. Jesus had 12 disciples and they were the pillars, or the founding fathers, of the Church. You need to get into a church where you can be fed and trained by God. Once you are baptized and know the power of the cross, the Spirit of God will begin to move in your life to quench your thirst and the thirst of others.

The number 70 represents elders in the Bible. God will bring people to us to help us and to train us. Elders are God's chosen people in the Church; they represent the pastor and the congregation.

And the palm tree speaks of righteousness and the righteous people of God in the Bible. Psalm 92:12 says, *"The righteous shall flourish like a palm tree, he shall grow like a cedar in Lebanon."* And Isaiah 61:3 says, *"That they may be called trees of righteousness, the planting of the Lord, that He may be glorified."*

They did not do anything to get there. The *Lord* led them to Elim, which was an oasis in the desert. We cannot do anything to earn anything from God. He blesses us because He is good and kind—our salvation is not based on our good works. We have to receive the righteousness of God in order to be used by God. We will be tested in this area. It is our choice whether we want to depend on our righteousness or God's righteousness. God is not pleased with self-righteous people.

We all need "Elims" in our life, where we are refreshed and restored from the toxins and pain that trials bring. It is a place of rest before we embark on our next mission in life. God has prepared an Elim for you. Some of you are there right now, for others it is on the horizon. You will be there very soon as you continue your journey in the wilderness.

One of the most difficult things for some of us is to trust God to meet all of our needs: emotional, spiritual, physical, and financial. We get panicky when things do not go the way we want or expect. Trusting in God is the foundation of our growth as believers. If we cannot trust God, we will not obey God. That is the next test.

Wilderness of Sin: The Test of Obedience

From Elim, they departed and reached the Wilderness of Sin, which is between Elim and Mount Sinai (see Ex. 16:1). Then Exodus 16:2-3 says:

> *Then the whole congregation of the children of Israel complained against Moses and Aaron in the wilderness. And the children of Israel said to them, "Oh, that we had died by the hand of the Lord in the land of Egypt, when we sat by the pots of meat and when we ate bread to the full! For you have brought us out into this wilderness to kill this whole assembly with hunger."*

This was the second test God had for them. Exodus 16:4 tells us the purpose of the test, *"That I may test them, whether they will walk in My law or not."* One thing we need to know for sure is that God knows every situation we face and is aware of all of our needs. He does not always respond or react the way we do or the way we would like Him to; He responds according to what is best for us in the long run.

We see in the life of these people that after God rescued them from one situation, they totally forgot about it when they faced the next one. That is what God hates the most. The sooner we learn this lesson, the better it will be for us.

They were faced with a shortage of food, but did not even try to remember what God had done for them so far, or to trust Him for anything. God wants us to fully trust in Him for all of our needs. We will likely go through hunger and lack, so we need to know how to trust God completely. If we are to walk in God's ways, we need to exercise self-control concerning our emotions and various appetites of the flesh. It is noteworthy that all of these tests occurred in the natural realm and related to the needs of the flesh and body.

God provided them with manna from heaven, but the people disobeyed God there by not listening to Moses and Aaron (see Ex. 16:20-27). When the people collected manna, they were given the specific instruction that no one should keep any leftovers for the next day. Moses said, *"Let no one leave any of it till morning.' Notwithstanding, they did not heed Moses. But some of them left part of it until morning and it bred worms and stank. And Moses was angry with them"* (Ex. 16:19-20). They would not obey God completely.

The second instruction God gave was that on the sixth day they needed to collect enough for two days because the seventh day was the Sabbath—no one should go out to collect because there would be no manna on the seventh day. *"Now it happened that some of the people went out on the seventh day to gather, but they found none. And the Lord said to Moses, 'How long do you refuse to keep My commandments and My laws?'"* (Ex. 16:27-28).

It is imperative that we listen to the specifics of God's directions. We should not try our own way; we need to live and function in His way. They failed to trust God for their provision and His direction and did not believe in His promises.

Rephidim: The Retest of Trusting in the Lord

From the Wilderness of Sin, they departed and reached Rephidim, which means "beds or place of rest" (see Ex. 17:1). We need to learn to rest in God, knowing that He is going to take care of us no matter how the circumstances look. They could not rest because they had already failed some of the previous tests.

Once we fail one of the tests, life will continue to move forward, but no matter what point we reach, we cannot make any progress because we are not prepared or matured enough to be in a new place spiritually. When we pass each test, God increases His favor and anointing over our lives. Each new level in life needs a new and increased level of God's favor and anointing. When we fail one test and move to the next stage in life, we do not have the favor and anointing to face those challenges, so we become weak and discouraged because we are not able to make progress the way we would like.

That happens to many people in the body of Christ. Their life is moving forward but they do not seem fit or prepared for the task that is before them. They have not passed the previous tests and they feel inside that something is missing, or they feel like they have lost the inner strength to be at the place they are right now. The Israelites were supposed to rest in God because they had seen and experienced enough to know that God was going to take care of them.

Unfortunately, their maturity had not reached that level and they contended with Moses for water. Before, they complained to Moses, but this time they contended with him.

> *Then all the congregation of the children of Israel set out on their journey from the Wilderness of Sin, according to the commandment of the Lord, and camped in Rephidim; but there was no water for the people to drink. Therefore the people contended with Moses, and said, "Give us water, that we may drink." So Moses said to them, "Why do you contend with me? Why do you tempt the Lord?"* (Exodus 17:1-2).

Rephidim was a second chance to pass the same test they failed at Marah. When we fail in one area, God will give us another chance and let us go through the same problem again in our lives. May the Lord give us wisdom to know His paths and understand His ways.

Instead of making progress, these people were on a downward spiral and getting worse than before. Once we fail a test, the strength and maturity we were supposed to gain from passing that test is not available to us to support our forward movement. So we spiritually get weaker and become more vulnerable to the enemy's attack. We are supposed to go from strength to strength and from glory to glory, but if we fail, we go from weakness to weakness.

When we have a church full of people who have failed their spiritual tests, instead of having a spiritual feast, we will have a feast of self-pity and carnality. They will contend with everything the leader is trying to do and they will stand against the move of the Holy Spirit.

God provided them with water from the rock, and they moved to the next place. We see in all these that God did not fail to provide His part. He always remains faithful and takes care of us. Still, their situation had not changed because their attitude did not change.

Mount Sinai: The Test of Delayed Gratification

From Rephidim, they came to Mount Sinai and encamped there according to the commandment of the Lord. *"For they had departed from Rephidim, had come to the Wilderness of Sinai, and camped in the wilderness. So Israel camped there before the mountain"* (Ex. 19:2). This place was a major stop on their journey.

They came to Sinai three months after they left Egypt and encamped there for 11 months (from Exodus 19:1 to Numbers 10:10). A total of 59 chapters were recorded about the events that took place at Mount Sinai. Moses received the Ten Commandments, the Law, the pattern for the tabernacle, the feasts, offerings, sacrifices, and all other ordinances while they were at Sinai.

Sinai is a place where you receive the power from on high and it is a type of Pentecost, where you receive the baptism of the Holy Spirit. At this point, the people were failing in their relationship with God and in their personal lives. God wanted to empower them with His Word so He gave them His commandments to help them walk uprightly. That did not help them though, because while they were camped at Sinai they went through and failed some major tests.

Moses was called up onto the mountain to be with the Lord for 40 days and nights. The people waited but did not see him return as soon as they expected. They asked Aaron to make a golden calf to lead them on their way and to worship as their god. They were being tested in the area of patience and delayed gratification of what they needed.

Exodus 20:20 says, *"And Moses said to the people, 'Do not fear; for God has come to test you, and that His fear may be before you, so that you may not sin.'"* This was the third test God gave them of delayed gratification. Moses did not come down from the mountain at the time they expected. *"Now when the people saw that Moses delayed coming down from the mountain, the people gathered together to Aaron, and said to him, 'Come, make us gods that shall go before us; for as for this Moses, the man who brought us up out of the land of Egypt, we do not know what has become of him'"* (Ex. 32:1).

They became impatient, took their life in their own hands, and began to play God. There will be times in our life when we will not get answers to our prayers when we expect them. Things will not always happen the way we want or when we want. It does not matter how serious the situation is, we need to develop our patience. That is one of the main purposes of spiritual tests (see James 1:2-3).

When we fail the test of delayed gratification and fail to wait for God's timing, we always get into something that is not God's perfect will. When we step out to do something that is not in conjunction with the will of God for our lives, it will bring situations and results that we cannot easily get rid of, or things we did not expect or want in the first place will suddenly manifest.

One thing to know in the Christian life is that everything we *think* is a need in our life may not be a need at all. We need to learn to differentiate a need from the desires of the flesh. We need to mortify the desires of our flesh. These days, people will get into all sorts of trouble to meet their so-called *needs* and step out of the will of God.

Self-control is a fruit of the Spirit, a must-have if we are going to fulfill our destiny on this earth. God does not *control* us; He *guides* us. That is why it is called *self*-control and not *God*-control.

The price we pay for not walking in self-control will be heavy. Some of the results will make us unhappy and will stay with us for the rest of our life. God will redeem us from situations, but sometimes the consequences of our mistakes will linger with us to remind us and to keep us humble.

Aaron made a golden calf and the people began to worship and party around this idol. Moses came down and saw the abomination the people had brought upon themselves. He threw down the tablets of stone and destroyed the golden calf. He then gave a command to kill everyone who committed sin. About 3,000 people were killed that day (see Ex. 32:27-28).

It is interesting to see that Moses went to the mountain to receive the Law from God to help the people walk more closely and uprightly before Him. The Law, though, brought death instead of life. Paul calls the ministry of the Law, the ministry of death (see 2 Cor. 3:7). It is a prophetic type of Jesus going to heaven and sending the Holy Spirit upon the believers. Moses went up the mountain and came down with the Law and 3,000 people died on the same day. When Jesus went to heaven and sent the Holy Spirit on the day of Pentecost, 3,000 people were saved.

Some people, when they receive the baptism of the Holy Spirit, become prideful and arrogant toward authority figures. They tend to think that they do not need to be submissive to their leaders anymore because they can do certain things by themselves. That is one of the gravest mistakes anyone can make. God gives you the power from on high to serve Him and His people. They failed that test and the wrath of God was kindled against them so that many died.

Every believer needs to receive the baptism of the Holy Spirit and serve in a local church. The baptism of the Holy Spirit is not the end of your Christian journey; it is a new milestone and a divine empowerment to serve the Lord and others. You will enter into a new level of authority and maturity when the Holy Spirit comes, and you can overcome the temptations the enemy brings to cause you to stumble in your walk.

They built the tabernacle during this time and entered into a new level of relationship with God. With a new level of relationship with God comes a new level of discipline, order, increased intimacy, and a new way of thinking. They began to worship Him in the tabernacle and they witnessed the glory of God. A new order of camping and marching was set in motion at this point. Mount Sinai was a new beginning in many ways.

Wilderness of Paran: The Test of the Lust of the Flesh

They set out from Sinai and came to the Wilderness of Paran, meaning "beauty, glory, ornament" (see Num. 10:12). After you receive the baptism of the Holy Spirit, you will receive the gifts of the Spirit, which are like ornaments, or the glory of God functioning in your life. There are different kinds of ornaments just like there are different kinds of gifts of the Holy Spirit. This was the next level they were supposed to go to, but they were not yet prepared.

Instead of receiving the beauty and glory of the Lord, the people began to complain. And Numbers says, *"Now when the people complained, it displeased the Lord; for the Lord heard it, and His anger was aroused. So the fire of the Lord burned among them, and consumed some in the outskirts of the camp"* (Num. 11:1).

From here onward we see God judging His people for their sins. Now the Bible does not even say why they complained. I think complaining became second nature to them and they did not know anything else to say. They again cried out for meat and began to weep and crave for it. The Lord was displeased by this and wanted to destroy them. But Moses interceded for them many times and stopped the wrath of God from bursting toward them.

Another major incident took place while they were in Paran. There was a mixed multitude (who came out from Egypt) among them, and they began to exceedingly lust for meat. The psalmist describes the situation this way: *"They soon forgot His works; they did not wait for His counsel, but lusted exceedingly in the wilderness, and tested God in the desert. And He gave them their request, but sent leanness into their soul"* (Ps. 106:13-15).

The word for *leanness* in Hebrew is *razown*, which means, "leanness, scantiness, or wasting by disease."[1] *Scantiness* means excessively frugal, having a small or incomplete supply. God's Word Translation says it this way: *"He gave them what they asked for. He also gave them a degenerative disease"* (Ps. 106:15).

This was the fourth test God gave them. Their appetite and lust for food spiraled out of control and began to work against them. God provided them quail and, while they were eating, the wrath of God came upon them and many died because of the plague (see Num. 11:33). They were tested again to control their appetite, but they were not willing to discipline themselves. One of the tests we see the people of Israel going through more than once is in the area of food and drink. It is one area in which they refused to trust the Lord. They got nervous and became anxious that they were going to die if they did not eat or drink.

Each test is geared toward teaching us to trust God for our different needs. We find that when they repeatedly failed the same test, other aspects of their life were affected. One of the main areas of their life that was affected was their health. God sent leanness to their soul, which means their soul became impoverished and they stopped prospering. I believe there is a spiritual root to most physical and mental (soul) sicknesses.

The Bible says we prosper according to how our soul prospers (see 3 John 2). It is true that some sicknesses are caused by things we eat—either by eating the wrong things or by over-eating. I found that in my own life, when I am depressed and my soul is not prospering, I tend to eat food that I am not supposed to eat and I eventually gain weight. When I am depressed, I lose the discipline in my life and I get to a place where I have an *I-don't-care-anymore, what's-the-use* attitude. There is a divine protection around those who walk in God's will.

Even those people who are being used by God mightily can miss Him in their lives, and shortcomings will beset anyone. There is a common trend among believers that if the leader they look up to as an example gets sick, or if some evil thing happens in his or her life, they wonder, "How could this happen when they are the 'Most Holy Servant' of the Lord?" The truth of the matter is this, although he or she is anointed, these believers may have no idea what their leader does in his private life or what happened to him or her in their personal life.

When people are depressed, they are constantly looking for something that will get them out of that depression. Many people turn to things such as food, TV, sleep, drugs, alcohol, wrong relationships, or other things that will keep them engaged or help them forget their pain. Depression is caused by constant disappointments, trauma, emotional pain, etc. in life. It affects the function of your brain and you lose the power to shift from one mood to another so you constantly stay gloomy.

The fear of losing one's livelihood is one of the main fears that keep people from stepping out to fulfill their call. They are afraid that if they leave the security of their job, they will die. That was the same fear the Israelites had. They said that when they were in Egypt, they knew they were going to have food to eat, but since God delivered them, there was no security in that area.

They had to trust God for their daily provision. That is what God wanted them to do, but they failed to put their trust in Him. It is also interesting to notice the world system today is set up in a way that most people would not dare leave a job because of the fear of losing their home, cars, children, etc.

I believe the Israelites received that mindset while they were slaves in Egypt. Slaves did not get enough food. It was provided to them at a certain time of the day, and only a certain amount, and if they missed it they had to go hungry for the rest of the day. So, every day when it was time for food, they would rush and become anxious as if they were not going to have enough, or they feared they were going to die. That fear was the reason some disobeyed God's command and tried to collect extra manna and keep it for the next day.

When God gave them manna, they were told not to collect more than they could eat for a day. Some did not listen to that and collected more than they were supposed to—that was the same anxious mindset about food showing up in their actions. They were not able to pass that test in the wilderness.

The dead bodies of the people were buried in Kibroth Hattaavah, which means the "graves of lust" (see Num. 11:34).

Jesus told us not to worry about what we are going to eat or wear. The nations of the world are seeking those things rather than the Kingdom of God (see Matt. 6:25-34).

Hazeroth: The Retest of Submission to Authority

They encamped next at Hazeroth, which means "village or palace." It was time for them to live either in villages or palaces. It was their choice. Believers will come to a place in their life where they must choose whether to live in the Kingdom or according to the standard of the world. God said He places before us blessings and curses, life and death, and we have the freedom to choose either one (see Deut. 11:26-28).

Jesus said that if we seek His Kingdom first, then all material things we need in our life will be added to us (see Matt. 6:33). We should not go after material things. Materialism is a dangerous thing and very easy to fall prey to. There is a fine line between materialism and true prosperity. If we are not careful, we will be caught in the trap that destroyed many mighty men and women of God.

Before God promotes us and trusts us with responsibilities, He will test us by putting us under authority to serve and obey another person. That person may not be someone you want to submit to and may not possess the qualities you want in a leader. But you need to submit to him or her because it is God's order and He is testing you.

This was where Miriam and Aaron rebelled against Moses, and Miriam was judged by God and became leprous. There are many lessons we can learn from this experience. They were having a family problem—Moses, Aaron, and Miriam were from the same family and Aaron and Miriam became jealous of Moses and the woman he was married to.

I believe every family that is used by God will go through this struggle, especially if the person who is used by God has other siblings. We see this in the life of Moses, David, Joseph, Jesus, and many present-day ministers.

I have a word to siblings of those who are used by God. If you are a brother, sister, father, or a relative, and the one that is being used by God is younger than you, you need to respect and obey that person as your spiritual leader regardless of their age or look. God is not a respecter of person or age. We need to respect and submit to those whom God chooses and anoints to do the work. If we fail to do that, there will be grave consequences to our rebellion.

Once God blesses you and you live in a palace, you will tend to think that you are just like your spiritual leaders and that God can use you the same way He is using them. We need to be very careful here. Whether you live in a palace or a hut, you will never outgrow your spiritual leader in position. If they are anointed and appointed by God, you need to respect their position and anointing until one of you dies.

Miriam was struck with leprosy and was put outside the camp for seven days. They did not pass this test either, so they went back again to the wilderness of Paran a second time (see Num. 12:16). They were going back to the same place they had just left!

Kadesh: The Test of Fear and Unbelief

They reached Kadesh, in the Wilderness of Paran, one of the pivotal stops of their journey, similar to the one at Mount Sinai (see Num. 13:26). Kadesh means "holiness" and Kadesh-Barnea means "holy place of the desert of wandering." The people kept going back and forth between Egypt and Canaan. When everything was well and good, they wanted to go to Canaan; but when things became difficult, they wanted to run back to Egypt. One of the most dangerous traps of the enemy is inconsistency, or double-mindedness. The Bible says double-minded people do not receive anything from God (see James 1:6-8).

One thing to notice in all this is that God was faithful to His commitment to take them to the Promise Land. He did not change His mind ten times. It was the people who could not catch the vision God had for their lives. They were tossed around with their feelings and sabotaged the plan of God.

They came to Moses and told him to send some people to check out the land, to see if it was real and whether all God had been promising was true or not. God did not want them to do this. Though we read in the book of Numbers that God told them to send the 12 spies, it was not His idea. All He wanted was for them to trust His Word. But God told Moses to select 12 leaders of the tribes and send them to spy out the land (see Num. 13:1-16; Deut. 1:22).

Ten of them came back with a negative report and confused the people. They became fearful and were not willing to go down to the land God had promised them. God had to make a very difficult decision here: the decision not to take them into the Promise Land. All of the adults that came out of Egypt, except Joshua and Caleb (the two spies who gave a positive, godly report), were destroyed in the wilderness.

Another important principle we can learn from this is that God is willing to take you and me only to the level we believe Him for. We will never go beyond the point of our faith. They wanted to spy out the land because they did not trust what the Lord promised them. They wanted to explore and see if it was really true. This was birthed out of fear and unbelief.

We all have to make a very difficult decision in our walk with the Lord to either depend on our feelings or trust in His holiness to fulfill what He has promised us. Moses's sister Miriam died in Kadesh. Two of the most painful challenges every leader may face are rebellion from his immediate family and rebellion from the people he is leading.

At Kadesh, God pronounced the judgment that they would wander in the wilderness for 40 years; one year for each day they took to spy out the land (see Num. 14:28-34). There are decisions that we make that carry the power to alter our destiny. At our Kadesh moment, we decide whether we are going to fulfill the plan God has for us, or allow fear to take over and follow the secondary (permissive will) plan He has for us.

The Test of Submission to Authority/
The Test of Serving

When your leaders make a mistake, it does not give you the right to judge them or rebel against them. They are still your leaders until God removes them. Be careful what you say about your leaders and their weaknesses. You will be judged in the same area, sooner or later.

While they were in Kadesh, they went through another major test. Two hundred and fifty key leaders and princes of the people rebelled against Moses and Aaron.

> *Now Korah the son of Izhar, the son of Kohath, the son of Levi, with Dathan and Abiram the sons of Eliab, and On the son of Peleth, sons of Reuben, took men; and they rose up before Moses with some of the children of Israel, two hundred and fifty leaders of the congregation, representatives of the congregation, men of renown* (Numbers 16:1-2).

There are three qualities the Bible attributes to these people:

1. They were leaders of the congregation, meaning they were elders or leaders of the people. They were appointed by the leadership and held certain responsibilities the common people did not have. They had influence over people; when they spoke, people listened.

2. They were famous in the congregation (see Num. 16:2 KJV). Everyone knew these people; they were famous for their position, power, and ability. One of the tactics the devil uses to bring down a nation, church, or family is that he always goes to the top, or to people of influence, trying to deceive them. If he can bring them down, it will affect the entire congregation because they look up to these people for guidance and leadership.

3. They were men of renown: the Hebrew word for *renown* is *shem*, meaning reputation, fame, glory, monumental, the Name (as designation of God).[2] These were people of reputation and high status among the men of Israel. People have a tendency to say, "If they can do it, then we can also do it."

These kinds of people are always a target for the enemy and are vulnerable to his deception. They need to constantly watch their attitudes and hearts to see if any pride is building up. These people have a natural tendency, because of their pride, not to submit to their spiritual leadership.

We know the end of the story. God judged them and the earth opened and they were swallowed up alive. Not just the men, but God destroyed their families as well, along with all they possessed (see Num. 16:31-32).

One of the things people who are called to leadership must take to heart is that before God places us in leadership, He will allow us to serve others who are in leadership. He will test our attitude and submission to their authority. If we fail, He will not promote us. Some will even try to take their position by force and jeopardize their life.

Wilderness of Zin: A Third Chance to Pass the Test of Trusting the Lord

Once again they reached a place where there was no water. Zin means 'buckler or coldness."

> Now there was no water for the congregation; so they gathered together against Moses and Aaron. And the people contended with Moses and spoke, saying: "If only we had died when our brethren died before the Lord! Why have you brought up the assembly of the Lord into this wilderness, that we, and our animals, should die here? And why have

you made us come up out of Egypt, to bring us to this evil place?" (Numbers 20:2-5).

Regarding the issue of water, they were tested one more time in the Wilderness of Zin and, once again, they failed. Not only did they fail, but Moses and Aaron disobeyed God and they also lost the opportunity to enter the Promise Land. The Lord told Moses to call all of the people together and to take his rod and command the rock to bring forth water (see Num. 20:7-13). But Moses hit the rock, not just once, but twice, and did not honor God.

This is an interesting thing to see: the first time God provided them water from the rock, He told Moses to smite the rock once to bring out the water (see Ex. 17:5-6). But the second time God told him to only command the rock, not to strike it.

We have to be careful not to form a mindset or doctrine based on a single experience with God. People form traditions and doctrines based on someone else's experience or a one-time incident in the Bible. We have to listen to God each time for specific instructions and never move in pretense or assume that we already know how God is going to work in a particular situation. Each new season in our life requires a higher level of faith.

If we continue to fail the tests, our heart will grow colder or harder. As a result, we will lose our sensitivity to the things of God. They failed miserably in this test and even Moses was provoked to anger. He committed an unpardonable sin and lost the opportunity to enter the Promise Land (see Num. 20:12). This was called the water of Meribah, which means "dispute or quarrel" because they contended with the Lord (see Num. 20:13).

Mount Hor: The Test of Gratification or Thankfulness

One of the keys to being joyful is to have a thankful heart. When you thank God for the things He has done for you, you are positioning yourself to receive more.

From Kadesh they came to Mount Hor, which means "conceives or shows." Aaron died here (see Num. 20:28). It was time for them to conceive God's plan for them again. After we have been through some tests and fail them, there will be times that we feel like the vision has been lost or is dead, but it is just our imagination. Sometimes it happens because of our own disobedience and, at other times, it is a test to know whether we will love God, even if He never does anything for us or through us again.

Here the people began to complain against God and Moses:

> *Then they journeyed from Mount Hor by the way of the Red Sea, to go around the land of Edom; and the soul of the people became very discouraged on the way. And the people spoke against God and against Moses: "Why have you brought us up out of Egypt to die in the wilderness? For there is no food and no water, and our soul loathes this worthless bread"* (Numbers 21:4-5).

God gave them manna from heaven and they called it "worthless bread." God calls it "angels' food." What is your attitude toward the blessings God has given you? It may not always be the things we dreamed of, but if we have more than we had before and are in a better place now than when we started our journey, we should be thankful to God for that.

The psalmist reminds us: *"Yet He had commanded the clouds above, and opened the doors of heaven, had rained down manna on them to eat, and given them of the bread of heaven. Men ate angels' food; He sent them food to the full"* (Ps. 78:23-25).

This was the fourth chance God gave them to pass the test of trusting in the Lord for their daily provision, but again they missed it. I believe that we Christians will go through more than one experience when we need to learn to trust the Lord for our next meal or provision. There will be times coming in our life when it will seem there is no way out financially. In each of those times, we have to trust Him to get us through and to provide for us. I have failed this test many times, and eventually passed it. I have also seen God provide miraculously for the need. Lord, please give us the grace and wisdom to trust you all the time.

Manna is a type of God's Word. There will be times in life when the only thing we will have as an evidence for the things we believe will be the Word of God. We should not say in our heart, "Oh, it's only the Word," or, "I am tired of believing the Word." I am guilty of this in my own life and have had to repent many times. Now I am at a place where I do not need any more physical signs. All I need is His Word.

Shittim: The Retest of Overcoming the Lust of the Flesh

The word *Shittim* means "thorns." This was the last stop the people of Israel made before they reached the Jordan River. Balak, king of the Moabites, heard about the Israelites and was afraid. He called Balaam, a seer, to curse the Israelites. God did not let Balaam curse them; but instead of cursing them, He caused Balaam to bless them (see Num. 22:1–24:10).

The king of Moab was very displeased, but Balaam gave him counsel, which caused great trouble for the people of Israel. He told them to invite men of Israel to join the Moabites in offering sacrifices to their gods. The name of one of their gods was Baal-peor, which means, "lord of the opening," and they joined the Moabites to offer sacrifices. The people of Israel then began to commit harlotry with the women of Moab because the ritual of worship to this god involved immoral acts.

> *Now Israel remained in Acacia Grove* [Shittim], *and the people began to commit harlotry with the women of Moab. They invited the people to the sacrifices for their gods, and the people ate and bowed down to their gods. So Israel was joined to Baal of Peor, and the anger of the Lord was aroused against Israel* (Numbers 25:1-3).

And Revelation 2:14 says:

> *But I have a few things against you, because you have there those who hold the doctrine of Balaam, who taught Balak to put a stumbling block before the children of Israel, to eat things sacrificed to idols, and to commit sexual immorality.*

The anger of the Lord was kindled against Israel, and 24,000 people died that day because of the plague (see Num. 25:9). They failed to overcome the lust of the flesh and were never given another chance—their time was up.

The people who failed these tests did not enter the Promise Land. They all died in the wilderness during the 40 years and a new generation was raised up by God to enter the Promise Land.

OVERCOMING THE WILDERNESS YEARS

Dear brothers and sisters, what I am talking about is not a joke. We all will go through or may have already gone through these tests. The reason the body of Christ is not effective today is because most believers have failed their tests and are wandering around looking for their next miracle. Others are fed up and their hearts are hardened. Still others have lost their joy and anointing and are barely hanging in there.

Salvation is by grace and is a free gift from God. Walking in God's ways and fulfilling our purpose can be challenging at times, and we have to pay a heavy price for it. That is why Paul encouraged us to work out our salvation with fear and trembling (see Phil. 2:12).

Unless we pass the tests in the wilderness, we will not enter the Promise Land where we will begin to fulfill our destiny. If we cannot overcome the challenges in the wilderness, we will not defeat the enemies in the Promise Land. Many people try to inherit their promises before they pass through the wilderness. They step out of

God's order and timing and start ministries and businesses only to get whipped by the enemy.

The wilderness is a place where God teaches you to overcome yourself. If you cannot overcome yourself, you will never overcome your enemies. The seven tests that we learned about need to be passed in the wilderness because there are seven enemies (nations) in the Promise Land that we need to dispossess. Each of these tests equips us to overcome a corresponding enemy.

Seven Enemies to Be Overcome

There were seven nations in the Promise Land that the Israelites needed to overcome in order to inherit their blessings.

> When the Lord your God brings you into the land which you go to possess, and has cast out many nations before you, the **Hittites** and the **Girgashites** and the **Amorites** and the **Canaanites** and the **Perizzites** and the **Hivites** and the **Jebusites, seven nations** greater and mightier than you... (Deuteronomy 7:1).

Also, in Acts 13:18-19, we read, *"Now for a time of about forty years He put up with their ways in the wilderness. And when He had destroyed seven nations in the land of Canaan, He distributed their land to them by allotment."*

We do not fight a physical battle as they did. We are fighting a spiritual battle. To a believer in Christ, each of those nations represents a demonic spirit that we need to overcome.

Jesus talked about a demon bringing back seven other spirits:

> When an unclean spirit goes out of a man, he goes through dry places, seeking rest, and finds none. Then he says, "I will return to my house from which I came." And when he comes, he finds it empty, swept, and put in order. Then he goes and takes with him **seven other spirits** more wicked than himself, and they enter and dwell there; and the last state of

that man is worse than the first. So shall it also be with this wicked generation (Matthew 12:43-45).

Why does the demon go and call seven other spirits? Because that is the number of demonic forces we need to overcome. There is another incident we see in the Gospels where Jesus cast seven spirits out of a woman: *"And certain women who had been healed of evil spirits and infirmities—Mary called Magdalene, out of whom had come **seven demons**"* (Luke 8:2).

I believe there is a strong connection between the seven nations and the seven demonic spirits mentioned here. In order to overcome these seven demons, God has given us His seven Spirits.[3]

Overcoming Seven Deadly Emotions

The wilderness is a place where we learn God's wisdom and His ways. The tests in the wilderness also enable us to conquer seven deadly emotions. Each of these emotions is connected to a demonic force. When we are tested, depending on which test we are going through, each of these emotions will surface in our life. Each test will bring to the surface one of these emotions. The purpose of the wilderness tests is to help us overcome these emotions.

One of the purposes of the tests is to reveal what is really in our heart. Unless we are tested, these emotions will not surface. When they manifest, we will be surprised that they are coming from our heart. Unless we learn to control these emotions, we will fall prey to the enemy in the Promise Land. These emotions are as follows:

1. Worldly Sorrow (see 2 Cor. 7:10)—Under worldly sorrow works anxiety, worry, stress, impatience, frustration, greed, and depression.

2. Bitterness (see Heb. 12:15)—under bitterness works hatred, offense, jealousy, and envy.

3. Anger (see Eph. 4:26)—under anger works wrath, regret, strife, retaliation, and vengeance.

4. Lust (see 2 Pet. 1:4)—under lust works the lust of the eye, the lust of the flesh, and the pride of life.

5. Pride (see 1 Tim. 3:6)—under pride works rebellion, deception, arrogance, and selfishness.

6. Condemnation (see Rom. 8:1)—under condemnation works guilt, self-pity, rejection, and apathy.

7. Fear (see 2 Tim. 1:7)—under fear works doubt, self-reliance, insecurity, retaliation, and all other bondages.

When we overcome the seven tests, the seven deadly emotions in the wilderness, and the seven enemies in the Promise Land, God will give us seven feasts to celebrate.

Our God is merciful and kind. Let us ask Him to show us where we have failed and show us how to get back on track. The time is short and we are in the last semester of our time on this earth.

Please pray this prayer with me:

Lord, please show me where I have failed You. Take me back to the place where I lost the head of my ax. Teach me how to rectify situations and get right with You. Please forgive me for those times I rebelled against Your Holy Spirit and disobeyed Your voice. Restore my soul and spirit. Heal my body and relationships. Forgive my pride and unthankful heart. Forgive me for not completely trusting in You. In Jesus's name I pray. Amen.

ENDNOTES

1. James Strong, Strong's Exhaustive Concordance of the Bible, Hebrew #7332.

2. Ibid., Hebrew #8034.

3. We will learn more about this in Chapter 13, "Wisdom: The Key to Passing Tests."

Chapter 8

THE SEVEN WILDERNESSES OF LIFE

As God prepares us to fulfill His purpose in our lives, He will take each of us through our own wilderness experience. It is important that we learn the principle of "wilderness" so we will not make the same mistakes the Israelites made. The intention behind God taking us through a wilderness experience is to teach us to trust Him, without fear or doubt, in everything and for everything, and in all circumstances. When we are able to trust Him and His Word in one area of our life, we will come out of the wilderness in that area.

God said through Hosea, *"Therefore, behold, I will allure her, will bring her into the wilderness, and speak comfort to her"* (Hos. 2:14).

I want you to know regardless of what you are called to do, right after you receive your call or are filled with the Spirit, straight away God takes you into the wilderness. He will take away the very thing you most trust, things you believe are the most essential for your livelihood, because He wants you to trust in Him wholeheartedly.

Before we go into the seven wildernesses of life, we are going to look into why God takes us through a wilderness experience. Below are some of the reasons.

PURPOSES OF THE WILDERNESS

To Develop Godly Character

Just as we chastise our children when they are little, God chastises us when we are young in the spirit. No parent chastises his matured child. God wants us to develop our character. The wilderness is the way God trains us to learn His ways. We discipline our children to teach them the right way of doing things.

The Bible says God corrects the ones He loves and not to rebel when He chastises us: *"Thou shalt also consider in thine heart, that, as a man chasteneth his son, so the Lord thy God chasteneth thee"* (Deut. 8:5 KJV). How does He "spank" us? He takes us through experiences that we don't like so our attitudes and emotional stability become tuned to His Spirit. He wants to develop the fruit of the Spirit in us.

If God is to trust us with His spiritual treasure, we have to possess some spiritual qualities. The Bible says, *"He has blessed us with all spiritual blessings in heavenly places"* (Eph. 1:2).

There are two main reasons God allows us to go through our wilderness. The number one reason is to teach us humility.

Receive, please, instruction from His mouth, and lay up His words in your heart (Job 22:22).

Listen to my instruction and be wise. Don't ignore it (Proverbs 8:33 NLT).

As many as I love, I rebuke and chasten. Therefore be zealous and repent (Revelation 3:19).

O Lord, do not rebuke me in Your anger, nor chasten me in Your hot displeasure (Psalm 6:1).

The Lord has chastened me severely, but He has not given me over to death (Psalm 118:18).

One of the most powerful lessons we can learn from the incarnation of Christ comes by studying the way He came down to fight the devil. He didn't come as an arrogant tyrant who was going to blow up the enemy's camps with mortar and shells. Jesus was just the opposite of what everyone expected from a king. He came to fight a spiritual battle. He came as a humble servant.

The number one piece of armor we need for our spiritual fight is humility. Jesus laid aside all of His heavenly glory and majesty and took the form of a servant (see Phil. 2:7). Many go to battle with the pride and arrogance of their race, status, money, and intelligence, and they get whipped and ripped by the enemy.

We are to have the same mind that Christ had while He was on this earth. The key to Jesus's victory over the devil was His humility, not His power. Power without humility is like fire in the hands of a 3-year-old. This is why we often feel aggravated with people while we are going through our wilderness training.

God is trying to deal with our pride and ego. He will let us work with people we don't like to be around, especially those people who know how to push the right buttons. He will take us places we don't want to go.

In the wilderness, everything was in the open; there was no privacy and there were no secrets. Everyone had the same clothes and the same shoes. We have to learn to love the people we don't like. We have to accept them and show them the love of God. When you are able to do that, you are ready for something big.

God was the One *"who fed thee in the wilderness with manna, which thy fathers knew not, that He might **humble** thee, and that He might prove thee, to do thee good at thy latter end"* (Deut. 8:16 KJV).

To Teach Us Patience

The second reason God takes us into wilderness training is to teach us patience. Some people, as soon as they hear that word, feel irritated. I had a friend in Bible school and we called ourselves "long distance friends" even though we lived in the same building. The reason was we just had opposite temperaments. We couldn't be near one another without making the other irritated. How many people might have achieved great things in their life if they had a little more patience?

The Bible says, *"That ye be not slothful, but followers of them who through **faith and patience** inherit the promise"* (Heb. 6:12 KJV). How does God develop patience in us? It is through making us do the same thing again and again. Other times it is through making us wait for His timing.

The Israelites didn't have very many choices in the wilderness. They had to have the same food, the same water, and the same people around them all the time. Can you imagine living like that for 40 years? But they still failed and didn't allow God to develop patience in them.

Do you sometimes wish you could just disappear and not have to deal with the situation you are in? Or, that the people who irritate your flesh would just disappear? Wait a minute! Maybe God is trying to work on your patience. I thought that many times in my life. I didn't know that what I was going through was intended to develop me. I thought it was the devil trying to destroy me. I didn't have anyone to come and tell me, or that I could go and ask. That is why He used me to write this book, to tell you why you are going through what you are going through.

Faith and patience always go together. If you want faith, you need to be patient. If you are to be patient, you need faith. *"For ye have need of patience, that, after ye have done the will of God, ye might receive the promise"* (Heb. 10:36 KJV). If you are to receive what God has promised you, you need patience.

One of the things that I learned about spiritual life is that what we gain through days of fasting, praying, and walking with the Lord can be blown apart by a minute of anger or impatience. Patience is a quality of the spirit, not the flesh.

To Teach Us God's Ways

In order to understand how God works and to pass spiritual tests, we need to know the ways of God. As I mentioned briefly in the previous chapter, God's ways are always higher than our ways. "God's ways" means the way He operates and does things.

How do we know God's ways? There is someone in the Bible to whom God chose to reveal His ways—Moses. If we study his life and what God did through him, we will learn about God's ways in great detail.

Usually, when we go through something difficult, we are looking for a way out. We get frustrated when God does not get us out of our challenge. What we should look for is His way of getting us out of that challenge. The "ways" of God and the "wisdom" of God are synonyms. They are different words, but their meanings are almost the same. To understand God's ways, we need the wisdom of God. And, if you *know* God's ways, you will *have* the wisdom of God.

If we are going to make it through this life victoriously, we need to learn God's ways. His ways are His methods of operation. We all have a particular way of doing things and so does God. Unfortunately, His ways are not our ways and His thoughts are not our thoughts. Isaiah declared: *"'For My thoughts are not your thoughts, nor are your ways My ways,' says the Lord. 'For as the heavens are higher than the earth, so are My ways higher than your ways, and My thoughts than your thoughts'"* (Isa. 55:8-9).

If God's ways and thoughts are higher than ours, just as the heaven is above the earth, is it possible for us to know them? Yes. He has made a provision for us to know His ways. He has chosen a person in the Bible to reveal His ways. If we study his life and ministry, we will understand the ways of God.

Psalm 103:7 says, *"He made known His ways to Moses, His acts to the children of Israel."* God revealed His ways to Moses. Many times, His ways and thoughts are just the opposite of our ways and

177

thoughts. God takes us to the wilderness to teach us His ways. What does that practically look like to us?

Below are some of the examples of people who were called to do great things but their present circumstances did not relate in any way to their call, or to what God told them.

- God has called you to be a father of many nations, but you are old and you do not have any children right now.

- God has chosen you to be the prime minister of the superpower nation of your day, but you are working as a slave.

- God has called you to be the deliverer of His people, but you are taking care of your father-in-law's sheep.

- God has promised you a life that flows with milk and honey, but right now you do not even have enough water to drink.

- You are the King of kings and the Lord of lords, but you are born in a manger.

- You are called as an apostle of the Lamb, but you are working as a fisherman.

I could go on and on about anyone who is used of God. But unless we learn God's ways, we will get discouraged and eventually give up.

To Teach Us to Trust in Him

Every human being on this earth trusts in something, or someone, for strength and help. Either we trust in God or in our own ability, money, relationships, self, or some other means. The Bible commands us to trust in the Lord with all our heart (see Prov. 3:5).

In Jeremiah, we read that those who trust in man are under a curse. God wants us to trust in Him. For the Israelites, their trust was in the Egyptians and the food they provided. For years they depended on the ration they received as slaves. For slaves, daily bread is life. They knew that if they did not receive that, they would die.

When they were in the wilderness, God let their supply of food run out. They became fearful and panicky. They thought they were going to die so they murmured against God and Moses. Instead of looking to God for help, they began to look to their strength to sustain them, and the result was failure. All they had to do was call upon God to provide for them; but instead, they complained.

God's purpose in taking His people through the wilderness was to teach them that man shall not live by bread alone, but by every word that comes from the mouth of God (see Deut. 8:3). The two most important words in this scripture are "bread" and "word." For the people of Israel, their bread was their life. In the natural, their survival depended on the bread.

What is the *bread* in your life? It will be the very thing that you think you cannot survive without. God will remove that from you or stop the supply of it to see whether you turn to Him or depend on yourself. Your "bread" can be a relationship, job, business, money, ministry, habits, etc. Only you know what constitutes the bread in your life.

We see a similar experience in the Gospels. Jesus's ministry was going so wonderfully and His followers multiplied with each miracle, especially after He provided them with bread and fish. Free food always attracts a crowd. Then He began to talk about eating His flesh and drinking His blood. They did not understand or digest what He was talking about. Many of His disciples left Him from that day onward (see John 6:66).

Jesus turned to His disciples and asked if they also wanted to leave. But Peter received a revelation and said, "Where should we go? You have the words of eternal life" (see John 6:67-69). He passed the test. There will be times in our life when the only thing we have to trust and hold onto will be the Word of God. You need to remain faithful to His Word if you want a good ending.

THE SEVEN WILDERNESSES OF LIFE

As we go through our Christian life, we will go through seasons that feel like wilderness experiences. We will experience wilderness-type events in different areas of our life. The Holy Spirit has shown me that there are seven different types of wildernesses that a believer will go through in their life and are according to a person's specific calling. We may not go through all of them, but there is a possibility we may go through more than one.

The wilderness is a season of life where we feel nothing exciting is happening on the outside; we feel dry and go from one challenge to the next. We are going to learn how different individuals in the Bible went through their wilderness experience and what they learned from it. I believe it will help us gain some wisdom for our own walk with the Lord. As one preacher said, "Everything great God has done came out of the wilderness."

Called, Chosen, and Faithful

There are three steps to receiving and fulfilling the call of God on your life: being called, chosen, and faithful. God's anointing is what places a call of God on your life. After you have been called, God starts the next process, which is to be chosen. To be chosen by God you need to pass some tests. When you reach the chosen step, what God has promised in your life will begin to manifest.

When you are called, all you will know is that you are called to do something great and you will have a picture of it in your heart, but will not know what to do about it. You want to try out different things but it will not go the way you want or expect. Sometimes, we fail and then wonder if we are really called.

Yes, you are called. That is why there is a desire in your heart to be used by God, but you are not yet ready. You need to pass some tests, especially the test of the wilderness. When you pass the wilderness, you will then be chosen. That is why Jesus said, *"For many are called, but few are chosen"* (Matt. 22:14). When you are chosen, you need to be faithful in what God entrusted to you in order to have a good ending.

> *These will make war with the Lamb, and the Lamb will overcome them, for He is Lord of lords and King of kings; and those who are with Him are **called, chosen**, and **faithful*** (Revelation 17:14).

Calling is an invitation for the interview test. If you pass the test, you will be chosen for the position. After you are called, you will enter a new season called the "wilderness experience." The wilderness is the University of God, where He trains His mighty men and women of faith. The season of our life we go through between called and chosen is called the wilderness, or the testing period.

God takes us into the wilderness after we are called, not before. Moses had to flee to the wilderness. Jesus was in the wilderness for 40 days just before beginning His ministry. John the Baptist was in the wilderness until he showed himself to Israel. The Israelites had to go through the wilderness before they could enter the Promise Land. The apostle Paul was in the wilderness before he entered his God-given ministry.

The wilderness is the place where He trains our patience and builds our character. It is the place of war between flesh and spirit. It is up to us to decide which one we will let win the battle. David was in the wilderness for 13 years. We need to know that this happened to him *after* he was anointed to be king. Many try to avoid the wilderness journey thinking that being anointed is sufficient, but they short-circuit their destiny. The duration of the wilderness varies from person to person and it depends on how *fleshy* we are.

Unfortunately, many try to function in their purpose as soon as they feel the calling. They try to make things happen only to end up in a deeper mess. The reason things are not happening in what you feel you are called to do is because you are not yet chosen. Many quit at this level and do not fulfill the call of God on their life.

When you are chosen, everything God promised will begin to manifest in your life. After you are chosen, you need to be faithful to God in order to remain in that office. In that way, you will be promoted to higher levels.

1. The Wilderness of the Children of Israel: How to Trust God (see Ex. 15:22; Deut. 8:2-3; Ex. 2:15; 3:1)

I dedicated an entire chapter to this so I will not repeat it in detail.[1] All that was required of the people of Israel was to trust God and believe that He was able to perform what He promised. That is what is required from each of us. It is human nature to take things into our own hands when they become difficult or uncertain.

The whole sin issue came to this earth because man strayed away from trusting God and His Word, and took things into his own hands. Since then, we have a tendency to trust in our own ability to pull us through life's circumstances, which is not what God wants from us.

The Bible says to trust in the Lord with all our heart and not to lean on our own understanding. It does not say to trust in Him sometimes with just a little bit of our heart, but all the time with all of our heart (see Prov. 3:5).

It is easy to trust in Him when all things are going well, but when things are tough is precisely when we really need to trust Him. Listen to the testimony of a person who trusts in Him at all times.

Yea, though I walk through the valley of the shadow of death, I will fear no evil; for You are with me (Psalm 23:4).

The Lord is my light and my salvation; whom shall I fear? The Lord is the strength of my life; of whom shall I be afraid? When the wicked came against me to eat up my flesh, my enemies and foes, they stumbled and fell. Though an army may encamp against me, my heart shall not fear; though war may rise against me, in this I will be confident (Psalm 27:1-3).

God waited 40 years for Israel to trust in Him, but they did not. When challenges came, all they needed to do was to say, "We trust in God no matter what. He promised us great things and He is able to perform it." That would have taken them to the Land of Promise, but because they were in unbelief it did not come out of their mouth. The next time things do not go the way you expect, remember to trust in Him with all your heart. He is faithful and He will come through for you, no matter what.

2. The Wilderness of Moses: Character Development (see Ps. 15; 24)

God had a great plan for Moses, but He had to train him before He could use him. It took a long period of time to develop Moses's character. The reason for this wilderness is to develop godly character in us. What is godly character? It is the character of Jesus. The reason God allows us to go through this wilderness is to get rid of all of our personal ambitions and to fully surrender to do His will. After 80 years of training, Moses was ready to enter into his destiny.

There was no one more humble than Moses on the face of the whole earth (see Num. 12:3). He was faithful in all that was required of him. He did everything God asked him to do, showing total obedience. He spoke what God told him to speak. That is what God is looking for from each of us.

The Bible also says Jesus emptied Himself of all reputation and took the form of a servant, which happens to be the same attitude God wants in us (see Phil. 2:7).

183

3. The Wilderness of David: Obedience and Submission to Authority (see 1 Sam. 23:14-16; Ps. 63)

If anyone knows what it is like to go through a wilderness experience, it is David. I have dedicated a whole chapter to his experience, so please refer to that for more information.[2] He was chosen by God and anointed king of Israel. The anointing did not immediately give him the throne, but it took him straight to the wilderness for the next 13 years. He was going to be entrusted with great authority and he needed to know what it meant to be under authority. The greater the authority God is going to entrust you with, the more you need to learn to submit to authority.

God put David under a man to whom it was not that easy to submit. What would be your response to leadership that was trying to kill you? David endured it with great patience and God brought him to a great place. We will have to reach a place where we truly pray for and bless those who persecute us, then we will know if we passed this test or not.

4. The Wilderness of Jesus: Overcoming the Devil (see Luke 4:1)

Jesus came to this earth with a specific mission. One part of the mission was to take back all the devil stole from us. He had to overcome the enemy in order to do that. He was filled with the Holy Spirit and the Spirit led Him into the wilderness to be tempted by the devil. The enemy came to Jesus to tempt Him in one of His physically weakest moments, but Jesus spoke the Word of God and overcame him. You and I need to overcome the enemy if we are to fulfill our destiny. The Word of God, which is the sword of the Spirit, is our weapon against the enemy.

We have to reach a place in our life that, when we are tempted by the devil and this world, we respond with the Word of God. We need to train our mind to think accordingly because this does not come naturally. It is a discipline that needs to be developed.

The next time you are tempted but are able to speak the Word to your situation, you will pass this wilderness test.

5. The Wilderness of John the Baptist: New Revelation of God (see Luke 1:80; 3:2)

While we are on this earth, we are on a journey to know God intimately. God has to reveal Himself to us for us to know Him. There will be seasons in our lives when God will take us to a wilderness experience to speak to us things we otherwise would not know or hear from Him.

John was sent by God to be the forerunner of Jesus. He came to prepare the way for Him. He had a miraculous birth and was dedicated to God. Like Jesus, he also had to wait 30 years before he could start his ministry. The Bible says he was in the wilderness until he showed himself to Israel (see Luke 1:80).

6. The Wilderness of Paul: Intimacy With Jesus, Dying to Self (see Gal. 1:17)

There will be seasons in our lives where God will take us into a wilderness experience to help us develop an intimate relationship with Him—God longs to have intimacy with us. In fact, we were created for it.

God will separate us from all our close relationships and let us go through times of loneliness where we will long in our heart to love someone, or for someone to love us, but no one will be there. People with whom you long to have a relationship will be away from you or against you during this season. The only option you have left will be to look up and cry out.

When we are in intimate fellowship with people, we will not long for intimacy with God. That is why He separates us and, after we have developed an intimate relationship with Him, He will restore those relationships to us. Hosea says He will take us into the wilderness to speak comfort to us (see Hos. 2:14).

Paul was called to be an apostle. Though he was called, he had to experience the wilderness in his life before God could use him. The ultimate purpose of spiritual life on this earth is to have an intimate relationship with Jesus. We will all go through this wilderness until we find our identity and fulfillment in Christ. Many are busy doing things, but inside they are not satisfied. They are burned out and empty. The reason is because they are trying to find their satisfaction, fulfillment, and identity in what they do. It will not happen.

To such a crowd Jesus cried out, *"Come unto Me, all you who labor and are heavy laden, and I will give you rest"* (Matt. 11:28). There is a place in every human being where God is the only thing that can satisfy and bring fulfillment. Paul was busy, passionate, and was a man with a mission before he met Christ. But that was not enough to fulfill his call.

Likewise, God had to hold me back until I found my identity in Him, as His child, so He could use me. There was a vacuum in me because I grew up with a lot of insecurity and rejection. I was trying to find my identity from what I was doing, which was ministry. I wanted to be somebody, and wanted to do something great so people would respect me and think I was great. They were all wrong intentions that sprang up from my insecurity.

I had to go around this wilderness a few times before I really understood. I was passionate and zealous in what I was doing, but nothing brought me satisfaction and I always felt empty deep down inside, knowing that something was not right. God had to remove everything; He had to take everything away from me for a season to bring me back to Him.

God completely stripped Paul to the ground and everything he held precious or valuable was taken away from him—his purpose, his mission, his work, his ministry, his relationships—everything. When everything was taken away from him, he had nothing to look forward to except Christ.

If you come to a similar point in life, do not be dismayed. It is not the end of your world; it is the beginning of a new dawn. If you can make it through this season, you will be in a better place than before. Whatever you are doing—business, ministry, or whatever position you are in—these things will not give you what you are looking for. Only Jesus can satisfy the hunger in a human soul. Until that happens, we will feel like we are going through the wilderness, though we may have everything else.

Saul was very influential before he became known as Paul. He had a lot of friends and was highly respected among the religious leaders. After his encounter with Jesus, though, Paul thought what Jesus had promised him would come to pass right away. He did not have a full understanding of the process of God. He lost all his friends and the Christians were afraid to associate with him.

He had to flee to the desert of Arabia with no one to commune with except Jesus. He describes it this way:

> But when it pleased God, who separated me from my mother's womb and called me through His grace, to reveal His Son in me, that I might preach Him among the Gentiles, I did not immediately confer with flesh and blood, nor did I go up to Jerusalem to those who were apostles before me; but I went to Arabia, and returned again to Damascus (Galatians 1:15-17).

The time Paul spent in Arabia produced some good fruit in him. Christ was formed in him and he received the revelation of the Church and the end times while he was there. He would not have received that had he stayed in Jerusalem. There will be a season in life where God will separate us from our friends and family and we will be left alone. It is not that He does not like you; it is because He wants all of you. It is a wilderness experience where He wants you to get to know Him.

Paul prayed for the believers in Galatia: *"My little children, for whom I labor in birth again until Christ is formed in you"* (Gal. 4:19).

7. The Wilderness of the Rebellious: Death and Destruction of the Disobedient (see Ps. 78:17,40; 95:8; 106:14,26)

Though more than 3 million people came out of Egypt, only two of the men reached the Promise Land. The rest perished in the wilderness. Each time there was an opportunity to trust God, they rebelled against Him and against Moses, so God said they would not enter into His rest (see Ps. 95:10-11).

This is the end of everyone who will not pass the wilderness test.

HOW TO KNOW YOU'RE IN THE WILDERNESS

The wilderness is a place of survival—you will not be productive or fruitful. You know in your heart that you are created for something great and all the resources are available, but you are not walking in your calling. At times, the sins and the mindsets of the past may revisit you in the wilderness.

You live more by what you feel than what you know. One day you are excited about God and your future, and the next day you want to give up and run away. You will love your neighbor and your spouse today, and the next day you hate them. These are some of the signs that you are in the wilderness.

You want to self-promote and look for connections to make you famous. You will send your resume and hand out business cards to people, but you will not receive any response. Joseph tried this when he was in the prison. He told the cupbearer to remember him when he was restored to his office, but as soon as he was restored, the cupbearer forgot Joseph for two years.

In the wilderness we live by experience and not by faith. We are always looking for a miracle or a sign from God to encourage us in our walk with the Lord, where God is trying to teach us to live by faith. Such experiences will keep us encouraged for a couple of days, but we will be back to the same place we started in no time.

HOW TO SUCCESSFULLY COME OUT OF YOUR WILDERNESS

Get Familiar With the Word of God

God's principles are eternal. They don't change with the times. We can have complete confidence in His nature and principles. God gave the Israelites manna in the wilderness to eat. The first thing they said when they saw manna was, "What is this?" Why didn't they say, "Wow, what a nice-looking cake, can I have some?"

Manna was the bread from heaven. It represents the Word of God. They had to eat manna not just for breakfast, but also for lunch and dinner. They had to collect it in the morning before sunrise. Why did God do that? Was it not tiring? Yes, it was. The reason was that God wanted them to get familiar with the bread from heaven first thing in the day and put Him first before any other need.

The only thing exciting about manna was that every day they got it fresh from heaven, though it was the same thing. They were being prepared to live by the Word of God once they reached the Promise Land. He wanted them to meditate on His laws day and night.

The Word of God is the number one thing you need to get familiar with while you are in the wilderness. It may not be exciting in the beginning. I have heard from people asking the same question the Israelites asked about manna when they start to read the Word. They ask, "What is this? It does not make any sense! Why do I have to read the same Word every day, day in and day out?"

189

When you give God the priority in your life, He has something fresh to speak to you every day, and it all comes from the same Word. It may not look that appealing, and you may not feel the hunger, but you know it is from heaven and it is God's Word. You might say that you know all of the stories in the Bible, so what else is there to know? What about when the test or the temptation comes, do those stories help you to overcome?

Jesus told us to pray for our daily bread (see Matt. 6:11). Let me tell you, no one has even touched the surface of the wisdom that is hidden in those stories. It depends on what you are going through. Those same stories will have something new to say about every situation.

If you can read and meditate on the Word in the midst of stressful circumstances, your spirit man is stronger than your flesh. When things go wrong or when you get sick, if you turn to God first before you seek any other help, you are maturing in the things of God.

When Jesus was tempted, He spoke the Word to every opportunity the devil brought. That is how He overcame them. It is interesting to note that all of the scriptures Jesus spoke to the enemy were from the book of Deuteronomy.

Seek God First at the Beginning of the Day

The Israelites had to gather the manna early in the morning. If they waited and said they would sleep in, they missed their food for the whole day because the manna would melt away when the sun rose. Even if they cried and complained, they had to fast for that day. What a loss! I don't know how many blessings I might have missed by not starting my day with God. Everyone had to collect only what they needed for each day. One person could not gather for another.

If you study the life of David, you find that he had a habit of seeking God early in the morning. Just look up in a concordance the words "early" and "morning" in the book of Psalms and you will be surprised to see the heart cry of David. Take a look at these three scriptures:

O God, Thou are my God; early will I seek Thee: my soul thirsteth for Thee, my flesh longeth for Thee in a dry and thirsty land, where no water is (Psalm 63:1 KJV).

David sought God early in the morning not because he was in the most comfortable place in his life, but just the opposite. He was in a land with no water, a land that was dry and thirsty. He was not asking God to meet His material needs; he was longing for God because of his love for Him.

David also cried out:

Mine eyes prevent the night watches, that I might meditate in Thy word (Psalm 119:148 KJV).

I wait for the Lord, my soul doth wait, and in His word do I hope. My soul waiteth for the Lord more than they that watch for the morning: I say, more than they that watch for the morning (Psalm 130:5-6 KJV).

Listen to and Obey Your Spiritual Authority

Pride can do more damage than we realize, both to ourselves and to others. The Israelites were not that good at listening to Moses in the wilderness. Your spiritual authority is your pastor, your husband, mentor, or whomever God sends your way to help you grow spiritually.

Aaron and Miriam thought they also could do the things that Moses did. They knew the consequence of their actions. The Bible says that Moses had to intercede for Aaron's life, otherwise God was ready to take him (see Deut. 9:20).

Moses could have let God destroy the entire people. He was so meek and humble that he interceded for them again and again. Thank God for such leaders, but we do not have many like Moses today, so be careful about what you say and do to the people who have spiritual authority over you.

> *Obey those who rule over you, and be submissive, for they watch out for your souls, as those who must give account. Let them do so with joy and not with grief, for that would be unprofitable for you* (Hebrews 13:17).

And Galatians 6:6 says, *"Let him who receives instruction in the Word* [of God] *share all good things with his teacher* [contributing to his support]*"* (AMP).

We find this stunning truth in First Samuel 15:23, *"For rebellion is as the sin of witchcraft, and stubbornness is as iniquity and idolatry. Because you have rejected the word of the Lord, He also has rejected you from being king."* Wow! When we are stubborn and rebellious, we are worshiping ourselves.

Crossing the River Jordan

Crossing the River Jordan is the final test of finishing God's training in the wilderness. Crossing the river was a unique experience for the people of Israel. It was a paradigm shift from the past 40 years. They were coming to the end of their wandering in the wilderness.

In the wilderness, they marched along with the cloud by day and fire by night. There was something supernatural to look up to and move after. It didn't take much faith. They could see the presence of God with their natural eyes.

They were walking by sight, not by faith. God provided their daily food every morning. They didn't have to worry about what they were going to eat. The Rock was following them from which they drank water. God was not working in their spirit while they were in the wilderness; He worked on their flesh. God knew that only after they learned how to conquer their flesh would they be able to exercise their spirit and move forward.

They remembered that God parted the Red Sea when Moses stretched out the rod. Here, Moses had died and it was now through their new leader that the River Jordan was going to part. Joshua didn't have a rod like Moses had. The cloud was not there to direct them. Once they crossed over, there would be no more visible, supernatural signs to look upon. There wouldn't be any free food every morning. Joshua even told them to prepare food before they crossed over (see Josh. 1:11).

They couldn't complain or murmur once they crossed over. We don't see any reference that they complained or murmured against Joshua after they crossed the Jordan. It was a change of government. It was a change of mindset. They had to look at the Ark of the Covenant of the Lord.

> *And they commanded the people, saying, When ye see the ark of the covenant of the LORD your God, and the priests the Levites bearing it, then ye shall remove from your place, and go after it* (Joshua 3:3 KJV).

In the wilderness, when the people rebelled against God, He sent plagues and consumed them with fire. After crossing the Jordan, God trusted the people to make the right choice. They had to exercise their faith. The priests and the Ark were at the center of this act. Joshua was merely a facilitator of this miracle. Crossing the Jordan represents crossing from our flesh to life in the Spirit; crossing from the law to the free gift of God's grace.

Two and a half tribes didn't want to cross the Jordan. They settled for less because they didn't receive God's vision beyond the river. Their vision was limited. Like many in the Church today, they opted for a mediocre life. You cannot do anything with them; you cannot force them to grow up. As someone said, "You can only bring the horse to the water, but you cannot make him drink."

Only after you cross the Jordan are you qualified to fight your enemy. Many have received a word from the Lord and years later they are still waiting for its fulfillment. Many have finished their wilderness journey but have not yet crossed their Jordan. They still need some visible evidence or feeling to do what God has asked them to do. They are not able to exercise their faith. If we are to walk in God's destiny, we need to walk by faith and not by sight.

Walk in the Spirit

Walking in the spirit is comprised of different elements. It means you listen to your spirit and obey its promptings above your body and soul. If you have no specific leading of the Spirit, do what the Word says. That is the simple solution for coming out of your wilderness. Whenever circumstances arise, you respond to them with your spirit and not with your soul or body. Learn to trust God at all times regardless of how intense or impossible things look in the natural. Obey immediately the promptings of the Holy Spirit. We are going to look into different elements that comprise walking in the spirit.

Walk by Faith and Not by Sight

As Christians, we do things differently than other people on this earth. To walk by faith means you live by the convictions of your heart and not your circumstances. It means you believe and live by the Word of God (the promises God gave you), regardless of what your life is like in the natural. God has put a picture of your destiny in your heart and you follow it. You speak positively about your life and your circumstances.

Love Your Enemies

This is a command of Jesus. It is easy to hate our enemies, but if we want to come out of the wilderness, we need to learn how to love our enemies and to bless those who persecute us. We should not revile those who revile us. Instead, we should commit it to God and trust Him to take care of these situations. It takes a lot of patience to love our enemies and to wait for God's intervention. We want to kill those who persecute us or want to see God's immediate judgment coming upon them. God often does not move in the way we would like and in the timing we expect. He will surely vindicate you against your enemies.

Give and Bless Others

Giving is the nature of God. We need to learn to be pliable in the hands of God when He tells us to bless someone. The reason God blesses us is for us to bless someone else. We are channels of His blessings. We should not delay when He asks us to give something away. We should give without grudging.

Do What is Right, Whether You Feel Like It or Not

This is a big test of maturity. Do you want to know how mature you are in the things of the spirit? Check your life and see if you are able to do the right thing even when you do not feel like doing it. If you can pray, love your spouse and children, give, and worship when you do not feel like it, you are qualified to be used by God. Many live in the feeling realm and never enter into the realm of the spirit. The realm of the spirit does not fluctuate according to what we feel. It always remains the same. Our feelings change and that is why we at times feel closer to God than at other times.

Believe, Speak, and Do What the Word Says When You Are Under Pressure

Do you want to know what you are made of and what is really in your heart? Listen to what comes out of your mouth when you are under pressure, disappointed, or angry. We have to discipline ourselves so that when we are under pressure only God's Word comes out of us. It is hard, but it is possible.

God told Joshua to meditate on the Word day and night and not let it depart from his mouth and he would have good success (see Josh. 1:8). It is easy to jump and shout when we are in the church, but our real life starts when we leave the church. We come to church to be trained to live in the world.

EIGHT MISTAKES TO AVOID

Here are eight mistakes you want to avoid when going through a wilderness experience.

1. Avoid Impetuous Actions and Words

The flesh is the enemy of the spirit, as is the devil. The devil works through our flesh to get to our spirit. When we are going through a test, all of the challenges, pressures, impatience, and irritation we feel are of the flesh. When we give in to those impulses of the flesh, our spiritual life gets affected.

Moses was appointed by God to take the people of Israel to the Promise Land. It was not an easy task for him to lead close to 3 million people through the wilderness. There were times when he lost his patience, and other times when God was done with the people and wanted to destroy them. But Moses interceded for the people more than once and they were spared.

They reached a place where there was no water for the people to drink, and so they murmured against Moses. God spoke to Moses to take the rod and speak to the rock to bring forth water.

Then the Lord spoke to Moses, saying, "Take the rod; you and your brother Aaron gather the congregation together. Speak to the rock before their eyes, and it will yield its water; thus you shall bring water for them out of the rock, and give drink to the congregation and their animals" (Numbers 20:7-8).

God only told Moses to take the rod and speak to the rock. Why would He ask Moses to take the rod to speak to the rock? It was a test for Moses; being the final test for him before he could enter the Promise Land. Moses lost his patience and allowed his emotions to control his actions. Instead of speaking to the rock, he angrily struck the rock with the rod:

So Moses took the rod from before the Lord as He commanded him. And Moses and Aaron gathered the assembly together before the rock; and he said to them, "Hear now, you rebels! Must we bring water for you out of this rock?" Then Moses lifted his hand and struck the rock twice with his rod; and water came out abundantly, and the congregation and their animals drank (Numbers 20:9-11).

Moses's actions displeased the Lord and he lost the opportunity to take the people into the Promise Land. One impetuous action in the midst of your test can alter the course of your destiny, so please be careful about what you say and do when you are tested. As I said earlier, when you are tested, the real you will come out!

Then the Lord spoke to Moses and Aaron, "Because you did not believe Me, to hallow Me in the eyes of the children of Israel, therefore you shall not bring this assembly into the land which I have given them" (Numbers 20:12).

2. Do Not Make Any Permanent Decisions

Know that every season you are going through in life is only temporary. What you feel emotionally while you are going through a test is not permanent. Usually, a test happens in a moment in the spirit, then for us to go through it emotionally may take a while, but most end within 24 hours. When we fail a test, it may take a few days or weeks to recover and get restored.

When you are going through a test, you will be tempted to make permanent decisions. When the Israelites were in the wilderness, God tested them, and many times they were tempted to go back to Egypt. They expressed that desire often with their words and God was not happy about it. I know many people who made permanent decisions when they were tested; when their marriages were tested they made unwise decisions, which they regretted later but could not reverse.

When Esau was tested, he made a permanent choice to sell his birthright to his younger brother. He sought to repent afterward, but could not be restored (see Heb. 12:17). He lost his eternal blessings for one stomach's worth of stew.

3. Avoid Pride

The reason we are tested is to remove the evil nature and conform us to the image and likeness of God. Pride is an enemy of God. There is no such thing as good pride and bad pride; every form of pride is evil and it comes from the devil. In the West, people usually use phrases like, "I am proud of my country," or, "I am proud of my children," without fully understanding what they are saying. Just because everyone is saying something does not make it right. Or just because we have been doing something for centuries does not mean it is good.

When Jesus was baptized, the Father spoke His approval. He did not say, "You are my beloved Son, I am so proud of You." No, He said, "I am well pleased." All forms of pride come from the devil and it comes from his nature. God hates pride and everything we have is because of His grace.

Pride brings rebellion and rebellion causes disobedience. When you are tested, make sure you do not act or do anything because of your pride. We see in the wilderness there was a group of people that rebelled against Moses because of their pride. The Lord destroyed them.

> Now Korah...took men; and they rose up before Moses with some of the children of Israel, two hundred and fifty leaders of the congregation, representatives of the congregation, men of renown. They gathered together against Moses and Aaron, and said to them, "You take too much upon yourselves, for all the congregation is holy, every one of them, and the Lord is among them. Why then do you exalt yourselves above the assembly of the Lord?" (Numbers 16:1-3).

And the story is summed up at the end of the chapter:

> Now it came to pass, as he finished speaking all these words, that the ground split apart under them, and the earth opened

its mouth and swallowed them up, with their households and all the men with Korah, with all their goods. So they and all those with them went down alive into the pit; the earth closed over them, and they perished from among the assembly (Numbers 16:31-33).

Their pride and rebellion was immediately judged.

4. Avoid Sexual Sins

When you are tested, you will feel like giving up because you will be under a lot of emotional pressure. You will feel like doing the craziest things on earth. You will feel like your dream will never come true and that God does not care. That is the moment the enemy comes to you with long-awaited opportunities to tempt you.

Many have made mistakes here, especially committing sexual sins. Potiphar's wife tempted Joseph in this arena. She compelled him to sleep with her. He could have thought, "What is the point of holding onto any dream? I was cast into a pit, now I am a slave and I will be a slave for the rest of my life, so let me be like others and enjoy life a bit." By the grace of God, he did not do it. He held onto his faith in God and fled.

When you are tested, you will feel like it is the end of your life and nothing good will ever happen again. That is just a lie from the enemy himself and you need to reject and renounce it. *"For we have become partakers of Christ if we hold the beginning of our confidence steadfast to the end"* (Heb. 3:14).

5. Avoid Strife

When you are tested, your patience level is so thin that you just need a spark to cause an inferno. You will be tempted to fight with people and your flesh will come up with all kinds of reasons to cause strife. It will tell you that you are being mistreated and they have no right to do that to you, etc. You need to have the self-control to say no to any strife. If you enter into strife, you will fail the test.

When Abraham left to follow God's plan for his life, his nephew Lot went with him. On the way, they both had a lot of livestock and servants and strife broke out between their servants. It could have been a genuine reason for Abraham and Lot to fight. Abraham avoided it and gave Lot the first chance to choose the land he liked. It was a test for both of them. Abraham passed the test, but Lot, in choosing for himself the best land, failed the test.

6. Never Quit

We will undoubtedly make mistakes while we are in the wilderness being tested. When you fail, the most important thing you should do is not quit. You will feel like quitting and forgetting every dream and promise. As age-old wisdom says, "Winners never quit and quitters never win."

Once you fail, you need to ask God to forgive you. He will, and He will give you another chance to pass that test.

7. Watch What You Say

Your thoughts and words control your destiny. What caused the Israelites to die before they entered the Promise Land was their words. Though God had done everything He should, the people could not come into alignment with His thoughts and words for them. Finally, God said He would do exactly as they had spoken.

> Say to them, "As I live," says the Lord, " just as you have spoken in My hearing, so I will do to you: The carcasses of you who have complained against Me shall fall in this wilderness, all of you who were numbered, according to your entire number, from twenty years old and above. Except for Caleb the son of Jephunneh and Joshua the son of Nun, you shall by no means enter the land which I swore I would make you dwell in" (Numbers 14:28-30).

8. Do Not Make Any Critical Judgments Against Others

When we are tested, the flesh wants to strike back because the whole purpose of the test is to crucify the flesh in order to live in the spirit. We will not be happy about ourselves and, because we are not happy about ourselves, we will be tempted to express that toward others. We will be tempted to criticize, judge, and mar others with accusations.

When you are tested, you will feel highly critical of others and want to judge them. In many events, what you see in others is a reflection of your own heart. Looking at other people can be like holding a mirror to our own heart. Proverbs 27:19 says, *"As water reflects a face, so a man's heart reflects the man"* (NIV).

While they were in the wilderness, Aaron and Miriam criticized their brother Moses concerning the woman he was married to. The judgment of God fell on them. God spared Aaron because of His high priestly anointing, but Miriam became a leper and had to stay outside of the camp for seven days.

In life, you will become what you hate the most. You will end up doing what you criticize others for doing, and you will be judged with the same judgment with which you judge others.

RESULTS OF PASSING THE WILDERNESS TEST

Increased Favor

Jesus increased in wisdom and in stature and in favor with God and man (see Luke 2:52). You can grow in the favor of God and man. Jesus went through some spiritual testing while He was on this earth. Every time we pass a spiritual test, the favor of God increases in our life.

We see this clearly in the life of Joseph. Every time he endured a test without reviling his brothers, God promoted him. First, he became a manager for Pharaoh's captain. There also he was tested and he became the manager of the whole prison, and from there he became the prime minister for the whole land of Egypt. We can see an increase in the prosperity and influence in Joseph's life. He did not become the prime minister overnight, though it seems that way. He had to go through about 17 years of testing and trials to get there.

We need God's favor to live and be successful on this earth.

Increased Anointing

David was anointed when Samuel poured the oil on his head, but that anointing did not make him a king overnight. He had to go through some testing in his life. Each time he passed a test, the manifestation of that anointing increased in his life.

Elijah put the mantle on Elisha as soon as he saw him. The mantle represents the anointing. Elisha did not become a miracle-working prophet on the same day. He stayed with Elijah and served him until Elijah's departure, then the power of God began to manifest in Elisha's life. He was like a servant to Elijah and did everything he was asked to do. Bible scholars say that he served Elijah for 12 years.

Increased Spiritual Maturity

As I mentioned before, one of the key purposes of all spiritual tests is to mature us in our character and patience. Just as every parent wants their children to grow up, take responsibility, and be productive, our heavenly Father wants each of His children to grow up, take responsibility for our walk with Him, and be productive for the Kingdom. It is so easy for us to get comfortable in our little corner and pretend to be spiritual. Unless we are growing daily and bearing fruit in our lives, we have not matured.

New Revelation of God and His Ways

Each test is designed in a way that, when we pass it, we will know God a little more than we knew Him before. Knowing God and His ways is essential to our success in this life. be a person of good character, but if you do not know how God operates, you will fail. A good education alone does not qualify you to be used by God.

More Faith

Our faith grows as we use it. God does not want you to be on the same page all your life. There are new horizons He wants you to conquer. There are more mountains you need to move. We are commanded to walk by faith and each new season in our life requires a new level of faith.

Increased Financial Blessings

Often, when you pass a test, you will be blessed financially. It is God's desire for you to increase more and more in every way. Financial blessings are a reward for those who solve a problem or for those who overcome something. The next time you need a financial miracle, ask God for a problem to solve or to send you someone with a problem. Or overcome that same battle that you have been going through again and again.

Love From a Pure Heart

Paul writes to Timothy, *"Now the purpose of the commandment is love from a pure heart, from a good conscience, and from sincere faith"* (1 Tim. 1:5).

It is easier to say to someone, "I love you," than to walk it out in practical living. One of the most difficult tests is the test of love—to love someone who does not deserve to be loved by our standard. Spiritually speaking, we did not deserve to be loved by God. We were by nature enemies of God, but He still chose to love us and gave His only begotten Son so that we could love Him.

We are commanded to love people with the same love that God loves us. We are also to forgive one another as God in Christ forgave us (see Eph. 4:32).

More Patience and Endurance

One of the prayers the apostle Paul prayed for the believers in Colosse is mentioned in Colossians 1:9-11:

For this reason we also, since the day we heard it, do not cease to pray for you, and to ask that you may be filled with the knowledge of His will in all wisdom and spiritual understanding; that you may walk worthy of the Lord, fully pleasing Him, being fruitful in every good work and increasing in the knowledge of God; strengthened with all might, according to His glorious power, for all patience and long-suffering with joy.

This is one of the most powerful prayers any believer can pray for themselves and for others. The result of being filled with the knowledge of His will and with the power of His might is to be patient and long-suffering with joy. That is what God expects from us. How do we know if a person is matured in the things of the spirit? It is relative to the level of his or her ability to patiently endure hard times without changing their attitude.

When we come out of spiritual tests, we will be able to go through hard times and still do what we are supposed to do without getting upset and offended. Children get offended quickly and throw a temper tantrum because they lack patience. When they are upset, they will not fulfill their responsibilities or do their chores with a joyful heart.

God allows us to go through some tough times in order to make us strong so He can entrust us with more. More blessings mean more responsibility. More responsibility means more challenges and testing.

Death to Self

Another main purpose for wilderness tests is to redeem us from our fallen nature. In each of our lives, there are areas that need to be brought into total submission to God. Because we will try our own way and do our own things, God has to let us face some roadblocks and setbacks so we will realize who is really in charge of our lives. If we are to come to a place of total surrender, we need to come to a place of total brokenness.

PASSED THE TEST

Here are a few ways to know if you've passed the spiritual test successfully:

- You are promoted from your current position, both spiritually and financially.

- You know God in your heart more intimately than before.

- You have more confidence in God than before.

- Your influence in the Kingdom has increased.

- You have more freedom in the Spirit.

- Your love for God and His people has increased.

- You are more excited about God than before.

ENDNOTES

1. See Chapter 7, "The Tests of the Israelites in the Wilderness."
2. See Chapter 9, "David and His Seven Tests."

Chapter 9

DAVID AND HIS SEVEN TESTS

David is a key person in the Bible from whom we can learn many spiritual lessons. His journey through triumphs and mistakes in life are always an encouragement. One of the reasons he is an encouragement to us is because he went through more than the average person will go through in life. That is one of the signs that you are called to do something extraordinary. The higher you want to go, the more battles you will face in life. The more you want to achieve in life, the more challenges you will face.

David is the only person in the Old Testament who was anointed three times. The places and circumstances he went through have much to teach us in our walk with the Lord, even in this era. We are going to look into some of those experiences and places and learn the principles so we can apply them to our life today.

When we study his life, we see the trials he went through and the tests he faced as he progressed to become the greatest king Israel ever had. Nobody becomes great overnight. There is always a series of incidents that person went through before he or she became great. If we learn from their experiences, it will help us understand how life functions on this earth so that we may avoid some mistakes. There are two ways to learn in life, either by making mistakes or learning from someone else's mistakes.

There are seven places and seven tests David went through before he became the king of Israel and built the city of David, which is called Zion. I will give a short synopsis of each of those places, its spiritual significance, and the tests he went through in those places. The name of the place is very important in this study so I will mention that instead of the particular test he went through.

BETHLEHEM: HOUSE OF BREAD— THE BIRTH OF VISION

David was born in Bethlehem, a small town in the hill country of Judah. It is a place of small beginnings. It is a place where people know you and treat you based on your family history, not based on your purpose or assignment. It is a place where people form an opinion about you based on your childhood. It is where people do not recognize your call or anointing; a place of tradition and bondage.

It is also the place of our initial anointing, where we recognize the call of God on our life. It is a place of menial tasks where God lays the foundation for our life. Everything begins in Bethlehem and the rest is a continuation of whatever we do there.

Proverbs 20:11 says, *"Even a child is known by his deeds, whether what he does is pure and right."*

We all have a Bethlehem in our life. David was the youngest in a family of eight boys. His job was to feed the sheep owned by his father Jesse. A time came when God told Samuel to go and anoint one of Jesse's sons as the next king of Israel. God did not tell Samuel the name of the person. We read in First Samuel 16:1 that God said to Samuel, *"Fill your horn with oil, and go; I am sending you to Jesse the Bethlehemite. For I have provided Myself a king among his sons."*

Samuel reached Jesse's home and he called all of his sons (except David) to have dinner. I believe that this entire time Samuel was trying to discern in his spirit by listening to the talk and looks of each of Jesse's sons, wondering whom he should anoint. The Lord rejected each of them and, finally, Samuel asked if there was anyone left. Jesse said, *"There remains yet the youngest, and there he is, keeping the sheep"* (1 Sam. 16:11).

David was called to come home and as soon as Samuel saw him, the Lord said that he was the one to anoint. Imagine, Jesse did not even think it was necessary to call David for this very important dinner. Having Samuel over for dinner with them was like the greatest spiritual leader of our day coming to our house for dinner. We would call all of our family members together if they were reachable.

When David reached home, he would have been surprised to see the preparation and commotion in the house—and would immediately know that he had missed something great. I believe the first test he had to overcome was rejection by his own family members. He was not considered important or valuable, just a shepherd boy. The rest of his brothers were smarter and stronger in their outward appearance and were soldiers in King Saul's army.

Unless God spoke to us directly, David was not the person we would choose if we were looking for a new king. However, in God's sight he was smart and he had the right heart for the job. Samuel anointed him before his brothers and that was the initiation of David's call. He was anointed, but he was not yet ready; his time had not yet come to be the king of Israel. He had to go through various other tests before he could walk in the fullness of what God had called him to do.

Afterward, Goliath, one of the giants of the Philistines, came and challenged the army of Israel to fight with him. No one dared fight this giant, but David arrived on the scene and immediately confronted him. His brothers again mocked him saying, *"Why did you come down here? And with whom have you left those few sheep in the wilderness? I know your pride and the insolence of your heart, for you have come down to see the battle"* (1 Sam. 17:28).

David was appointed and anointed by God to defeat this giant, but his brothers rejected and looked down on him. His brothers and family members did not recognize the call of God on his life. You and I may go through similar situations in our own life. The Bible does not tell us of David's reactions toward these kinds of incidents. He somehow learned to deal with it and did not let it affect him.

We need to learn how to overcome rejection if we are to fulfill our call. Otherwise, it will keep us bound and looking inward for strength and confidence instead of looking to God. We will seek for acceptance and validation from other people instead of God. David had to overcome rejection in his heart before he could go on the mission God had for him. His attitude toward his brothers was good and he did not render evil for evil. He overcame evil with good (see Rom. 12:21).

GIBEAH: HILL—SUBMISSION TO AND RESPECT FOR AUTHORITY

After David defeated the giant with God's help, his fame reached the palace and he was brought before King Saul. Saul appointed him as one of his assistants to take care of affairs in his palace in Gibeah (see 1 Sam. 18:2-5).

Gibeah was the place King Saul lived and reigned (see 1 Sam. 15:34). David was behaving wisely in the palace and did everything Saul asked him to do. Very soon he became more popular in Israel than the king (see 1 Sam. 18:7,30). This generated jealousy in Saul's heart and he became afraid of David (see 1 Sam. 18:12). God allowed an evil spirit to torment Saul because of his attitude toward David. He became so angry at times that he looked for an opportunity to kill David.

Gibeah is a place of promotion and praise. It is a place God uses to teach us the skills that we need for the future, the place where we do what we can do but not what we are supposed to do. We have to watch our heart and attitude because God is going to test us there. Other people are going to be jealous of our blessing, and how we react to them determines our promotion to the next level.

David had to flee from the palace because Saul was determined to kill him. For the next seven years, he was chased by Saul and ran for his life. All this time David did not commit a sin against Saul. He was determined to respect and obey his king. He was tested to the utmost in the area of submission to Saul's authority. It is easy for us to submit to our leaders and say nice things about them when they are nice to us. What if they fire us for no reason and they are wrong? What will our attitude be then?

Gibeah is a place where God teaches us how to submit to and respect authority. God will allow situations like that in our life. In this place we will be mistreated by people to whom we have done no wrong, but only tried to help and bless. Those times are very important in the spirit because they are spiritual tests God allows in our lives for our good.

CAVE OF ADULLAM: REFUGE—LOVE AND COMPASSION

David fled from Saul and found himself a place to hide in the cave of Adullam:

> *David therefore departed from there and escaped to the cave of Adullam. So when his brothers and all his father's house heard it, they went down there to him. And everyone who was in distress, everyone who was in debt, and everyone who was discontented gathered to him. So he became captain over them. And there were about four hundred men with him* (1 Samuel 22:1-2).

It is interesting to see that he was trying to run from his own pain and fear and now all these people were coming to him for help. I do not know what happened to his brothers and parents, they might have sold everything they had and moved in with David. Or Saul might have attacked them and destroyed everything because he could not get David. Or they might have run away for fear of Saul. Whatever the case, David now had over 400 people to care for.

Adullam is the place where God will test our heart. He will send troubled people who need our help even when we are going through our own trouble. When we can care for others in the midst of our own pain, it shows we are ready to move on with God. But if we chase them away, we will lose the blessings. Some of these people will turn around and bless us as they did to David. They became his mighty warriors and brought great success to his life when he became king.

Adullam is a place where God prepares our heart. It is a place where we do not feel like helping anybody. When Jesus was on the cross, He was still asking the Father to forgive those who crucified Him and mocked Him. He also showed mercy to one of the thieves on the cross.

WILDERNESS OF ZIPH: REFINING—ENDURANCE

David was tested more than once in the same area when he was running away from Saul. I believe this happened to develop his patience and endurance because he needed those qualities when he became king. James says that the testing of our faith produces patience (see James 1:3).

It was also a test of obscurity where no one knew him as the anointed man. He was escaping from one place to another like a thief who stole something. We will face this in our life as well. You will be anointed to do something, but right now no one knows you or cares about you.

God will hide you for a season before He reveals you before the people. When you are hidden, God teaches you some important principles. He will teach you about love for people and some leadership principles. David became captain over a bunch of bandits but some of them later became his mighty men when he became king.

Joseph was hidden in the prison of the house of Pharaoh, but he was a leader in the prison over other prisoners. The outside world did not know him as a leader or a minister. We need to be faithful even when we are obscure in order to be revealed in a later season.

It is also the place you hit bottom and discouragement floods your heart. David said, *"Now I shall perish someday by the hand of Saul. There is nothing better for me than that I should speedily escape to the land of the Philistines; and Saul will despair of me, to seek me anymore in any part of Israel. So I shall escape out of his hand"* (1 Sam. 27:1).

But we see that Jonathan, who is a type of the Holy Spirit, came to David to encourage him:

> *Then Jonathan, Saul's son, arose and went to David in the woods and strengthened his hand in God. And he said to him, "Do not fear, for the hand of Saul my father shall not find you. You shall be king over Israel, and I shall be next to you. Even my father Saul knows that"* (1 Samuel 23:16-17).

Without the help of the Holy Spirit, it is impossible to come out of some of these tests.

We learn the following principles from Jonathan's relationship with David that will help us in our relationship with the Holy Spirit:

1. To inform you of the enemy's move—Jonathan promised David that when Saul made a new plan to attack him, he would send someone to inform him so that he could escape (see 1 Sam. 20:12-13). The Holy Spirit reveals to us the plots of the enemy, protects us, and gives us victory over every attack. The Holy Spirit will show us things to come (see John 16:13).

2. To encourage you in the time of distress—Jonathan often came to encourage David when he was discouraged (see 1 Sam. 23:16-17). Praying in the Holy Spirit is the best way to encourage yourself, for His name is Comforter (see John 14:16 KJV).

3. He intercedes on your behalf—Jonathan interceded for David to his father. He told King Saul about the good things David did and tried to support him (see 1 Sam. 20:24-32). One of the ministries of the Holy Spirit is to intercede for us (see Rom. 8:26-27).

4. He is interested in your destiny—Jonathan was supposed to be the next heir to the throne, but he sacrificed that for David because he recognized that David was supposed to be the king (see 1 Sam. 23:17). When things get difficult, the Holy Spirit will encourage you by reminding you of your destiny and the promises God gave you. He will show you things that are given to you by God (see 1 Cor. 2:9-10).

5. He will stand beside you during the time of trouble—Jonathan risked his own life to protect David and stood with him all the way (see 1 Sam. 20:32). The Holy Spirit will never leave us nor forsake us. He is called the *Paraklete*, One who is called to stand beside. The Holy Spirit is with you and in you (see John 14:17).

6. It is a covenant relationship—Jonathan and David made a covenant relationship to protect one another (see 1 Sam. 20:13-16). The Holy Spirit is a gift to those who are under the New Covenant and no one can annul that covenant.

7. He did not leave David when things got difficult—Jonathan was faithful to David until the end

(see 1 Sam. 20:42). The Holy Spirit will not leave us, no matter what we go through (see Isa. 43:2-3).

8. He was truthful and a man of integrity—Jonathan did not side with his father Saul because he was the king or because Jonathan was ambitious to be the next king. He did not violate his own conscience and had integrity of heart. The Holy Spirit is the Spirit of truth so you can always trust His voice (see John 14:17).

ZIKLAG: PRESSED DOWN BEYOND MEASURE—BROKENNESS

This was one of the major tests David encountered before he became king. When he and his men were staying in Ziklag, the Amalekites invaded, taking all the women and children captive, and setting the city on fire. When David and his men came back, they saw the devastation and were totally shattered (see 1 Sam. 30:1-8).

> *Now David was greatly distressed, for the people spoke of stoning him, because the soul of all the people was grieved, every man for his sons and his daughters. But David strengthened himself in the Lord his God* (1 Samuel 30:6).

In our walk with the Lord, we will reach a place where we think all is lost and the enemy has come and devastated everything. But God is able to restore all we have lost and more. Ziklag is a place where we will be pressed down beyond measure. It is a place of loss, of people who are close to us, finances, credibility, health, resources, etc. People in whom we put our trust might betray us. There will only be one place you can go for help—the Lord. *"But David strengthened himself in the Lord his God."*

In the end, David recaptured everything he lost plus he spoiled the enemy and plundered their goods. When he came back, David sent gifts to all the elders in that region and his reputation was stronger than ever.

Now when David came to Ziklag, he sent some of the spoil to the elders of Judah, to his friends, saying, "Here is a present for you from the spoil of the enemies of the Lord" (1 Samuel 30:26).

Every great man and woman of God reaches this place before they are used by Him. In truth, this marks the end of human effort and the beginning of the true work of God. Many times we think we are serving God or doing ministry, but we are really doing what we want to do in the way we want to do it. Ziklag is a leveling of the field. We lose everything and come down to nothing to begin the real life with God.

Jacob was a deceiver who cheated his brother out of his blessing, but then had to run away for his life. The only thing he had was the staff in his hand. That was the real beginning of Jacob's life.

HEBRON: ALLIANCE—PROMOTION

When you finish all of the tests, God will bring you to Hebron, a place of alliance. He will connect you with some people who will help you to fulfill your destiny. You will enter into an alliance with people who are committed to support you. David and his men went to Hebron by the direction of God and that was the beginning of David's glory. *"Then the men of Judah came, and there they anointed David king over the house of Judah"* (2 Sam. 2:4).

This was the second anointing David received in his life. The anointing comes to our life in stages. The more we are faithful and pass the tests, the more the anointing in our life will increase. The tests did not end here for David. The battle between his house and the house of Saul continued for a long time: *"Now there was a long war between the house of Saul and the house of David. But David grew stronger and stronger, and the house of Saul grew weaker and weaker"* (2 Sam. 3:1).

Hebron is a place of increased responsibility, increased accountability, increased anointing, increased power, and increased wealth.

It is a place of restoration and honor. David reigned over Judah for seven years. He was faithful and executed justice and righteousness to the people. That promoted him to the next level.

> *Therefore all the elders of Israel came to the king at Hebron, and King David made a covenant with them at Hebron before the Lord. And they anointed David king over Israel.*
>
> *And the king and his men went to Jerusalem against the Jebusites, the inhabitants of the land, who spoke to David, saying, "You shall not come in here; but the blind and the lame will repel you," thinking, "David cannot come in here." Nevertheless David took the stronghold of Zion (that is, the City of David).*
>
> *So David went on and became great, and the Lord God of hosts was with him"* (2 Samuel 5:3,6-7,10).

Hebron is also a place of promotion. David received his third anointing to be the king over all of Israel while he was in Hebron, as we read in the above scriptures. It also shows the three anointings of Jesus Christ: that of King, Prophet, and Priest. David is the only king who functioned in these three levels. Through Christ, we receive the same anointing if we go through the tests and come out victorious.

ZION: FORTIFICATION—FULFILLMENT

Zion was the ultimate goal; David settled down from all his wars and God gave him victory over all his enemies (see 2 Sam. 7:1). David built his palace and his house and reigned as the mighty king of all Israel. Zion is a place of fulfillment, peace, victory, fame, and a place of glory and honor that has been prepared for all of us. All of our dreams come to fruition in Zion.

But Zion is also a place of great temptation. As leaders, when we reach that position of fame and glory, we tend to ignore our weaknesses and the path that brought us there. There is a tendency to think that we are immune to all attacks and can do anything.

We might feel we have the power and money to do anything we want. That is not true at all.

If we are not careful, we can fall from glory to the deepest pit of failure. Just because we are successful does not mean we do not have any weaknesses. David failed to overcome the lust of his flesh and committed a hideous sin.

He looked at a woman bathing and was tempted. He gave in to the temptation and committed adultery, and to cover that act, he committed murder and then lied about it. This one series of unwise decisions marred his name and brought shame to the whole nation (see 2 Sam. 11:1-27).

When we are successful, we will be tested, and if we are not careful, we can experience a tragic fall. When we fall when we are successful, it affects more people than when we fall when nobody knows us. When we are successful is not a time to slack off; it is imperative to fortify our lives with greater strength and vigilance.

I have seen that many great, anointed men and women also had great weaknesses. I was wondering why God did not take away those weaknesses. Moses had an anger problem and it cost him the privilege of entering the Promise Land. David had a problem with his flesh. I found that it is our responsibility to take care of our weaknesses once we recognize the call of God on our life. They will try to creep in on us as long as we live in this earthly suit.

There is a final test that David went through in his life. I will explain it in Chapter 15, "The Final Test."

Chapter 10

AREAS OF OUR LIFE IN WHICH GOD TESTS US: PART I

In the following pages we are going to learn some of the major areas in which God will test every individual He chooses to utilize toward fulfilling His purpose. The list is not exhaustive in any way. I have listed and explained them based on the wisdom and understanding God has given me. Some of them I have made into individual chapters, while others are just headings throughout this chapter. I believe God will use this to bless your life in a mighty way.

TEST OF THE GOOD VS. THE BEST

We have heard that good is the enemy of the best. In life, we will have opportunities to do many good things, but that does not mean they are all part of God's will for our life. As you move forward in the Lord, there will be many good things.

People will come your way with opportunities and you will be tempted to accept them all, but if you do so without consulting God first, they could be a trap to keep you from the best plan He has for you. You will be tied up with all good things, and when the time comes to do the best and to have the best God has for you, you will not be prepared to accommodate it.

I have seen in the Bible, as well as in my life, that whenever you are close to having the best God has for you, there will always be a good opportunity that shows up at your door to tempt you and distract you from making the step toward the best. As human beings, we like to choose the path of least resistance. But, if you want to have the best of something, you need to pay a little extra for it.

In the spirit, if you want to have God's best, you need to go through some extra struggles where you will learn to wait and develop patience. The enemy is very smart and very good at bringing shortcuts to fulfill our dream or vision. Jesus came to take back the authority over the whole earth from the devil. He was fasting and about to enter into the ministry the Father had for Him. The devil offered Him a shortcut to have all the glory and the kingdoms of the earth. What he was telling Jesus was that it was not necessary to go through all the pain and struggles. "Just look," he said, "here is an easy way to achieve Your purpose. You do not need to go to the cross, You can have it now."

That is the path of least resistance and it might have looked like a good idea, but it was not what the Father had for Him. Jesus denied the good in order to have the best. I have been deceived a few times. When I got close to having God's best in my life, the enemy came with a good idea and I was distracted. Good ideas are counterfeit opportunities of God's best.

The Israelites came to the border of the Promise Land that they had been waiting 400 years to enter. They only had to cross the Jordan River to enter. They had some conquests and victories over on this side of the Jordan, but the best was waiting for them on the other side.

Gad, Dan, and half of the tribe of Manasseh were tempted by the good things they had seen on one side and they decided to stay there and not cross over. At that time they thought it was a good idea, but they did not realize it was a trap and a big mistake. They were disobeying God by doing that and missed the best God had for them.

We know from history that they were the first ones to be carried away into captivity when the enemy came. That is what happens every time we choose the path of least resistance and trouble. In the beginning it will look easy and comfortable, but we will pay in the end. The difference between the good and the best is quite noticeable when you pay the price. For the best, you pay the price (go through struggles) in the beginning and enjoy the rest of life. For the good, you enjoy the temporary comfort right now and pay later—sometimes you pay for the rest of your life.

Another incident we see in the life of Jesus occurred in the middle of His earthly ministry. He fed the 5,000 and the 4,000 on two separate accounts. He healed the sick and comforted those who were mourning. The people saw Him as a great leader and tried to make Him their king. It was a good idea, but not the best or God's will for Jesus at that time.

The Jewish people were under the Roman Empire and they were not happy about it. They were waiting for their Messiah to come and redeem them from Roman rule. They wanted Jesus to set up an earthly kingdom and reign as their king.

It was not for this purpose that Jesus came to the earth, however. Though He is the King of the Jews, He was not establishing an earthly kingdom at His first coming. We need to be very careful in our own life because these ideas are not always bad ideas. But they are always the enemy of the best. We will not think there is anything wrong when these ideas and opportunities come to us. They will almost look and feel like the best thing to do at the time, but you will not have an inner witness in your spirit.

Abraham and Sarah are another example of those who chose the good over the best. God promised them a child and they waited for many years with no sign of the fulfillment of God's promise.

Suddenly, Sarah had a "good" idea to give her maid to her husband for them to have a child together. You and I both know now how costly that choice was.

They did not feel anything wrong at that time because they thought it was a good idea. Sarah might have thought, "God promised Abraham and it does not matter through whom he will have a child." She was excluding herself from the promise of God. That was not God's will for them. When God gives a Word to the husband, it very much involves the wife and also their children.

In each new season you reach in life there will appear an opportunity that will look good but will keep you from entering into God's best. Many people will seize that moment and will think, "Wow, I have been waiting for something like this for a long time," and then will jump in without looking to the left or right. After they have jumped, they will realize that it was not God's best for them and they will ask for help to be rescued from that situation.

All the men and women that God used faced this test in their life. Do not settle for the mere good. Keep moving until you have God's best in every aspect of your life. Life is too short and we do not have time to do everything we would like to do on this earth. We need to keep our focus on the purpose God has for us and fulfill it at any cost. God did not promise us an easy road, but He promised to be with us always.

The Bible says in Proverbs 14:12, *"There is a way that seems right to a man, but its end is the way of death."*

If you are in full-time ministry, please be careful that you are not driven to do too many good things. As ministers, there is always a temptation to do a lot of good things. Make sure you hear from God before you begin any major projects or goals in your ministry. I believe the best is God's perfect will for you and the good is God's permissive will for you.

TEST OF DELAYED DELIVERANCE

God will deliver you from some things as soon as you ask Him. There are other areas that we ask Him, we fast and pray, we get prayed for by others, and we confess the right thing, but it seems for some reason the deliverance is not happening. Sometimes you will walk around with the same struggles for many years.

The reason God lets us go through the fire instead of delivering us from it instantly is so that when we come out we will be able to strengthen others who will go through similar problems. Unless we go through something, we cannot teach others about it. Having head knowledge about something is not the same as having heart knowledge. Head knowledge comes through education and heart knowledge comes through experience and revelation.

Jesus told Peter that Satan asked to sift him like wheat, but Jesus prayed for him that his faith would not fail. Jesus did not pray that he would not go through the sifting, but that he would come out of it and be in a position to strengthen the brethren (see Luke 22:31-32).

God will let you go through the test until His purpose is accomplished and you have learned the lesson. Many important things God teaches us *about* life come by way of the things we go through *in* life. Jesus learned obedience through the things He suffered (see Heb. 5:8).

When people go through a difficult situation, all they usually ask is for God to deliver them from it or get them out of it. God might have taken us into that situation to teach us some valuable lessons. Instead of delivering us from the situation, He will walk us through it so that many will be blessed at the end and His name will be glorified.

This was true of Daniel in the Old Testament. He was a God-fearing man whose associates became jealous of him and falsely accused him. The king decreed that he be thrown into the lion's den. God could have delivered him, but He did not. He actually let him be cast into the lion's den, only to miraculously preserve him so that, in the end, Daniel was blessed and God's name was glorified throughout the whole kingdom.

We read about the same thing with the three young men in the book of Daniel: Shadrach, Meshach, and Abed-Nego. They went through the fire and God received much more glory through that outcome than if He had helped them to not go through it in the first place.

We focus on the result and desire it so desperately that we try to get there as fast as we can in our own way. God focuses on the process because it is in the process that our character and patience are developed. During this time, the best thing to ask God is not to deliver you from it, but ask Him, "Lord, what do You want me to learn from this? What are You trying to teach me? Please give me the grace to cooperate with You and to learn from You."

God told the Israelites that He would cast out the nations before them little by little and not have them destroyed all at once (see Deut. 7:22). The reason was so the beasts of the field would not increase. That is what I call delayed deliverance.

TEST OF FAILURE

There will be times in life when we step out to do things we believe we heard from God, but they will not end up the way we expected. Those are hard times in life because we believe we tried to obey God's voice, but we ended up in a great trial or difficult situation.

Peter heard the voice of Jesus calling him to come out of the boat and stepped out to obey Him. When he began to walk on the water, everything seemed to be working and he thought he was doing well. But the closer he drew to Jesus, the more he began to lose his focus and sink into the water. He might have thought that he would die right there and that would be his last day. He cried out to Jesus for help and Jesus lifted him out of the water (see Matt. 14:28-30).

When you and I step out to obey God, it will be the same. There will be nothing and no one to rely on. We will be alone in the midst of the storm. Imagine Peter, he was in the water and there was nothing he could hold on to. He might have thought that he failed or that his faith did not work. In those moments, you will not even know how to trust God anymore.

You will question God's character and your trust in Him. But when you look back on that experience after a while, it will be the single most significant element God used to build your faith and your trust in Him.

There will be different occasions when you will go through such times in your life. I have gone through it myself many times. He lets us go through these incidents to show us what is really in us. Peter might never have thought that he had issues with fear in his life. But when he was on the water walking, and when he saw the wind and the waves, they brought out the fear that was already in his soul. I believe it gave him an opportunity to deal with his fear; otherwise, it would have affected him later in his life and ministry.

There is no word called *failure* in the dictionary of God. He uses all of our circumstances to teach us His ways. He calls it the process, or preparation, for His purpose.

TEST OF TIME

Every purpose under heaven has an appointed time. God is a God of timing. He is never too late and never comes a minute early. Humans are impatient in nature and look for instant gratification. We are not naturally trained to wait, but this is a discipline we need to develop if we are to walk with God. It is called the *discipline of delayed gratification.*

I have learned from experience and from the Word of God that God speaks to us concerning our life and purpose long before He ever decides to fulfill them. God will tell you something today that He is planning to fulfill 15 years from now. You might wonder why He should speak that to you *now*.

Well, welcome to the club. You are not alone in this. Remember, when God told Abraham that he was going to have a son, he was 75 years old at that time. God was not planning to fulfill this promise right away, but when Abraham was 100 years old. Twenty-five years is a long time to wait for something.

Many saints of God make mistakes here. They hear from God and jump out ahead of His timing. They will be on an airplane the next day and arrive at their destination a few years early. They arrived at the right destination, but not at the right time. What is waiting for them there? Trouble. Or they get married too soon. It may even be the right person but it is the wrong time.

The reason God speaks to you ahead of time is so you can prepare for it. What does that mean? If God has spoken to you that you are going to be the prime minister of a country, well, don't you think you might need some education and training? If God comes, tells you today, and puts you in that position tomorrow, guess what will happen? You will not last too long. If He called you into a ministry that is going to touch millions of people around the world, you need a long time of preparation to get ready for it.

Then the question becomes, "If God called me to do something, will He not anoint me to do it? Why should I prepare for ten or twenty years? Isn't His anointing supposed to enable me with everything I need?" God can anoint you only to the extent that you are prepared. Anointing is the "ignition" in the automobile, and we know that an ignition itself will not make an automobile run. It takes a long time to design, plan, and build an automobile.

God will not build an automobile. He will give you the wisdom and understanding, but you need to do the work.

The enemy likes to push you and make you feel that it is getting too late and you do not have much time left. Learn to be patient and rest in His promises.[1]

TEST OF FEELING

We are emotional beings as well as spiritual beings. Have you heard someone say lately, "I feel like doing something," or, "I don't feel good"? There is a realm of feeling and that is the natural realm. God does not operate in the realm of feeling. Just because we feel something does not mean we have to do it or say it. Feelings are of the body, or flesh. Emotions are of the soul. But truth is of the spirit.

Proverbs 29:11 says, *"A fool vents all his feelings, but a wise man holds them back."*

In our Christian walk, we need to mature beyond our feelings in order to grow spiritually. There are times in life when we need to do the right thing whether we feel like it or not. If we depend on our feelings, we will not make much progress in life.

It takes a lot of discipline to say "No" when you feel strongly to do or say something that is not right. I know from my own experience that a lot of problems in family life come because people do not know how to control their feelings. They say things they should not say—you do not need to express everything you feel, especially when you are upset with someone.

Impetuous actions cost us dearly. There will be times we feel something really is from God but it may not be God's will for us. We need to wait until our feelings calm down so we can evaluate the situation before we act on those feelings.

We have to reach a place in our Christian walk where we are not driven by feelings. Feelings should not determine our actions or reactions. We should do things out of discipline, character, integrity, and by the love of God. People who are led by their feelings will not reach maturity in Christ.

There will be times when we really feel like doing something and will almost feel like God is speaking or orchestrating the situation. Beware! Wait another two hours or a day and then check it out to see whether you still feel the same about that particular situation. If God is speaking to you, it will be consistent. There will be no variation in the intensity of the voice or feeling.

TEST OF DESIRES

The test of desire has to do with our emotions. Most things in life will not happen when we would like them to happen, or in the way we think they should happen. When I was a teenage boy, I desired so badly to have a stereo. One of my uncles was working in the Middle East and when he came home he brought two or three stereos. I asked him if I could have one. He said, "No," and instead sold them to someone else.

I remember coming home with my feelings so hurt that I cried bitterly that day. I could not believe I did not have a stereo. When I grew up and became an adult, God blessed me financially and I could buy ten stereos if I wanted. But I do not need them anymore.

It is not God's will for us to have all that our heart desires. We have to be very careful about following our feelings and emotional drives. When I was 17, I told my mother that I wanted to get married. Thank God she did not listen to me and that I did not get married. I was married when I was 26 and I had to go through a maturing process to have and live with a wife. When I was 17, I thought marriage was about having sex with a woman.

Many times, we will kick, scream, and ask God why He is not answering our prayers when we want. We think the situation is so bad and we need an answer from God right away. But God does not see things that way. We need to learn to see things from His perspective.

TEST OF SACRIFICE

If we are to accomplish anything that is valuable or anything that is going to last, there must be a sacrifice made on our part. What this generation does not like is sacrifice. They want everything for free and someone else to pay the price. When we have a whole generation with that mindset, the society ceases to develop and begins to degenerate.

Sacrifice means you are willing to delay and avoid temporary gratification and luxury for a greater purpose and for a later time.

SACRIFICE OF TIME

In order to accomplish any task, we need to invest our time. If you want to be a piano player, you need to set aside time to practice every day. There will be times when you will not want to practice or do the things you should. You need to discipline yourself, sacrifice other things, and commit yourself to practicing the piano. After a few years, you will become an excellent piano player and will be happy for the time you sacrificed.

For me to write my books is a sacrifice. God had me write seven books in one year. Some days all I do is sit in my chair and type on my laptop. After I completed each one, I felt joy in my heart from seeing the finished product.

Prayer is one of the major areas where we need to sacrifice our time. We may not immediately see the results of our prayers, but the years of invested time in prayer will give us a great return in due time.

SACRIFICE OF WORLDLY PLEASURES

To live godly in our society these days, we need to sacrifice the pleasures that are available in the world. They may look so alluring and tempting, but we need to resist and say, "No." The apostle Peter exhorts us to run from the lust that is in the world, which leads to corruption (see 1 Pet. 2:11).

Moses is an excellent example of someone who sacrificed worldly pleasures for a divine call and purpose:

> *By faith Moses, when he became of age, refused to be called the son of Pharaoh's daughter, choosing rather to suffer affliction with the people of God than to enjoy the passing pleasures of sin, esteeming the reproach of Christ greater riches than the treasures in Egypt; for he looked to the reward* (Hebrews 11:24-26).

God will ask you to sacrifice time and things, anything and everything for you to achieve your dreams on this earth.

SACRIFICE OF CONVENIENCE

Many times God will ask us to do things that are not convenient for us or in the time we would like to do them. Many miracles took place in the Bible because people were willing to go out of their way and obey what God told them to do. It was not convenient for them, but they did it and received the miracle.

Naaman the Syrian did not like what the prophet Elisha told him to do to receive his healing. He was told to dip himself seven times in the Jordan River. He became furious and refused, but later submitted to Elisha's direction after receiving good advice from his servant (see 2 Kings 5:1-19).

Jesus said that if someone asks us to go one mile with them, we should go two miles (see Matt. 5:41). Reading and studying the Bible every day is not an easy task. Some days it will not be convenient to do, but we have to do it in order to grow spiritually and stay on the course God called us.

TEST OF WAITING AND FRUSTRATION

The Bible says they that wait upon the Lord shall renew their strength (see Isa. 40:31). Waiting is a spiritual thing and delay is a natural thing. Waiting is when God gives us a promise and we have no idea when He is going to fulfill that promise. So we wait for His timing.

We see another sad incident in the book of First Samuel. God appointed Saul as king of Israel. The prophet Samuel was his spiritual advisor and spiritual covering. King Saul was not keen on obeying the voice of God; he wanted to be popular. One day Samuel told him to wait until he arrived to offer the sacrifice. Saul waited for a couple of days and lost patience.

Saul went ahead and offered the sacrifice, and the moment he did, Samuel showed up. That one incident caused God to reject Saul from being the king of Israel. His kingdom was taken from him and was given to David. We should not give in to our feelings when God has told us to wait or when He has given us a word.

Saul did not wait patiently as the psalmist exhorted us to do: *"I waited patiently for the Lord; and He inclined to me, and heard my cry"* (Ps. 40:1).

TEST OF HUMILITY

Humility is not pretending you do not have what you have. It is not misrepresenting your personality or position. True humility is being real and true. There is a false humility among religious people, falsely showing themselves to be so pious and spiritual. They call themselves worms and the dust of the earth.

There is a constant fight in us to degrade ourselves. Very few people are willing to admit who they really are. They are either too high-minded or they are too low-minded. If God called you to be an apostle, there is nothing wrong with being addressed as an apostle. Paul did not deny his apostleship for the sake of humility. Every time he wrote to the churches, he wrote as Paul the apostle. Paul said: *"For I am the least of the apostles, who am not worthy to be called an apostle, because I persecuted the church of God. But by the grace of God I am what I am, and His grace toward me was not in vain"* (1 Cor. 15:9-10).

Jesus did not deny His position as the Son of God. He was humble, and we need to have the same mind that Jesus had. It is not denying our call or position on this earth. Humility is staying within the limit of the call, position, and authority God has given us.

We will be tested in this area. Many people are trying to be somebody and do things God has not called them to be or do. It does not matter how blessed we are, we need to know that it was God who blessed us and gave us what we have. A humble person always acknowledges his dependency on God, that He is the source of every blessing he or she receives.

TEST OF BETRAYAL AND REJECTION

The test of betrayal is perhaps one of the most painful things we will ever go through in life. It wounds the soul and heart more than anything else. Believe it or not, we will be betrayed by our close friends and, sometimes, close relatives and family members.

Paul said that all of his partners in Asia deserted him (see 2 Tim. 1:15; 4:16). Paul spent a majority of his time and ministry in Asia Minor and its surrounding region. Toward the end of his ministry, his testimony was that everyone in Asia deserted him. That is not an easy thing for any leader to swallow. When you have spent your life and resources to train up people and, in the end, they betray you and go with someone else, it is heartbreaking to go through.

David was betrayed by his son Absalom; his close friends betrayed him; he even says in Psalm 41:9, *"Even my own familiar friend in whom I trusted, who ate my bread, has lifted up his heel against me."*

Jesus was betrayed by two of His apostles. Peter and Judas denied Him, but Peter repented and was restored. When this happens, we should not take things into our own hands. We need to trust God to take care of us and deal with the circumstances. We need to make sure we do not hold any bitterness or vengeance against that person.

There is a slight difference between betrayal and rejection. Betrayal is rejection from someone you love and trust, while rejection can be from people that you know but not necessarily love or trust.

TEST OF PERSECUTION

You will be persecuted for your faith in Christ. Anyone who lives a godly life in Christ will face persecution (see 2 Tim. 3:12). I know many precious brothers and sisters in India who have been rejected and disowned by their families and communities because they chose to believe in Christ.

When we face persecution, we should not lose our hope. Those moments can serve as opportunities to draw closer to Him and to know Him in ways that we did not know Him before. Persecution can come in many forms. It can be emotional or physical abuse. Many have lost their lives because of their faith in Christ.

The Church was founded upon the blood of the martyrs. If they had not stood strong for their faith, we would not be enjoying the freedom and blessings we now enjoy.

TEST OF PRAISE

The test of praise is the opposite of the test of rejection. Here we will be praised by people instead of being rejected by them. We need to make sure we do not do anything to receive praise from men. We need to divert all the praise, honor, and glory to God who enables us to do anything good.

There is a possibility that the same people who praise us today will reject us tomorrow. When Jesus came into Jerusalem, the people shouted, "Hosanna, blessed is He who comes in the name of the Lord." A few days later they were shouting, "Crucify Him. We have nothing to do with this fellow."

We should not fall prey to the praise of men. People will come to you praising, but their heart may not be with you. Psalm 62:4 says, "*They only consult to cast him down from his high position; they delight in lies; they bless with their mouth, but they curse inwardly.*"

We need to make our heart "praise proof" and give all the praise and glory to God alone.

TEST OF OBSCURITY

When God calls us, He separates us from some people and trains us for our future. The greater the call on your life, the greater and longer the preparation will be. He will put the vision and dream in our heart from a young age and we will think it is going to happen within the next two years or less; whereas, in God's timetable, He might be thinking 20 or 30 years.

During this season, He will put us in close proximity with other great men and women from whom we should learn about life. Elisha was appointed as a prophet after Elijah. God asked Elijah to find him and train him. Elisha was serving Elijah for a long time before he ever did any ministry—he was pouring water for Elijah (see 2 Kings 3:11).

David was put in King Saul's palace as a musician so he could learn how kings administrate a kingdom. It was not the best atmosphere for him to learn, but it gave him access to people and places he otherwise would not have been able to experience.

We will be as obscure as dust and no one will ever recognize that we are created to do anything great. Moses was feeding the sheep of his father-in-law in the desert for 40 years before he had an encounter with God.

The world will not even know that you exist. Do not try to make things happen or build your organization in the wilderness.

Do not build anything permanent in the wilderness, because the wilderness is not your permanent place.

The vessels God puts out for people to see have to be flawless. That does not mean we need to be perfect before God uses us. God will keep us obscure until He thinks we are ready. We may feel we are ready to take on the world and do anything for God, but He sees the things that need to be worked on in us. So He will take us through some more fire until all of the dross has been burned and what remains is pure gold. One thing you can be sure about God is that He is never late.

You might feel you are more anointed and more capable than the leader you are serving—that is only a temptation of the flesh. Yield to the process and God will bring you out when He thinks you are ready.

One of the best modern examples I can think of is Pastor Joel Osteen of Lakewood Church. He was a cameraman for his father for many years and he never thought that one day he would be preaching and pastoring a megachurch. He was faithful and committed to what he was doing. No man knew him or noticed him during those days. People might have thought he was just a cameraman. God promoted him from that place to a place of influence, and now people all over the world know him.

TEST OF PROMOTION

There is nothing more dangerous than to be promoted in the Kingdom before the right time. Our flesh wants things to happen now and does not like to wait for God's timing. People will also influence us to act prematurely. We all like to speed up our lives and events.

David was anointed to be the king of Israel, but it was not until 13 years later that he actually became king. In between, he had many opportunities to promote himself and become king. King Saul was trying to kill him. He could have led a coup and killed Saul and overthrown his kingdom. People who were with him encouraged him to do so, but he denied them and waited for God's timing. Some of his sons did not learn that lesson from their father. They promoted themselves and declared to the world that they were kings and destroyed their lives.

There was a time in Jesus's ministry when people tried to make him a king over them. He went away from them and avoided popularity. Very often, after He performed a major miracle, He charged the person not to publicize it. He did not want the praise and adulation from people.

You might be called to do great things or to run great organizations, but now you are serving someone else and nobody knows you or recognizes you. Do not be disappointed. Wait for the right time. You do not need to influence any human being to get promoted by God.

There will be times when we will be tempted to promote ourselves because the people who could promote us do not even recognize us or our ability. We will be frustrated and feel like taking things into our own hands. We need to wait until God promotes us, whether in ministry or in the business place. Our flesh wants to find shortcuts for promotion, which usually brings regrets later.

TEST OF FAITH

The test of our faith is more precious than the gold that perishes (see 1 Pet. 1:7). Faith alone will not produce much long-lasting fruit. Faith needs to be mixed with love and patience. It takes time to develop our patience. There is only one kind of faith that does not fail; that is faith that works by love (see Gal. 5:6).

TEST OF LONELINESS

All servants of God go through this particular test. It has been said by someone, "It is lonely at the top." When we walk with the

Lord, there will be times we feel like God has left us or forsaken us. What we feel is not exactly true. God will test us to see how we will react to this test.

We will go through a mountaintop experience and then walk right into a season where we feel God has left us. Elijah had a great breakthrough on Mount Carmel, and the next day He was running away, totally lonely and afraid for his life. When you are lonely you will feel like you are the only one who is going through what you are going through.

The disciples had a great time feeding the 5,000 with Jesus. After that miraculous experience, Jesus told them to go to the other side of the lake. Jesus went to pray, and while they were traveling, the storm came and beat on their boat. They were terror-stricken and afraid they were going to die. Jesus was not going to let that happen, but they forgot about the miracles and the promise when they were in the midst of the storm.

God is a God who hides (see Isa. 45:15). Why does He hide? It is because He wants us to seek Him and find Him. The psalmist laments, *"Loved one and friend You have put far from me, and my acquaintances into darkness"* (Ps. 88:18).

TEST OF LACK

When the Israelites came out of Egypt, they had to go through the wilderness to reach the Promise Land. After traveling for three days, they ran out of water. God provided them water, and three days later they ran out of food.

Though they were free from the bondage of Egypt, they still had to overcome lack in their lives. Why does God test us with lack? He wants us to know that we should not trust in food or anything else for our satisfaction, but in Him and in His Word.

The Bible tells us the reason God let them hunger and thirst was to teach them they should not live by bread alone, but by every word that proceeds from the mouth of God (see Deut. 8:3).

When we experience lack, we need to be thankful to God and share with others who are in need. When we are in lack we may have access to other people's money or God's money and may be tempted to steal it. God will test you with someone else's wealth before He will entrust you with your own. He will test us with unrighteous mammon before He entrusts us with true riches (see Luke 16:11-12).

When the Israelites reached the Promise Land, the first city they possessed was the city of Jericho. God instructed them, specifically saying all of the gold and wealth from that city belonged to Him. One man named Achan stole some of the wealth that belonged to God and buried it in his tent. He was caught and judged by being stoned.

We need to remain faithful with the little we have and know that God will bring the increase at the right time.

TEST OF DISAPPOINTMENT

There will be times when we believe God for things and feel in our heart that He is going to meet that need but, when the time comes, what we believed will not come to pass. We will feel disappointed in God. We need to get past that stage and trust Him during those times.

When you are disappointed, be careful about the words you speak. We need to discipline ourselves to have self-control so that we will not say words that displease God. When you reach that place, you have overcome the test of disappointment.

TEST OF THE WILL

The second greatest power on earth, behind God's power, is human willpower. Demonic forces have more power than human beings, but until they can channel their power through a human being, they cannot do much on this earth. It is like a nuclear power station, which produces millions of watts of power. Unless we channel it through cables, it won't benefit us. Unless we say yes or agree with the devil, he cannot do anything on this earth.

One of the things the enemy tries to do is weaken our will and make us feel like we have no power over anything and are not able to make decisions for ourselves. He uses the demon of addiction to bind many people and, once they are addicted to something, they lose their willpower over it. They become a victim of that habit and are unable to break off from it until they believe they can have power over it.

One of the key areas where we need to have victory and self-control is in the area of speaking. The Bible says the tongue is a small member but it controls the entire body (see James 3:2-5). We need to exercise our willpower over our words if we are to live victoriously.

One thing about God is that He prepares us before we go through a test. He will give us the tools (His Word and revelation) to pass the imminent tests.

One morning I was reading the Bible and my attention fell to Psalm 17:3, where it says, *"You have tested my heart; You have visited me in the night; You have tried me and have found nothing; I have purposed that my mouth shall not transgress."*

And Isaiah 44:26 says, *"Who confirms the word of His servant, and performs the counsel of His messengers; who says to Jerusalem, 'You shall be inhabited,' to the cities of Judah, 'You shall be built, and I will raise up her waste places.'"*

I did not realize at that time why God brought those two scriptures to my attention. The next two days I felt so irritated and angry that every time I opened my mouth I wanted to speak negative words.

My circumstances aggravated me so much and I could not remember a day I felt like that before. One night I had to ask my wife to pray for me so I would feel normal again. On the third day,

I realized that I was going through a test about using self-control in speaking.

If you are anointed, the words you speak with your mouth have power. God will confirm the words that we speak and perform our counsel (see Isa. 44:26). All that God has to work with in order to perform what we need in our life is our faith, and the words we speak.

> *If anyone can control his tongue, it proves that he has per-*
> *fect control over himself in every other way. We can make a*
> *large horse turn around and go wherever we want by means*
> *of a small bit in his mouth. And a tiny rudder makes a huge*
> *ship turn wherever the pilot wants it to go, even though the*
> *winds are strong. So also the tongue is a small thing, but*
> *what enormous damage it can do. A great forest can be set*
> *on fire by one tiny spark. And the tongue is a flame of fire.*
> *It is full of wickedness, and poisons every part of the body.*
> *And the tongue is set on fire by hell itself and can turn our*
> *whole lives into a blazing flame of destruction and disaster*
> (James 3:2-6 TLB).

> *For the Scriptures say, "If you want to enjoy life and see*
> *many happy days, keep your tongue from speaking evil and*
> *your lips from telling lies. Turn away from evil and do good.*
> *Search for peace, and work to maintain it"* (1 Peter 3:10-11
> NLT).

A will that is not surrendered to God will always get entangled with the things of this world. They will always look for something new to do because the will is like a hungry wolf looking for food. But when your will is surrendered to God, it will be like a child that is weaned, calm and peaceful (see Ps. 131:2).

ENDNOTE

1. Please read my book *Recognizing God's Timing for Your Life* to understand and learn more about the importance of timing.

Chapter 11

AREAS OF OUR LIFE IN WHICH GOD TESTS US: PART II

TEST OF SUBMISSION AND REBELLION

One of the main areas in which people fail is submission and obedience. We have all inherited rebellion from the devil as part of our nature. He succeeded in convincing Adam and Eve to rebel against God's authority. We bought the lie that God is not just and that He is holding back the best we deserve.

Most people, deep down in their heart, deal with this problem, saying, "If God is good, He would not have allowed..." Or, "If God is just, He would answer my prayer."

We all have a rebellious part in us that does not want to submit to God's authority. It cries out to God, saying, "He is not just. He is not fair." So God will let us go through the valley of the shadow of death for us to deal with that rebellion. Some will get angry and bitter at God, thinking He is not fair in dealing with them.

He is letting us go through such places and events to help us get rid of that rebellion. God is not angry or upset with us when we express our true feelings. He knows the feelings in our heart. He is just working on us for our good and His glory.

TEST OF TRUST

There will be times when everyone we thought who was close and loyal to us will disappoint us. We will go through the pain of rejection and mistrust. Things that we thought could never happen will happen in our own closest relationships.

David describes his experience in Psalm 55:12-14:

For it is not an enemy who reproaches me; then I could bear it. Nor is it one who hates me who has exalted himself against me; then I could hide from him. But it was you, a man my equal, my companion and my acquaintance. We took sweet counsel together, and walked to the house of God in the throng.

Jesus had the same experience with Judas. The only difference was that He knew beforehand what was going to happen. But it didn't make the pain or experience any less real.

After we go through the betrayal, it will be hard for us to trust anyone. There is a saying in my language, which goes like this, "The cat that fell into the hot water is afraid when he sees the cold water." It means, because the cat went through one painful experience with water, it is afraid of any kind of water; it does not matter if it is hot or cold.

People we think will be with us until we die will pack up and leave in a day. People who said they would never do anything bad to us will suddenly stand against us.

TEST OF COMMITMENT

Most people are excited to start new projects, ventures, businesses, or even ministries. But few like to stick around to complete the job when it is no longer fun. We will be tested in our commitment to tasks we undertake and relationships we are in.

For me, the test of commitment to long-term projects comes when I hit the five-year mark. In the fifth year, I will be hit with the temptation to discontinue or run away from it. But I have to make the decision to stay with it whether I feel like it or not.

The test of a new relationship comes after one year. Something will seem to go wrong in the relationship, and I will be tested to continue that relationship or not. Most of the time, those relationships are important to me and I need them for the long run.

After we go through the test and come out on the other side, the relationship will always be better than when it first began. One of the reasons God tests relationships is to bring things out that need to be brought to light. If we do not address these issues, they will hinder us from having a deeper relationship in the future. Tests will always bring things to the light that we never thought were there.

The night Jesus was betrayed was a test of commitment for the disciples. They never thought they would betray Jesus or run away from Him. They did not recognize their own weaknesses. Only tests will reveal our weaknesses. As a result, they realized how weak they were.

Things will happen in our life that will make us feel a legitimate reason to quit, but we need to stick with it whether we feel like it or not. Our flesh is too weak to keep any commitment. We need the grace of God to keep the commitments that we have made to ourselves and to others.

TEST OF FAITHFULNESS

One of the reasons God does not entrust us with much is because we are not faithful with the little He has given us. God will entrust us with small responsibilities to see how we handle them. If we are faithful with the little, He will entrust us with more (see Matt. 25:29).

I have heard the stories of many great preachers. When they started their ministry, they would go to small meetings and preach like they were preaching to thousands of people. They would do the same preparation to preach to a group of five people as they would if they were going to preach to a crowd of 5,000.

God will test us with a little—a little money, a little responsibility, a little anointing, a little ministry, etc. We're not to despise the days of small beginnings (see Zech. 4:10).

TEST OF ATTITUDE

Attitude is the hidden state of our heart when we do a job, help someone, or go through something. God discerns the intentions of the heart (see Heb. 4:12). This is one of the common tests we all go through often. The Bible says whatever we do should be for the glory of God, to please Him and not to please man (see Gal. 1:10; 1 Cor. 10:31).

TEST OF RETALIATION AND VENGEANCE

God will allow other people to take advantage of you, cheat you, insult you, and revile you, to see whether you will hand the matter over to Him or try to handle it yourself. When Jesus was persecuted and abused, He could have called millions of angels to support and protect Himself, but He gave it to the Father.

It is human tendency to react, retaliate, and pay back those people who offend and revile us. We need to learn how to control those emotions and not react in anger toward other people. God will allow those situations to happen in our life time and time again until we are mature in that area and ready to manifest divine character.

If Jesus had retaliated on those who beat and spat at Him, He would have failed in His mission. He handed it over to the Father who judges righteously. Even though David was treated unjustly by King Saul, he still developed maturity in that area and passed the test.

Peter writes:

For God called you to do good, even if it means suffering, just as Christ suffered for you. He is your example, and you must follow in His steps. He never sinned, nor ever deceived anyone. He did not retaliate when He was insulted, nor threaten revenge when He suffered. He left His case in the hands of God, who always judges fairly (1 Peter 2:21-23 NLT).

And again:

Finally, all of you be of one mind, having compassion for one another; love as brothers, be tenderhearted, be courteous; not returning evil for evil or reviling for reviling, but on the contrary blessing, knowing that you were called to this, that you may inherit a blessing (1 Peter 3:8-9).

TEST OF VISION

The vision God gives us belongs to God. Sometimes we try to take it as ours and try to make things happen, and in so doing, that vision becomes an idol to us. God will come in and obstruct things, causing you to be stuck in the middle of something without being able to go forward or backward.

In that time, we need to surrender our vision to God and say, "Lord, it is Yours, I am Yours, and if You do not want something, I do not want it." Laying your vision at the altar may be one of the most painful experiences you have to go through, but it is a necessary step.

Some people call it the death of vision. The vision never dies, but goes back to whom it rightfully belongs. We did not create the vision, it was implanted in us by God through His Holy Spirit. God implants the Word in us and the Holy Spirit brings that Word into manifestation.

Our focus should never be on the vision, but on Jesus only. We are to set our eyes on Jesus (see Heb. 12:2).

TEST OF LETTING GO

We will all reach a point in life where we need to let God have complete control. When we are first saved, we accept Jesus Christ as our Lord. That means we are letting go of the control of our life and giving it to Him. Many people do not realize this. They just think they have done God a favor by saying the Sinner's Prayer. From that point, the requirement is that there is only one Person in charge of our life. Either we let Him control our life, or we continue to control it ourselves. It is our choice.

What does Jesus being in control of our life mean? There are two types of control. One is self-control, which is our part. Though we accept Christ as our Savior and Lord, He does not take over and make us do everything in our life. God did not create us to be robots. He created us with free will. We need to take care of our health—what we eat, where we go, and everyday decisions are still in our control. We still also have to control our emotions, actions, and words.

He will be in control of our life in those areas we let Him have control. He is not a tyrant who will force us to do things we do not want to do. This test is, for many, one of the hardest to go through.

Once we are saved, we step into the purpose God has for us, which He created before the foundation of the earth. In Him, all that concerns us was completed before the age began. As human beings, it is not easy for us to believe and not feel any anxiety about how things are going to work out.

We get tense and worry every day about how things are going to happen and how the great plan God has for us is going to take place. One thing we should know is that it is God who called us, it is God who gave us the purpose, it is God who gave us the promise, and He is able to complete it.

What we need to do is relax and daily enjoy fellowship with Him and walk through the doors He opens for us. We are not supposed to create anything or make anything happen.

It is so difficult for us to get to that place. We like to figure things out and see how something will work out before it actually happens, so we tend to step out of God's timing and start things that God did not want us to start. But God is faithful to fulfill what He has promised, and He will complete the good work He has begun in us (see Phil. 1:6).

We need to learn to relax, love Him, and walk in the Spirit. I used to be so worried and anxious about how things would work out. I tried to make things happen by my own effort and the results were always the same: tired, financial loss, stressed out, frustrated, angry at myself and bitter toward God, feeling He did not help when I needed Him.

I encourage you to let go and take your hands off of what God has promised you. Let Him guide and lead you. Let Him be the navigator of your life. If He has not asked you to do anything, spend your time reading and studying His Word and worshiping Him.

The sooner we let go, the better it is for us. You have not wasted any time. It does not matter how many years have gone by, God will complete what He started.

Do not fret, do not be anxious for anything, do not worry; these are some of the commandments in the New Testament. Your time will come. Kicking and screaming will not make anything happen faster than it ought to happen. God has not gotten any faster—He still moves at the same speed as when He began with Adam. The world has gotten faster and we think spiritual things need to get faster too, but they will not.

Let Go of Our Control

God will not force us or control us. He has given us free will. We have to choose to allow Him to guide us—and He promises to do just that: *"I will instruct you and teach you in the way you should go"* (Ps. 32:8).

249

Every day we need to choose to let Him guide us. We need to ask Him to lead us.

Let Go of Our Vision

God has given us the vision we have, and He is responsible to fulfill it. We need to prepare and plan and do all of those things, but we are not supposed to try to make things happen. We are supposed to walk through the doors when He opens them. We remember the story of Paul just after he believed. He tried to make things happen and tried to become a great preacher, but realized that he could not do it and had to wait for God's timing.

Sometimes the very vision God gave us can hinder Him from working through us. If we start to do things on our own and do not wait to hear from Him, we can get into big trouble.

So Paul had to spend some time (years) alone with Jesus to get His plan and strategy. Many people I know are busy helping God. They are promoting themselves and trying to be number one. Their motivation is, "I want to do this," or, "I want to do that." Everything is focused on the "I." It takes them a while to realize that things do not run the way they thought.

God loves us so much and He is waiting patiently for us to ask for His help and guidance. He already planned out everything concerning how to fulfill the vision He has given us. He already has all of the resources and the people we need. Nothing can stop Him from performing His purpose.

Many people try to do many things to get anointed. They try to squeeze it out of themselves as if the anointing is coming because of their self-discipline or performance. The Bible says, *"Not by might nor by power, but by My Spirit,' says the Lord of hosts"* (Zech. 4:6).

God is faithful to fulfill His Word. When Solomon dedicated the temple, he declared to the people the faithfulness of God: *"Blessed be the Lord, who has given rest to His people Israel, according to all that He promised. There has not failed one word of all His good promise, which He promised through His servant Moses"* (1 Kings 8:56).

That is a wonderful testimony about our God. There has not failed one word of all of His good promise. All of His promises are good. All of His promises are yes and amen in Christ Jesus (see 2 Cor. 1:20).

THE TEST OF TRIALS AND TEMPTATIONS[1]

James writes:

Blessed is the man who endures temptation; for when he has been approved, he will receive the crown of life which the Lord has promised to those who love Him. Let no one say when he is tempted, "I am tempted by God;" for God cannot be tempted by evil, nor does He Himself tempt anyone (James 1:12-13).

Temptation is of the flesh and always prompts us to do something to gratify the desires of the flesh. Trials are obstacles, challenges, delays, offenses, misunderstandings, and whatever pricks our heart and soul. Temptation comes from our own desires and from the enemy.

James goes on to say:

But each one is tempted when he is drawn away by his own desires and enticed. Then, when desire has conceived, it gives birth to sin; and sin, when it is full-grown, brings forth death (James 1:14-15).

When we are in the middle of a trial and do not understand the purpose of it, it means God is teaching us to be patient in an area of our life that is weak. We need to ask God for wisdom to understand the purpose of the trial. That is why James 1:5 says, *"If any of you lacks wisdom, let him ask of God, who gives to all liberally and without reproach, and it will be given to him."*

We need the wisdom of God to come out of trials victoriously. When we are tempted, we need to endure it. I used to lose heart when I encountered trials, and I would get discouraged, moody, and irritated because my patience was not developed to the level where I could rejoice. Now I am in a better place by His grace. Many people have given up on their faith and stopped walking with the Lord. Others do not believe that Christians go through any trials at all; they are in denial or think it is the enemy coming against them.

But James 5:13 asks, *"Is anyone among you suffering? Let him pray."* This scripture does not say if anyone is suffering, let him fight the enemy; it says to pray and seek God.

THE TEST OF MATERIAL WEALTH AND EARTHLY RICHES

As we grow spiritually, God will bless us materially. We need to make certain that our focus does not change from God to the material things. We should not regard the gifts more than the Giver. We will be tested to see whether we will serve God or money—or to see whether we are serving God for money.

It is easy to fall prey to the allure of money, influence, and power. It is easy to take the money God gives us and build personal wealth. Our focus should be winning souls for His Kingdom. God is not against us having wealth and money, but what is most important to Him is the motive of our heart.

There will come a time in life when we have to make a choice between God and material wealth. Gehazi was the servant of Elisha the prophet. I believe he could have been the successor of Elisha, but he lost his focus and failed the test. He regarded material wealth above the anointing of the Holy Spirit. Instead of the anointing, he and his descendants inherited Naaman's leprosy.

If God gives you wealth, make sure you have the right perspective and use it for the right cause, which is to expand the Kingdom of God on this earth. Do not be hasty to be wealthy. Those who try to be rich will fall into various temptations and shipwreck their lives: *"But those who desire to be rich fall into temptation and a snare, and into many foolish and harmful lusts which drown men in destruction and perdition"* (1 Tim. 6:9).

We have to make sure our earthly blessings are not given more importance than heavenly things. It is so easy to get caught in the trap of material wealth and abundance and forget the purpose of our existence on this earth. We are not on this earth right now to accumulate material wealth. Jesus said a man's life does not consist of the abundance of his goods (see Luke 12:15).

It is sad that in many circles all we hear about is money and material abundance. Many misunderstand the teaching of Jesus and use godliness for their own profit. Jesus promised us abundant life. What is abundant life? Many think it is talking about material abundance or earthly riches. If that was so, all of the disciples and apostles of the Lamb did not receive abundant life because they did not own multimillion dollar homes or expensive cars or ships. In fact, they never preached to any of the believers about material wealth or gave sermons on how to be rich.

Jesus promised us abundant life, not abundant stuff! Today, we see people with abundant stuff, but they are spiritually wretched and their life is a mess. They drive luxury cars, but their handbag is full of medication and tranquilizers to numb their pain.

They cannot even overcome a headache by faith, let alone a demon! The problem with the Church today is that we misunderstand the difference between this world and the Kingdom of God—we mixed them and it is almost impossible to know which one is which. Jesus's Kingdom is not of this world and it does not come by observation. It is not made of material stuff. His Kingdom is a spiritual kingdom. We cannot build God's Kingdom with gold and straw.

Many preachers are sleeping in the bosom of this world, the great Babylon, and they do not think about the wrath of God that is going to come upon them. No apostle in the New Testament preached about giving an offering and receiving the anointing or a financial breakthrough. That was not the subject of their preaching. They preached Christ and Him crucified. Do not misunderstand me: of course Paul wrote about giving in the Epistles, but it was not a gimmick of sowing a $1,000 and getting your debt cancelled.

We need to be aware of the deceitfulness of riches. Mammon, the spirit that works behind the monetary system of this world, is a controlling force. We should not base our spiritual life on earthly blessings. That should not be the goal of the Christian life. If you have or do not have, praise God. The teaching of the Bible is that if you have enough to eat and be clothed, be content; any desire to have more than that has its root in this world. Paul wrote, *"For we brought nothing into this world, and it is certain we can carry nothing out. And having food and clothing, with these we shall be content"* (1 Tim. 6:7-8).

Every man and woman of God will be tested in the area of material wealth and earthly riches. We need to walk away from them and avoid the trap of the enemy. Many are caught in it and have destroyed, or will destroy, their lives.

They teach that Abraham, Isaac, and Jacob were rich so we are also supposed to be rich. Where do we read in the Bible Abraham, Isaac, or Jacob teaching or preaching about their material wealth, or giving a lesson to their servants about how to reach millionaire status? We do not see that anywhere in the Bible. The wealth they had was given to them by God, but that was never their focus or intention. What about us? If God gave you material wealth, praise Him for it. If not, do not strive to be materially wealthy. Strive to be closer to God every day.

In the West, people work most of their lives to pay off the loan on their material possessions. Are those things worth spending a lifetime for on this earth? Is that all we value before we die? What do we tell Jesus when we meet Him? The majority of our time, energy, and money went toward something that is going to be burned in fire!

Oh, Lord, have mercy on us. Give us wisdom to count our days on this earth. And teach us how to live productively. Deliver us from the bondage of this spirit called *mammon*. Help us to work for things that are eternal. Deliver us from the deceitfulness of earthly riches. Conform us to the image and likeness of Your Son, Jesus.

If we love the world and the things in it, the love of the Father is not in us (see 1 John 2:15). Those who love the world are enemies of God (see James 4:4)—they have no part in the Kingdom of God. What are we doing in our churches today? We teach people how to become materially wealthy. Many are broken emotionally, their relationships are in shambles, their children are not walking in God's ways, but as long as they pay their tithe and come to church on Sunday, we call them good Christians.

We are the only "Jesus" the world can now see. Do people want to know Jesus after they see our lives, the way we conduct our lives? If not, woe to us because we have fallen from grace. We need to get back to our first love. Jesus said that if anyone does not forsake everything, they cannot be His disciple. We teach the opposite.

This is a trap of the enemy and he has blinded our eyes from seeing the truth. Abundant life means that we have the life of God overflowing in us: rivers of life flowing from our belly. What is flowing from our belly now? Worldly sorrows, depression, and the lack of love, joy, and peace? Christians grope in the darkness like the people in the world. Only in name are we different from them!

Run, dear children of God. Run away from this wretched world and its lusts. Do not get entangled with it. Many have fallen prey to the deception of the enemy. It is time to wake up. It is high time to wake up from our sleep. Beware of covetousness, which the Bible calls idolatry (see Eph. 5:3; Col. 3:5).

The Church in the West talks about idolatry in places like India, and yes, of course there is idolatry in India. But if someone is covetous and their main goal is to make money, they are no better than a Hindu who worships an idol.

The Church has been comfortably sleeping in the bosom of this world for too long. Most do not like anyone bothering them or saying it is wrong to do it. Are we married to the world or to the Lord? This is how you tell: if you lose every material thing you have and you still love Jesus, your life is founded in Him.

THE WORD TEST

When we receive a word from the Lord, we will go through a test to see whether we really believe that word. That is why many people get excited and jump up and down when they hear the Word preached. But, if you saw them the next day, you would realize nothing has changed in their lives.

The reason is that as soon as they reach home they will face a situation where they need to apply that Word, and instead of applying it, they will react to that situation as they always did and the Word they heard will not benefit them.

Jesus speaks to this type of person: *"Yet he has no root in himself, but endures only for a while. For when tribulation or persecution arises because of the word, immediately he stumbles"* (Matt. 13:21).

The reason the Word we receive does not benefit us is because we do not mix it with faith. Hebrews 4:2 says, *"For indeed the gospel was preached to us as well as to them; but the word which they heard did not profit them, not being mixed with faith in those who heard it."*

When you are waiting for the fulfillment of a promise, you will go through a period in your life where you will only have the word or the promise you received to hold onto and nothing else. You need to stay faithful during that time, without wavering. The word you received is a seed and it will come to pass.

TEST OF OPPORTUNITY VS. DESTINY

As we progress in our walk with God on this earth, one thing we need to learn is how to discern God's perfect will. One of the ways the enemy gets us sidetracked from God's perfect will is by throwing good opportunities in front of us. Those opportunities will be so alluring that it will almost look like the other twin of God's perfect will. But only when you step into it will you understand the pitfalls, and it will always end in regret and pain.

TEST OF OBEDIENCE AND GIVING

One of the main tests God uses to promote us in the spirit is the test of obedience, or the test of giving. I put both of these tests together because they are related to one another. When God tests us in the area of obedience, He also tests us in the area of giving. When we obey God, we have to give something to Him. It may not always be monetary things, but we need to give something from our heart to obey God. It could be pride, selfishness, our dream, passion, desire, our will, etc.

When God tests us in the area of obedience, we have to give up something that is precious to our heart, surrendering it to Him. Obeying God and the test of obedience are two different things. The test of obedience does not occur every time you obey Him or His Word. There will be special occasions when God tells you to do something just to check your heart to see whether or not you will obey Him.

Once He knows you are willing to obey Him regardless of what it is going to cost you, He will often give it back to you and say, "OK, I know you will not withhold anything from Me and that I am more important than anything you have, so I will bless you more."

Obeying God is a general rule to everyone, but the test of obedience is specific to each individual. What do I mean by that? When you repent of your sins, you are obeying God, but it is not a test of obedience. Every single person needs to repent of their sins. Likewise, giving is not a test because everyone is commanded to give.

For example, God asked Abraham to offer Isaac as a sacrifice. That was a test of obedience. You and I are not required by God to obey Him in that area unless He asks us specifically to give our sons as an offering, which I personally don't believe He will ever do again.

Even though God tested Abraham and asked him to offer his only son Isaac as a sacrifice, I believe God never wanted a human sacrifice and Isaac was the son of promise. God could not fulfill the promise if there was no Isaac. But He wanted to know that Abraham would obey Him even to the extent that he would give up the only son he had.

When Abraham laid him down on the altar and was ready to put the knife to Isaac, God intervened and stopped him from killing his son. God said the following words to Abraham:

> *Then the Angel of the Lord called to Abraham a second time out of heaven, and said: "By Myself I have sworn, says the Lord, because you have done this thing, and have not withheld your son, your only son—blessing I will bless you, and multiplying I will multiply your descendants as the stars of the heaven and as the sand which is on the seashore; and your descendants shall possess the gate of their enemies. In your seed all the nations of the earth shall be blessed, because you have obeyed My voice"* (Genesis 22:15-18).

Many people quote the above scriptures for their own selfish reasons, but do not understand how much it cost Abraham to receive that promise. As I said before, God uses the test of obedience to spiritually promote us. When you pass the test of obedience, you will come out with more of the power and anointing of God than before.

Before this incident, God never gave the promise of possessing the gates of their enemies to Abraham and to his descendants. This special promise was given as a result of passing the test of obedience.

I have had many incidents in my life where God asked me to give something to someone and I struggled in my heart for a while about it. I tried to negotiate with God, "Lord that is all I have, can I give something else or part of it?" Finally, I agreed and said yes, and suddenly a surge of peace flooded my heart. On one occasion, after I decided to obey, I heard Him whisper in my heart saying, "OK, you do not need to give it now."

An example from the life of Jesus illustrates this test: As Jesus was going along, a man came before him and asked Him what he could do to inherit eternal life. When Jesus told him to obey the commandments, he claimed he had kept them from his youth.

Then Jesus, looking at him, loved him, and said to him, "One thing you lack: Go your way, sell whatever you have and give to the poor, and you will have treasure in heaven; and come, take up the cross, and follow Me" (Mark 10:21).

The man went away sorrowful because he had great possessions. I love the attitude of Jesus here—He did not condemn him—instead, He loved him and gave him a test. He said to go, sell whatever he had, and give it to the poor. When the young man heard this, he became very sorrowful because he had great possessions and went away without obeying God.

This is a specific test of obedience Jesus gave to this particular person. If that was the requirement for everyone, not many would enter the Kingdom of God. Then, in the following verses, Jesus explained that this person's trust was in his riches and not in God. He wanted to see if the young man was willing to give up his trust in his riches and put his trust in Jesus. He could not do that and failed the test.

259

What if he had said, "Lord, all that I have is Yours, do what You please"? Jesus may have told him to go in peace and he would have inherited eternal life without selling his possessions. What if He required him to sell the possessions and give to the poor? Jesus gave the result in the following verses of the same chapter.

The disciples asked Jesus what they would receive because they gave up everything and followed Him.

> *So Jesus answered and said, "Assuredly, I say to you, there is no one who has left house or brothers or sisters or father or mother or wife or children or lands, for My sake and the gospel's, who shall not receive a hundredfold now in this time—houses and brothers and sisters and mothers and children and lands, with persecutions—and in the age to come, eternal life"* (Mark 10:29-30).

This was a test of obedience for this young man. Even if he had given away everything he possessed, he would have received it back a hundredfold in the days to come. So whenever God asks you to give anything, trust Him and obey His voice or you will end up at a loss in the end. God is good and loving. He will not test us beyond our capability and will always provide the grace to obey Him.

In the test of obedience and giving, God tests our heart to see whether we will put Him first and to see whether He is our first love. He wants to know that we will go to any extent to obey and follow Him. It is not because He needs something from us and it is not to put us through any pain, it is for our good that He tests us.

ENDNOTE

1. I have explained this in detail in Chapter 5, "The Test of Suffering."

Chapter 12

THE TEST OF LOVE AND RELATIONSHIP

TRUE LOVE'S RELATIONSHIP

Now we are going to learn about the test of all tests—the test of love. If you pass every other test but fail this one, you will not fulfill your destiny on this earth. In fact, this is the key to passing the other tests because all other tests depend on you passing this one. For that reason, this is one of the most difficult to pass.

Because of our fallen nature, our heart is deprived of true love, which most people did not receive during childhood. It is difficult to give love to someone else when we have not received it ourselves. It is difficult to forgive someone when you were never forgiven or do not know what true forgiveness is. The grace of God here is mandatory.

Relationships are of utmost importance in the Kingdom of God. Every blessing we receive comes through a relationship we have. Most of the problems we face on this earth will also be relational. God works out His purposes on this earth through the relationship He has with human beings. He works out our purpose through the relationships we have with each other.

Every relationship we have—particularly marriage, business, and ministry relationships—will be tested before we go to a new level. When we ask God to take our marriage to a new level, He will send a test. When we are tested, we might feel that the relationship is over. The test may come through a mistake or a wrong one person commits against the other. We may even have a legal right to break the relationship, but we should not. If we do, we will not prosper on this earth.

God had every legal right not to love us. Man is the one who broke the trust. But He chose to love us, and that is the example we need to follow. We are His children and we are commanded to imitate Him on this earth. There will be unusual circumstances where reconciliation in the natural will seem impossible, but still you need to hang in there and ask God for help. You may not want to associate with that person, but still you need to show love to them.

God will bring someone to our life who, based on normal human and religious standards, does not deserve to be loved, and He will ask us to love that person unconditionally. Humanly, it is impossible, but He has given us His love in our heart through the Holy Spirit that was given to us (see Rom. 5:5).

Unless we pass this test, no power will be released into our lives and we will not fulfill the destiny God has for us. Love is the foundation of Christian living and is the reason for our existence. God created us because He is love and wants someone to love and to love Him back. Because He loves us, He gave Jesus to redeem us and reconcile us to Himself so that we could fellowship with Him.

God expects us to give that kind of love to others because we were created in His image and likeness. Every great man and woman God used in the Bible was tested in this area.

HINDERED LOVE

The reason we are not able to love others is because our hearts are not clean and the flow of love is hindered by wounds and by scars. Many people are not able to love because they did not receive any love, or do not know how to receive it. They are not able to receive any love because they were not loved perfectly by their parents, or others, when they were growing up.

To bring us out of those experiences and to heal our hearts, God will bring people into our lives from whom we feel like running, but He will ask us to love them regardless of their behavior.

Four of the worst enemies of true love are self-righteousness, the religious spirit, a hardened heart, and legalism. When a person is influenced by any one of these, that person cannot truly love others the way God intended. That person might love people of the same feathers, but to love a person out of his or her self-righteous conscience is almost impossible.

COMMON CHARACTERISTICS

We are going to look at some biblical examples of how people passed the test of love and relationship in their life and fulfilled their destiny.

When we study the lives of mighty men and women of God in the Bible, we see some common characteristics. They were all very careful about their relationships. How they handled relationships was more important to them than their own lives. It seems like they all knew the secret of how much a broken relationship could hurt them. They knew that if there was a broken relationship in their life, God's favor would not be able to flow to them. They behaved wisely and carefully when it came to offenses.

We are going to learn how the patriarchs of our faith overcame this test. They are called fathers because they went before us in faith and in the knowledge of God. Children learn from their fathers and according to Galatians 3, Christians are the children of Abraham.

Our God is the God of Abraham, Isaac, and Jacob. They were not perfect, as we are not perfect, but we can learn from their examples and from their mistakes so that we will not repeat them in our own life. The foremost commandment in the Bible, both in the Old Testament and in the New, is to love God, and then to love others as we love ourselves (see John 15:12). When we love God with all our heart, we will not sin against Him. When we love others as we love ourselves, we will not sin against people. Jesus said that loving God and loving others fulfills the law and the prophets (see Matt. 5:17).

GOD OF LOVE

God is a God of love. He *is* love. He loved the world and sent His only begotten Son to save us. We are going to see how love has the power to overcome and break every curse and evil spirit. The Bible says that love covers a multitude of sins (see 1 Pet. 4:8) and that perfect love casts out all fear (see 1 John 4:18).

If sin and fear can be gone because of love, then with love in our life there will be no place for the devil to work. He can only enter our life through sin.

The devil often attacks those who have money in the area of relationships. He will try to bring offenses and broken relationships. Once we have a broken relationship with someone, we will not prosper as God intends.

Abraham was rich in gold, silver, and sheep. The problem came in Genesis 13:5-7, when there was not enough room for his herds and Lot's herds to dwell together. Strife broke out between their servants. How many of you know that when there is strife between your family members or associates, it affects you too?

> *"So Abram said to Lot, 'Please let there be no strife between you and me, and between my herdsmen and your herdsmen; for we are brethren'"* (Genesis 13:8).

Though Abraham tried to protect him, Lot was more interested in material wealth. So they had to go their separate ways. There was a breach in their relationship. Lot chose Sodom and Gomorrah. Whenever you go against the counsel of the people whom God has put over you, there is an open door for the enemy.

Abraham had God's promise to protect him, and Lot was protected as long as he was with him. When he left Abraham, Lot was open to the enemy's attack. He went away from his spiritual covering. Lot did not try to reconcile, His vision was to get rich and make money (as is common today).

Lot no longer cared about Abraham's call or mission; his eyes were on the wealth of the world (see 1 Tim. 6:9). In Genesis 14, we see that the heathen kings conquered Sodom and Gomorrah, looted the cities, and took Lot along with his family and their substance.

Someone informed Abraham about this. He could have easily thought, "Yes, I already told him that if you go away from me, you are on your own. Do not bother me anymore." He didn't think like many Christians do today. He did not say the usual, "I told you so." Or, "I will pray for you that God will send His angels." He had a compassionate heart, for he was called the friend of God. He did not stop loving his nephew just because Lot was gone.

TEST OF LOVE AND RELATIONSHIP IN ABRAHAM'S LIFE

Even though Lot went His own way, Abraham's love for him did not diminish. Even though we turn away from God, He does not stop loving us. We have offended Him in many ways, but He always comes to our rescue, even at times when we are living in sin. God took the initiative to redeem mankind, not us, though we were the ones who had strayed from Him.

That is why Christ gave us the command to go to the brother who offended us and be reconciled to him, not to wait until he or she comes to us. Abraham went with the mighty men from his own house. He was willing to sacrifice his own to redeem his nephew. He could have easily hired other people. He had the money to do it. Instead, he put his very life at risk and took his best men to save the nephew who had forsaken him.

We might have wondered or asked what we would get out of doing that since Lot was not even thankful for what had already been done for him. What if the lives of Abraham's servants were lost? That would affect the business. But Abraham had a different spirit. He fought with those kings and rescued Lot and all he had. Jesus said there is no greater love than a person laying down his life for his friends (see John 15:13).

This is the true test of every child of God: when you go out to bless or rescue someone who has not been nice or respectful to you. Or perhaps they spoke evil of you. When you do what is pleasing to God, all of heaven moves on your behalf.

A Righteous Judge

God is a righteous judge. He loves righteousness and justice. His justice, however, is a little different from what we call justice. He loves all of His creation. He is merciful and longsuffering (see Ps. 145:8; 86:15; Ex. 34:6), and when we express His nature in and through our life, we receive His favor and abundance in return. He will not withhold any good thing from us (see Ps. 84:11).

Now, when Abraham came back from the battle victoriously, something powerful happened in his life. Melchizedek came to meet him and saluted him. Many people discuss this event in the area of tithing, but they do not fully understand why Melchizedek came to meet Abraham.

When you move out to help your brother or sister who is in need and may not be your favorite, even kings will bow to you (see Gen. 14:17). Melchizedek brought bread and wine, and he was the priest of the Most High God. Abraham had communion with Melchizedek.

I believe it was Jesus Christ Himself who appeared to him. He blessed Abraham again. Once again, he discovered a divine secret concerning prosperity, health, and obedience. The curse of hatred and strife that was between Abraham and Lot was broken because

Abraham went the extra mile. I believe it was a big lesson for Lot to learn.

After this, God appeared to Abraham and said that He would be his shield and his exceedingly great reward (see Gen. 15:1). God Himself became his shield, not his money or servants. A shield is that which protects you from the enemies' assaults and attacks.

Abraham could now be safe and secure because God would be taking care of all of his affairs.

God of Relationship

God will fight for you when you show love and compassion to the needy. When God protects, everything you have is safe and secure. Jesus told us the parable of the Good Samaritan. It deals with the question of, "Who is our neighbor?" Whoever is in need is our neighbor, regardless of color, creed, religion, or nationality.

Our God is a God of relationship. His priority is relationship. Everything in the Kingdom of God flows through relationships. We are all members of the same body. Jesus said in Luke 17:1-2, *"It is impossible that no offenses should come, but woe to him through whom they do come! It would be better for him if a millstone were hung around his neck, and he were thrown into the sea, than that he should offend one of these little ones."*

Nothing is more important to God than our relationships with Him and with each other. Our victory or our defeat is based on our relationships. The enemy has worked a great breach in the Kingdom and the Church, dividing it into as many pieces as possible, with lots of little kingdoms and kings. Again, everything from God flows through relationships. We are supposed to be like God in relationship and unity (see John 17:23).

God of the Covenant

Because Abraham took that step to save his nephew, his life afterward was never the same. His relationship with God was never the same. It was only after this incident that God established His covenant with Abraham. Until then, it was just a promise.

In chapter 15 of Genesis, God established His covenant with Abraham and told him about his future. When you take that first step to mend that broken relationship, it is the first step to true prosperity.

When all of your relationships with others are based on God's Word, you are safe from all the attacks of the enemy. The enemy will not have any ground to launch an attack against you or accuse you before God. When there is no enemy, you live in peace.

The Bible says, *"If it is possible, as much as depends on you, live peaceably with all men"* (Rom. 12:18). Divorce and broken relationships are the means that create many offenses in the land and Church so that God's Spirit will be hindered from operating.

Now, as soon as Abraham took victory over that attack, the devil started causing trouble in his house. The devil brought an idea to Sarah to give her maid to her husband in order to bring forth a child (see Gen. 16:1-6).

Abraham, the man of faith, fell for this plan and slept with Hagar. Once the devil saw that his plan had worked, he came back to Sarah with guilt and condemnation. Once again, strife and contention began in their family life (see Gen. 16:5-6). So Sarah chased Hagar out of the house when she was pregnant with Abraham's son.

When Hagar was in the wilderness, God appeared to her and told her to go back and submit herself to Sarah and do whatever she said. That meant that if Sarah were to mistreat her, Hagar could not resist. Why? In His sovereignty, God knew that if there was strife and contention in Abraham's life, the promise could not be fulfilled.

Broken Relationships

God was about to move on behalf of Abraham after a long period of waiting. The devil has some understanding about God's timing and tries to bring a breach in relationships. Broken relationships open the door to the spirit of poverty in a person's life. There are two dangerous spirits that work under the spirit of poverty—abortion and barrenness. The purpose is to delay God's timing and abort His promises from being fulfilled in your life.

The spirit of abortion can abort your harvest, your divine appointments, relationships, etc. His plan is to abort in the womb before you give birth to God's vision. This spirit works to abort your breakthroughs in the spirit. If they are aborted in the spirit realm, you will never be able to see them.

They are like intercepting missiles that attack God's blessings in the air. God has blessed us with all spiritual blessings in Christ in heavenly places (see Eph. 1:3). God has already blessed you with every blessing you need or will ever need. Now they have to come to you by breaking through the enemy's barriers.

The devil is known as the prince of the power of the air. Demonic forces work in the air. Before the blessing gets to you, it can be intercepted, delayed, scattered, dried up, and exhausted. You need to recognize the enemy's plans and destroy them (see Jer. 1:7). We have authority over all the power of the enemy and are not ignorant of his devices (see 2 Cor. 2:11).

Plans and Purposes Delayed

God pronounced a blessing on Hagar's child also. Abraham was 86 years old when Ishmael was born to him. I believe that God's purpose and promise to Abraham was delayed because of a relationship. We may call it unbelief or disobedience. We do not hear of any conversation between God and Abraham for the next 13 years following Ishmael's birth.

But when he was 99 years old, God appeared to Abraham again. Maybe it took that many years to heal the wounds in their hearts. Two things that can stop us from hearing God are bitterness and hurt in our heart.

Matthew 5:8 tells us that the pure in heart shall see God. But, God is faithful to His Word even when we are unfaithful. What He said, He will do, if we allow Him to mold us and make us. Or we can also rebel against God's plan and miss it.

Abraham decided to settle for second best (see Gen. 17:18) and be mediocre. We can see the enemy's hand behind all of this, even though the Bible does not give any credit to the devil. In the same way, we should never give any credit to his ugly works; we are to destroy his works (see 1 John 3:8).

God gave the physical sign of circumcision to remind Abraham of His covenant. Every time he saw the circumcision, he thought about God's promises. Hagar and Ishmael stayed with Abraham until Isaac was born so there would not be a breach in any relationship.

In chapter 18 of Genesis, God appeared to Abraham again. Another test was brought before him in the areas of love and giving. Now three men stood by the way. Abraham invited them to his tent and showed again love and hospitality to the strangers, giving them the best he had. God blessed him again, and reassured His promise to him. The following year they saw the fulfillment of their long-awaited dream. It is astonishing to see that sacrificial giving precedes most of the miracles in the Bible.

TEST OF LOVE AND RELATIONSHIP IN ISAAC'S LIFE

Blessings are generational, as are curses. There are generational curses as well as generational blessings. One act of obedience will have eternal consequences; so also, one act of disobedience will have eternal consequences.

It is noteworthy that we tend to commit the same mistakes or sins that our fathers committed. There is a default setting in our nature that we inherited from our ancestors, to fail where they failed. Unless we take care of that purposefully and specifically, and destroy those settings in the spirit, things will not work out well.

When we study the patriarchs, we see that these principles manifested in their lives from one generation to the next. Abraham went to Egypt when there was a famine in the land. When Isaac faced the same problem, he was also planning to go to Egypt, but God intervened and stopped him. Abraham lied concerning his wife, Isaac did the same, and Jacob told many lies as well. Their wives Sarah (see Gen. 16:1), Rebekah (see Gen. 25:21), and Rachel (see Gen. 29:31) were all barren for a season.

We see that Abraham made a covenant with Abimelech, the king of Gerar (see Gen. 21:27). When Isaac's time came, the relationship with Abimelech did not work out well. When there was a famine in the land, Isaac sowed and reaped a hundredfold. God blessed him in everything he did (see Gen. 26:12-13).

The Philistines grew to envy him and his blessings. Today, many envy the ungodly when they see their prosperity. In Isaac's time, the ungodly envied him. Seeing Isaac's growth and prosperity brought fear to Abimelech, so he asked him to go away from the land: *"And Abimelech said to Isaac, 'Go away from us, for you are much mightier than we'"* (Gen. 26:16).

We need to remember that Abraham made a covenant with Abimelech, a covenant that is eternal and must not be broken. When a covenant is broken, favor lifts and poverty walks in. Until the covenant was broken, Isaac had no problems in his life—he was prosperous even in the time of famine.

But after he left Abimelech and tried to dig the wells that his father had dug, strife broke out between Isaac's servants and the men of Gerar (see Gen. 26:20). Strife is not a sign of blessing and favor. It opens a door for the enemy. They could not find water for them and the livestock.

Isaac had an encounter with God in the midst of this (see Gen. 26:24-25). Following this, Abimelech came back to meet Isaac.

Then Abimelech came to him from Gerar with Ahuzzath, one of his friends, and Phichol the commander of his army. And Isaac said to them, "Why have you come to me, since you hate me and have sent me away from you?" (Genesis 26:26-27).

Abimelech and his men came to reconcile and renew the covenant. They said, *"We have certainly seen that the Lord is with you. So we said, 'Let there now be an oath between us, between you and us; and let us make a covenant with you'"* (Gen. 26:28).

They made a covenant and restored the broken relationship. Favor was restored to Isaac's life. That same day, Isaac's servants came and told him they found water (see Gen. 26:32).

TEST OF LOVE AND RELATIONSHIP IN JACOB'S LIFE

By name, Jacob was a supplanter and a deceiver, but God had something different in His heart for him. Before God blessed him, Jacob had to pass the test of love to inherit the promise. Jesus said we are to love our enemies and bless those who curse us, and to pray for those that spitefully use and persecute us (see Matt. 5:44).

Jacob was a deceiver. He took advantage of his brother and stole his birthright, deceiving his father and inheriting the blessing. Esau was so angry toward him that he sought to kill Jacob. Esau said he would wait until the death of his father and then take his revenge.

Following his mother's advice, Jacob ran away from home and dwelt in Haran. He worked for his uncle feeding the flock. Laban was a subtle, conniving man and he made Jacob work for him for 14 years in order to marry his two daughters. Jacob began to reap what he sowed in his life and was deceived by Laban. He spent a total of 20 years with Laban in Haran: 14 years for his wives and 6 years for his herds (see Gen. 31:38,41).

How many of us know that we cannot run away from problems? Sooner or later, we have to face them. The problem we run away from will catch up with us in the future. Offense and hurt will not be healed by geographical change, because they are issues of the heart. Even though we can change houses or the place we live, we cannot change our heart.

The sooner we face these issues, the better our life will be. Before Jacob ran away, he talked to his father and made things clear. Isaac blessed him again and sent him away to Haran (see Gen. 28:1), but the issue with his brother remained unreconciled.

Twenty years later, when he departed from Haran, Jacob did not leave in peace with Laban. God, in His mercy, didn't let another offense come to his life. Laban came back to meet Jacob and they reconciled and made a covenant with each other (see Gen. 31:44).

Though he worked hard and earned some material blessings, Jacob had not yet inherited the promise God had made with his fathers. The spiritual breakthrough in Jacob's life had not yet come because the relationship with his brother had not been restored. The offense was still active between them.

Wrestling for Breakthrough

Jacob decided to return to his country and reconcile with his brother. As he was journeying to meet Esau, he had to cross a river called Jabbok. At evening, he let all his family, servants, and flocks cross the river ahead of him and he was left alone at the side of the brook. That night he decided to reconcile with his brother and a "man" came to wrestle with him until daybreak: *"Then Jacob was left alone; and a Man wrestled with him until the breaking of day"* (Gen. 32:24).

The wrestling lasted until early morning because Jacob would not let that Man go until he received the blessing. In reality, he was wrestling with God for his breakthrough. God was wrestling with him to change his nature. When God knew that Jacob was not going to let go, He blessed him and changed his name from Jacob to Israel, meaning, "Prince with God." *"And He said, 'Your name shall no longer be called Jacob, but Israel; for you have struggled with God and with men, and have prevailed'"* (Gen. 32:28).

The long-awaited breakthrough in Jacob's life came the very night he decided to reconcile with his brother Esau. Now he was going to meet Esau, not as the old Jacob, but as Israel.

When you release forgiveness and love to those who deserve it the least, you are demonstrating God's nature and likeness through your life. God will come down to honor you and lift you up to a new position and your long-awaited miracle will take place.

Do you see now why the enemy is so busy breaking relationships and bringing offenses between people? He comes to steal God's favor and blessing from you. He mostly does this through broken relationships, covenants, commitments, and promises. May the Lord open our eyes and help us to walk in love.

Blessing and Promotion

God will send you some Lots in your life. They have come not to hurt you, but to bless you. There will be some Esaus as well. They are there to change you and promote you. Without them, you cannot receive your blessing, you cannot have God's favor.

The people you thought who came to hurt you are actually there to bring blessings to you. They are the keys to open the doors that no one else can open for you. Everyone sees the rock, but few see the sculpture that is hidden inside the rock. All will pass by, but the man who will take the time to chisel away the extra pieces will have a beautiful piece of art.

God will send you a Judas as well as a Peter. Both are necessary for your growth and promotion. Without Judas, Jesus would have been unable to fulfill the Scriptures. Without Peter, the door to the Gentiles would not have opened. It is your responsibility to recognize the Peter and the Judas in your life.

Most people welcome Peter and try to avoid Judas, so they have one-sided blessings. If only one of your legs kept growing, what would happen? Both need to grow to be the same size. Many people know how to handle money but are poor managers of people. Others may be good with people but bad with money.

You need both the Word and the Spirit. Both need to be in balance in your life. I believe that God left the devil alive for a purpose—to keep us humble in spirit. That is why a messenger of Satan was given to Paul. If it were not for the devil, some of us would not even be Christians now. What the enemy has meant for evil, God will turn around as a blessing.

There are two kinds of enemies that will come against your life: one is to destroy you, but you need to destroy him first, but the other is to promote you. Even though you will receive blessings when you tackle both, many men and women of God have missed many blessings because they ill-treated their Lot, Judas, Saul, or Esau.

Saul was sent to David to promote him, not to destroy him. David could have been destroyed if he handled Saul with a wrong attitude. It is easy to bring down Goliath; you can kill him, but you cannot kill Saul. You have to love him.

You do not have to worry about these kinds of people. God will take care of them for He is the One who is sending them your way. If you treat them nicely, they will not destroy you. Instead, they will destroy themselves. Your response to them determines your destiny. You will be blessed without dealing with these people, but your blessing will be limited. Your influence in the Kingdom will be limited.

EXTRAORDINARY PEOPLE

Extraordinary people treat others extraordinarily and they achieve extraordinary things. There are not very many people who want to go all the way with God. As soon as they face a lion or a bear, they will retreat to their own cave. They will also try to keep others in the cave.

David's brothers tried to stop him from facing Goliath. They tried to fight and failed, and they did not want anyone else to try because they had already drawn the conclusion that Goliath was undefeatable. They had not killed their own lion and bear before. These are the people who are afraid and run from their lion and bear. But David had taken care of business before so he knew how to take care of Goliath—with God's help.

If you cannot defeat your own enemies, do not try to help others to overcome theirs. If you do, you will end up in great trouble. The proportion of love you will receive from God is the proportion of love you are willing to give to others. Many want big blessings from God but they give small blessings to others. You cannot pour four gallons of milk into a one-gallon bottle. It doesn't matter how you try to pour—three gallons will be lost.

The bottleneck of your heart is as big as the blessing you give to others. The same measure we meet with will be measured back to us (see Luke 6:38). Many people's hearts and minds are as big as a one-gallon bottle, but they ask God to pour into them more than they can contain. Enlarge your heart toward others and God will enlarge your blessing.

If you sow sparingly, you will reap sparingly. If you sow in plenty, you will also reap in plenty. If you sow large blessings to others, God will pour out extra-large blessings to you. If you are ready to show extraordinary love to others, God will show extraordinary love to you.

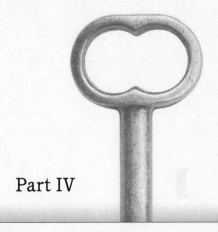

Part IV

KEYS TO VICTORY

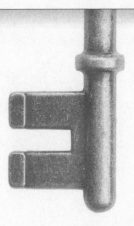

Chapter 13

WISDOM: THE KEY TO PASSING TESTS

WISDOM FROM GOD

It was 1993, the final year of my Bible School training in India. Each student got a chance to preach in one chapel session before he graduated. I thought about what I should preach and God gave me the subject: wisdom. I do not know what I preached that day because I did not know very much about wisdom, but it was a subject I always loved and wanted to learn more about.

If you and I are to come out of our trials and tests victoriously, we need the wisdom of God. There were many anointed men and women of God who failed when God tested them and, consequently, lost their anointing and the very purpose for their life. It is unfortunate that in the Church most people seek the anointing and the power of God but very few seek the wisdom of God. The anointing of God without the character and the wisdom of God will eventually destroy us.

The Bible says wisdom is the principal thing (not the power of God), and in all our getting, we need to get understanding (not the power of God) (see Prov. 4:7). If we understand the order of God and how He operates, then we will avoid unnecessary trouble in our life.

279

CHANGED BY THE POWER OF
THE WORD

We need a balance between the anointing and the character of God, and between the power and the wisdom of God. Anointing does not necessarily change a person's character. People are changed when they have an encounter with the person of God, not the power of God. God's character and nature are revealed in His Word. His power and glory are revealed through the anointing. We usually say things like, "We are changed by the power of God." But, truly, we are changed by the power of the Word of God.

If we study the Bible in-depth, we will see that God manifested His wisdom in His interaction with the earth and human beings more than His power. God is unlimited in His power and glory, and He channels His power through His wisdom. Electricity is power, and to make use of that power, we need to channel it through cables, wires, and switches. Otherwise, it will harm us.

Just because the electricity contains power does not mean it will benefit us. If we touch an electric wire without protection, it can endanger us. We need to know how to harness that power in ways that will benefit us. If we connect that electricity to an electric bulb, it will give us light; if we connect it to a refrigerator, it will keep things cold; if we connect it to a TV or computer, we can keep in touch with almost anything that occurs around the world.

The wisdom of managing electricity properly in ways to benefit humanity is called electrical engineering. God has power, and He has given that power to us, but we need to know how to use it; we need the wisdom of God. God taught Moses His ways and Israel His acts (see Ps. 103:7). His ways are His wisdom and His acts are His power.

WHY IS WISDOM SO IMPORTANT?

It was by wisdom that God established the earth.

O Lord, how manifold are Your works! In wisdom You have made them all. The earth is full of Your possessions (Psalm 104:24).

To Him who by wisdom made the heavens, for His mercy endures forever (Psalm 136:5).

The Lord by wisdom founded the earth; by understanding He established the heavens; by His knowledge the depths were broken up, and clouds drop down the dew (Proverbs 3:19-20).

If God created the earth through His wisdom, we definitely need wisdom to operate on this earth as well. It was the wisdom of God that manifested in Christ to save us from the enemy. Paul wrote:

*However, we speak wisdom among those who are mature, yet not the wisdom of this age, nor of the rulers of this age, who are coming to nothing. But we speak the wisdom of God in a mystery, the **hidden wisdom** which God ordained before the ages for our glory, which none of the rulers of this age knew; for had they known, they would not have crucified the Lord of glory* (1 Corinthians 2:6-8).

*To the intent that now the manifold **wisdom of God** might be made known by the church to the principalities and powers in the heavenly places* (Ephesians 3:10).

There are two men in the Old Testament whom God used to demonstrate His manifold wisdom to the principalities and powers. The first example is Job. The entire purpose of his affliction was to teach the devil that God is greater and that man's relationship with God goes much deeper than the presence or lack of material abundance in his life.

The second example is Solomon. The Bible says that all the earth came to Solomon to seek the wisdom God had given him (see 1 Kings 10:24). He was the world's wisest and most influential king.

WISDOM IN TRIALS

Why do we need to have wisdom when we are tested or going through trials? I have found that before God manifested His power in any situation, He always manifested His wisdom first. If you study the miracles in the Bible, before the power of God wrought the miracle, the wisdom of God manifested to set the stage for that miracle. *Wisdom is the forerunner of the power of God.*

It is a normal thing for people, when going through trials and testing, to ask God to deliver us or send a miracle to rescue us from it. But very few of us know what produces a miracle while we are going through our struggles.

Every trial or test is an opportunity for us to learn the wisdom of God. God's wisdom is hidden in each of life's trials. Most of us only see the trial, but God sees an opportunity to reveal His wisdom to us.

I have asked God for His power many times. Often, I felt the power of God but I did not know how to sustain that power so I lost it. Again, I would go to Him in tears and He would give me some more power, then I would lose it again. I was like a child who wanted candy. Later, I found out that instead of asking God for His power, I should ask for the wisdom to sustain that power.

Genesis 1:1 says, *"In the beginning God created the heavens and the earth."* That means everything related to the earth and the heavens was created at the same time (see Gen. 2:4). In the following verses, God was calling for those things He had already created in the beginning and put them where they belong. That is why He says, "Let there be"—He took six days to do this.

God declared the light to manifest on the first day (see Gen. 1:3). But He called forth the sun, moon, and stars on the fourth day. That means there was light on this earth before the sun, moon, and stars were put in place. What was that light He made on the first day? It was wisdom. The root word for *light* in Hebrew is the same as the word for *knowledge*, and the root word for *darkness* is the same as the word for *ignorance*. The root cause of all fear is ignorance.

There are many places in the Bible where God talks about light: "You are the light of the world," "Your light has come," "Let your light shine," etc. It has been said about Daniel that he had light in his life. The word *light* does not refer to electronic photons or rays; it talks about the life and wisdom of God.

> *There is a man in your kingdom in whom is the Spirit of the Holy God. And in the days of your father,* **light and understanding and wisdom**, *like the wisdom of the gods, were found in him* (Daniel 5:11).

> *That was the true Light which gives light to every man coming into the world* (John 1:9).

> *The entrance of Your words gives light; it gives understanding to the simple* (Psalm 119:130).

Before God began the restoration of this present earth, He first called forth wisdom to be His companion. Proverbs 8 says that God created wisdom before beginning His work of creation:

> *The Lord possessed me at the beginning of His way, before His works of old. I have been established from everlasting, from the beginning, before there was ever an earth. When there were no depths I was brought forth, when there were no fountains abounding with water. Before the mountains were settled, before the hills, I was brought forth; while as yet He had not made the earth or the fields, or the primal dust of the world* (Proverbs 8:22-26).

WISDOM AND MIRACLES

When the children of Israel were at the Red Sea and the Egyptians were behind them, God told Moses to stretch forth his hands to the sea. That was the wisdom of God in operation that brought the miracle-working power of God. When they were at Marah, the water was bitter and they could not drink it. God showed them a tree and told them to put its leaves in the water. That was the wisdom of God. When they did that, the water became sweet.

When Joshua and the people reached the Promise Land, the first city they captured was Jericho. This was no ordinary city. They could not just march in and take over. It was fortified and no one went in or went out. God told them to walk around the wall for seven days, and on the seventh day to walk around seven times and then shout. That is the wisdom of God in manifestation, which caused the wall to fall and they possessed the Promise Land. Wisdom is knowing what to do in the midst of a trial or a test. Wisdom prepares the way for God's miracle-working power.

In the New Testament, the first miracle Jesus performed was at a wedding. The host family had a crisis—there was no more wine. He asked the people to fill six jars with water before He initiated the miracle. Why did He ask them to do this? How did He know what to do at that time? What He asked them to do was the manifestation of wisdom. Jesus (Wisdom) knew what to do in the midst of a crisis.

In any miracle you see in the Bible, it was the wisdom of God that wrought that miracle. From now on, whenever you see a miracle recorded in the Bible, examine it and see how the wisdom of God operated to bring it about.

SUPERNATURAL IN THE ORDINARY

The key to your breakthrough or miracle is in your hand or home. It is not going to come from somewhere else, so stop looking.

We look for the supernatural and the spectacular and miss the significant hidden in the natural and the ordinary.

The widow in the book of Second Kings was faced with huge debt. Her husband had died and the creditor was going to take her two sons to be his slaves. She came crying to the prophet Elisha. The prophet asked what she had in her house, and she said she had nothing but a jar of oil (see 2 Kings 4:1-7).

The prophet instructed her in what to do and she received an extraordinary miracle. She had that jar of oil in her house all along, but it did not benefit her. Why? It was simply because she lacked the wisdom of God. God is not a debtor to anyone. He has already provided a way for you right where you are. The reason you do not see it is because your eyes of understanding are not yet opened.

Whenever we go through a trial or problem, we always look for a miracle from God. That is the wrong thing to look for. We need to ask God what He is trying to teach us and what He wants us to do in the midst of that trial.

MAKING KNOWN THE WISDOM OF GOD

The purpose of the Church is not to make known the power of God to the world and the demonic forces. But that is what we have been trying to do for centuries, while asking God to give us more power. The real purpose of the Church is to make known the manifold wisdom of God to the principalities and powers (see Eph. 3:10). That is why Paul prayed for the church in Ephesus to receive the spirit of wisdom and revelation (see Eph. 1:17-18).

First Corinthians 1:5-6 says, *"You were enriched in everything by Him in all utterance and all knowledge, even as the testimony of Christ was confirmed in you...."*

The Bible talks about different kinds of wisdom. Any invention or creativity in any field—science, technology, medicine, leadership, etc.—is the manifestation of God's wisdom.

285

In the book of Proverbs, wisdom is portrayed as a person. Proverbs says wisdom has two hands—in the right hand is long life, and the left holds riches and honor:

> *Happy is the man who finds wisdom, and the man who gains understanding; for her proceeds are better than the profits of silver, and her gain than fine gold. She is more precious than rubies, and all the things you may desire cannot compare with her. Length of days is in her right hand, in her left hand riches and honor* (Proverbs 3:13-16).

When God appeared to Solomon in a dream and told him to ask Him for whatever he wished, the young king asked for wisdom and understanding. God gave him what he asked for, plus riches and honor, which he did not ask for, because riches and honor come with wisdom. He became the richest man who ever lived (see 1 Kings 3:12-13).

WISDOM AND PATIENCE

When we are tested, there are only two things that will help us to come out of that test victoriously: wisdom and patience. The Bible gives more importance to wisdom and knowledge than to power and strength.

> *No king is saved by the multitude of an army; a mighty man is not delivered by great strength. A horse is a vain hope for safety; neither shall it deliver any by its great strength* (Psalm 33:16-17).

The reason we fail when we are tested is because we lack wisdom, not because we do not have strength.

> *Wisdom strengthens the wise more than ten rulers of the city* (Ecclesiastes 7:19).

> *There was a little city with few men in it; and a great king came against it, besieged it, and built great snares around it. Now there was found in it a poor wise man, and he by his wisdom delivered the city. Yet no one remembered that same*

poor man. Then I said: "Wisdom is better than strength" (Ecclesiastes 9:14-16).

We see something similar in the book of Second Samuel, where a woman saved a city and its people through her wisdom. When Joab, the captain of David's army, went to capture Sheba, who had rebelled against the king, a woman came forward to present a solution. Instead of his army killing an entire city, Joab listened to her, saving the woman and the rest of the people (see 2 Sam. 20:16-22).

IGNORANCE: A LACK OF WISDOM

There is only one real problem we have on this earth today: ignorance. How many of you would agree that if you had only known better, you would not have made the mistakes you made in your life? The same is true now. The problems you have right now in your life are because of a lack of wisdom and knowledge concerning those areas.

God said, *"My people are destroyed for lack of knowledge"* (Hos. 4:6). The Bible does not say God's people perish because of their enemies, or sin, or even the devil. God's people go into captivity because of ignorance.

Isaiah 5:13 says, *"Therefore My people have gone into captivity, because they have no knowledge; their honorable men are famished, and their multitude dried up with thirst."*

Most believers think the enemy is their problem. The Bible tells us not to be ignorant of his devices (see 2 Cor. 2:11; Eph. 6:11). The real problem is not the enemy, but ignorance of how he operates. The devil uses our ignorance to deceive us.

We do not have what we need in our lives because we lack wisdom; things are not the way we want in our life because we lack patience. Impatience causes irritation, agitation, and impetuous actions, and then we finally give up on dreams and projects, or do the wrong thing.

If you are struggling in any area of your life, you are struggling because you lack knowledge about that area. If you are facing problems in your family, it is because you lack knowledge concerning family life. If we are having financial problems, that means we lack wisdom. In the right hand of wisdom is long life, and in the left hand are riches and honor. We are paid for what we know. A doctor is paid for the knowledge he has, and a businessman is paid for what he knows.

If the enemy is our problem, the Bible says Jesus defeated the devil on the cross and took back all authority in heaven and on earth. He gave us authority over all the power of the enemy. If the enemy is defeating us, it is because we do not have enough knowledge of his devices, not because of a lack of the power of the cross.

If we are having family problems, it is because we lack understanding in that area. If the husband thinks the wife is the problem, then he lacks understanding about how to live with the wife (see 1 Pet. 3:7). If the wife thinks the husband is the problem, then she lacks wisdom because the Bible says the foolish woman tears down her own house (see Prov. 14:1).

BEING USED BY GOD

Anyone in the Bible who was powerfully used by God had the wisdom of God operating through them. Anyone in the Bible who made a national impact had the spirit of wisdom working in his or her life. Joseph was used by God to change the future of Egypt and the people of Israel, all through the wisdom of God.

> So let the king choose a man who is **very wise and understanding** and set him over the land of Egypt....So the king said to Joseph, "God has shown you all this. There is **no one as wise and understanding as you are**, so I will put you in charge of my palace. All the people will obey your orders, and only I will be greater than you" (Genesis 41:33,39-40 NCV).

And Stephen's sermon in the book of Acts says of this:

> *And the patriarchs, becoming envious, sold Joseph into Egypt. But God was with him and delivered him out of all his troubles, and gave him **favor and wisdom** in the presence of Pharaoh, king of Egypt; and he made him governor over Egypt and all his house* (Acts 7:9-10).

Moses and Joshua had the wisdom of God operating in their lives as well.

> *Now Joshua the son of Nun was full of the **spirit of wisdom**, for Moses had laid his hands on him; so the children of Israel heeded him, and did as the Lord had commanded Moses* (Deuteronomy 34:9).

> *And Moses was learned in **all the wisdom** of the Egyptians, and was mighty in words and deeds* (Acts 7:22).

David talked about wisdom in the Psalms (see Ps. 119:98).

> *To bring about this change of affairs your servant Joab has done this thing; but my lord is **wise, according to the wisdom of the angel of God, to know everything that is in the earth*** (2 Samuel 14:20).

> *One of them said he knew a young fellow in Bethlehem, the son of a man named Jesse, who was not only a talented harp player, but was handsome, brave, and strong, and had good, solid judgment. "What's more," he added, "the Lord is with him"* (1 Samuel 16:18 TLB).

Daniel had the spirit of wisdom and might in his life.

> *I thank You and praise You, O God of my fathers; You have given me **wisdom and might**, and have now made known to me what we asked of You, for you have made known to us the king's demand* (Daniel 2:23).

The first martyr of the Church, Stephen, had the spirit of wisdom working in his life.

> *And they were not able to resist the **wisdom and the Spirit** by which* [Stephen] *spoke* (Acts 6:10).

And the apostle Paul had wisdom operating in his life. Peter writes of him:

*And consider that the longsuffering of our Lord is salvation—as also our beloved brother Paul, **according to the wisdom** given to him, has written to you* (2 Peter 3:15).

We read that Jesus grew in wisdom and stature, and in favor with God and man. He grew in wisdom and stature *before* the power of God came upon Him. With any miracle we see in the Bible, it was the wisdom of God that brought the power of God. Knowing what to do in the midst of problems, challenges, and trials is the wisdom of God.

Colossians 1:9-11 talks about believers increasing in the knowledge of God's will in wisdom and in all spiritual understanding. In fact, each chapter of Colossians talks about the wisdom of God in some form.

INCREASE OF WISDOM

The Church today lacks the wisdom of God more than anything else. What we need to ask God for is more wisdom to influence our culture and nations. Paul wrote to the Corinthians:

For Jews request a sign, and Greeks seek after wisdom; but we preach Christ crucified, to the Jews a stumbling block and to the Greeks foolishness, but to those who are called, both Jews and Greeks, Christ the power of God and the wisdom of God (1 Corinthians 1:22-24).

Greeks sought after wisdom. Does that mean believers should not seek wisdom? No, the above scripture condemns seeking man's wisdom or the wisdom of this world instead of seeking the wisdom of God.

Many people have a lot of knowledge about many things, but they are not able to organize what they know and use it in a way that profits them. That is what wisdom does. Wisdom helps you organize and channel what you know to produce a desired outcome. Knowledge is raw power. You need wisdom to harness that power and make it productive.

Gasoline has explosive power contained in it, but that power is not useful to anyone unless we tap into it. It takes an engine to transform that power into a useful form of energy and regulate it according to our needs. An engine makes the power in the gasoline productive. God created each individual with great potential (power), but we need the wisdom of God to make that potential beneficial to us and to others. When we do that, we prosper.

Understanding is the bridge that connects knowledge and wisdom. I've known since I was 5 years old the scripture, "The Lord is my Shepherd" (see Ps. 23). I knew about sheep and shepherds, but I never knew what it meant to me personally, so it did not benefit me in any way. When I grew up, God gave me some understanding about that scripture, and suddenly there was a connection between my circumstances and the knowledge I possessed.

Using the example of the gasoline engine, people knew gasoline had power and that engines could be useful, but someone had to connect those two together. It took imagination, research, design, and scientific experiments to create an engine that runs on gasoline. It takes people with understanding to perform such tasks.

Revelation brings understanding. Engineers might have experimented hundreds of times before they could make an efficient engine. It was their understanding that converted the knowledge they had into the wisdom of making an engine, and what brought that understanding was revelation.

The fear of the Lord is the beginning of wisdom, not power (see Prov. 9:10). The wisdom of God is the greatest power against the enemy. People on this earth die and go to hell not because God did not forgive their sins, but because they do not *know* that God forgave their sins. They go to hell because of their ignorance.

Paul writes, *"Having their understanding darkened, being alienated from the life of God, because of the **ignorance** that is in them, because of the blindness of their heart..."* (Eph. 4:18).

THE GREATER THE TEST, THE GREATER THE PROMOTION

If we have problems in any relationship, it is because we do not have a full revelation of the love of God. We are supposed to walk in love. The distance between your present life and the future you dream is a problem. What stands between you and your Promise Land is a crisis. When you ask God for a promotion, He will send a test. When you overcome that problem, crisis, or test, you will be promoted to the next season in your life.

The connection between Joseph and his dream was the pit, the persecution, and the prison he endured. What promoted David to his next season in life was facing the giant. What killed Goliath was David's wisdom and skill in using a slingshot. When he demonstrated that wisdom, the power of God manifested.

Moses had to leave Egypt, his comfort zone, to go to the wilderness in order to enter into the next season of his life. Joshua and the Israelites had to overcome Jericho to enter the Promise Land. Shadrach, Meshach, and Abed-Nego were promoted in Babylon because they went through the fire. The greater the dream, the longer and more severe the crisis. The higher the promotion, the hotter the fire.

We have all asked God for a promotion, but when He sent a test, intending to promote us, we failed, and then blamed the enemy for messing up our lives because we lacked wisdom. If we are not careful, we can stay in this same rut for many years. To understand the solution to the problem we face, we need the wisdom of God. What brought the people mentioned above through their problems was the wisdom of God—the most powerful weapon against the enemy.

WISDOM COMES THROUGH TRIALS

In the book of James we read that when we go through various trials, we need to rejoice. When I read this, I wonder, "How can a person rejoice when he is going through trials, not just one, but various?" One of the major ways we grow spiritually is through the trials we endure.

That is why the Bible says to rejoice when you face challenges and hardships, because they are producing some good fruit in your life that otherwise would not be produced (see James 1:2-4).

The reason we get discouraged and irritated when we go through trials is because we do not understand and appreciate the benefits they bring to our lives. If we are to understand the purpose of trials, we need the wisdom of God. As I mentioned before, wisdom is knowing what to do when we go through a trial or test. One of the most difficult things to understand when you are going through a trial is the purpose of that trial.

James goes on to say, *"If any of you lacks wisdom, let him ask of God, who gives to all liberally and without reproach, and it will be given to him"* (James 1:5). That means that when you are going through trials and testing and do not understand the purpose of it, ask God for wisdom and He will show you the reason. Most of us do not rejoice when we go through a trial, forget about various trials, because we do not understand their purpose.

Joseph was promoted in Egypt because God gave him wisdom to help Egypt overcome a national crisis. God sent a famine to cause Pharaoh to promote Joseph to be chief minister of Egypt (see Ps. 105:16-17).

What promoted Joseph in Egypt was not the power of God— it was the wisdom of God. He overcame each test with the wisdom of God and, ultimately, he interpreted Pharaoh's dream, which is the manifestation of God's wisdom. He then taught the Egyptians the wisdom of God. Psalm 105:21-22 says of Pharaoh promoting

Joseph: *"He made him lord of his house, and ruler of all his possessions, to bind his princes at his pleasure, and teach his elders wisdom."*

In all our getting, we need to get wisdom and understanding. God's wisdom is manifested to us through His seven Spirits. God's wisdom is manifold and it is impossible to measure because His wisdom is unsearchable (see Rom. 11:33).

SEVEN PILLARS OF WISDOM

Wisdom is so important that God dedicated to it three books in the Old Testament and four books in the New Testament: Job (Job was chosen to make known the wisdom of God to the principalities and powers), Proverbs, and Ecclesiastes in the Old Testament; and First Corinthians, Ephesians, Colossians, and James in the New Testament.

That does not mean other books in the Bible do not talk about wisdom or that these books do not talk about other subjects, only that one of the main themes of these seven books is wisdom. Why did God dedicate seven books of the Bible to the subject of wisdom? The Bible says there are seven Spirits of God, which are connected to the wisdom of God.

"Wisdom has built her house, she has hewn out her seven pillars" (Prov. 9:1). What are these seven pillars of wisdom? There are seven churches that are mentioned in the book of Revelation. Each of these churches and its message represents a historic church that existed at that particular place and time, and also has a spiritual meaning to the churches that exist in different regions and nations on this earth.

If we study the churches that exist today in different nations, the messages that were written to those seven churches in the book of Revelation are relevant to them. One of the messages to the seven churches is applicable to the church that you are part of right now.

The Church is compared to a pillar in the Bible: *"But if I am delayed, I write so that you may know how you ought to conduct yourself in the house of God, **which is the church of the living God, the pillar and ground of the truth**"* (1 Tim. 3:15).

Each of the messages to the seven churches starts with a specific revelation of Jesus and represents one or more of the Spirits of God. Let us look at them right now:

1. *"To the angel of the church of Ephesus write, 'These things says He who holds the seven stars in His right hand, who walks in the midst of the seven golden lampstands'"* (Rev. 2:1)—the seven Spirits of God were released into this church.

2. *"And to the angel of the church in Smyrna write, 'These things says the First and the Last, who was dead, and came to life'"* (Rev. 2:8)—the Spirit of might, which caused Jesus to rise from the dead.

3. *"And to the angel of the church in Pergamos write, 'These things says He who has the sharp two-edged sword'"* (Rev. 2:12)—this is the Spirit of counsel.

4. *"And to the angel of the church in Thyatira write, 'These things says the Son of God, who has eyes like a flame of fire, and His feet like fine brass'"* (Rev. 2:18)—the Spirit of understanding was released into this church. Understanding is connected to how you see things. That is why Paul refers to the eyes of our understanding.

5. "And to the angel of the church in Sardis write, *'These things says He who has the seven Spirits of God and the seven stars: "I know your works, that you have a name that you are alive, but you are dead"'"* (Rev. 3:1)—to this church the seven Spirits of God were released.

295

6. *"And to the angel of the church in Philadelphia write, 'These things says He who is holy, He who is true, "He who has the key of David, He who opens and no one shuts, and shuts and no one opens"'* (Rev. 3:8)—the key of David is the Spirit of knowledge.

7. *"And to the angel of the church of the Laodiceans write, 'These things says the Amen, the Faithful and True Witness, the Beginning of the creation of God'"* (Rev. 3:14)—the beginning of the creation is the Spirit of wisdom.

When we study these churches, we will see that each of the seven Spirits of God has been working through them at different times in history and currently in different parts of the earth.

RECEIVING THE BENEFIT OF THE SEVEN SPIRITS OF GOD

We are going to look now at these seven Spirits of God that are revealed in His Holy Word and how receiving these can benefit our lives. It is impossible to fulfill God's purpose and overcome the enemy and the tests that come into our lives without the wisdom of God (see Rev. 1:4; 4:5; 5:6).

The book of Revelation is the revelation of Jesus Christ in His divinity. The Gospels are the revelation of Jesus Christ in His humanity. The purpose of the Church is to make known the manifold wisdom of God to the principalities and powers (see Eph. 3:10), and each of the churches in the book of Revelation was manifesting one or more of the seven Spirits of God during that age.

If each local church can figure out which Spirit(s) of God is being manifested through them in that region, they can also discover their corresponding weakness, which is mentioned in the book of Revelation as well. Each of those weaknesses is an attack of the enemy against the particular local church in a given region.

If they can overcome that weakness, that church will become a bride without spot and wrinkle, ready to face the Bridegroom.

God foresees what each local church will encounter in a particular region and equips them with the needed spiritual power through His Spirit. Through that church, He in turn, makes known to the principalities and powers the manifold wisdom of God. God is so smart and there is no one who compares to our God.

THE SEVEN SPIRITS OF GOD

You might be thinking by now that God has only one Spirit, which is the Holy Spirit. Who are these seven Spirits? Though God has only one Spirit, which is the Holy Spirit, He manifests in seven different forms. Isaiah 11:2 talks about these seven Spirits of God: *"The **Spirit of the Lord** shall rest upon Him, the **Spirit of wisdom** and **understanding**, the **Spirit of counsel** and **might**, the **Spirit of knowledge** and of the **fear of the Lord**."*

Each of these Spirits has a distinct manifestation, characteristic, and function in a believer's life. They bring the manifold wisdom of God into our lives. We are going to learn about each of them and what they bring into and through our lives.

In Paul's prayer for the Colossian believers, he included five of the seven Spirits of the Lord.

> For this reason we also, since the day we heard it, do not cease to pray for you, and to ask that you may be filled with the **knowledge** of His will in all **wisdom** and spiritual **understanding**; that you may **walk worthy of the Lord, fully pleasing Him** [fear of the Lord], *being fruitful in every good work and increasing in the knowledge of God; strengthened with all **might**, according to **His glorious power**, for all patience and longsuffering with joy* (Colossians 1:9-11).

In Paul's prayer for the Ephesian believers, he prayed they would have four of these Spirits:

*That the God of our Lord Jesus Christ, the Father of glory, may give to you the **spirit of wisdom** and **revelation in the knowledge of Him** [Spirit of knowledge], the eyes of your **understanding** being enlightened; that you may know what is the hope of His calling, what are the riches of the glory of His inheritance in the saints, and what is the exceeding greatness of His power toward us who believe, according to the working of **His mighty power**...”* (Ephesians 1:17-19).

In the following pages we are going to see how these seven Spirits manifest in our lives and what they bring to us.

1. The Spirit of the Lord

Jesus began His ministry by reading a scripture from the book of Isaiah:

The Spirit of the Lord is upon Me, because He has anointed Me to preach the gospel to the poor; He has sent Me to heal the brokenhearted, to proclaim liberty to the captives and recovery of sight to the blind, to set at liberty those who are oppressed; to proclaim the acceptable year of the Lord (Luke 4:18-19).

When you have the Spirit of the Lord, the following things will manifest in and through your life:

- Preach the gospel to the poor (spiritually poor)

- Healing the brokenhearted

- Deliverance to the captives

- Recovering sight to the blind

- Freedom to the oppressed

- Proclaim the acceptable year of the Lord (grace)

In the Old Testament, we read about the Spirit of the Lord coming upon people to empower them to do the extraordinary. Prophets prophesied when the Spirit of the Lord came upon them.

2. Spirit of Wisdom

When you have the Spirit of wisdom, the following things will manifest in and through your life, bringing invention, revelation, and favor.

- Victory over the oppression and bondage of your enemies (see Eccles. 9:13-15).

- Possessing your inheritance—God used Joshua to take the people into the Promise Land. The land was possessed and divided under his leadership because he had the Spirit of wisdom operating in his life (see Deut. 34:9).

- Solutions to personal and national problems (see Gen. 41:37-41).

- Riches, honor, and length of days (see Prov. 3:13-16).

- Leadership anointing (see Ps. 105:21-22).

- Revelation of your purpose, call, and the power of God (see Eph. 1:17-19).

- Invention and craftsmanship of new things (see Ex. 28:3; 31:1-6).

For all leadership positions, both in the Old Testament and in the New Testament, precedence was given to people with wisdom and understanding.

How can I alone bear your problems and your burdens and your complaints? Choose wise, understanding, and knowledgeable men from among your tribes, and I will make them heads over you (Deuteronomy 1:12-13).

Therefore, brethren, seek out from among you seven men of good reputation, full of the Holy Spirit and wisdom, whom we may appoint over this business; but we will give ourselves continually to prayer and to the ministry of the word (Acts 6:3-4).

Who has put wisdom in the mind? Or who has given understanding to the heart? (Job 38:36).

My mouth shall speak wisdom, and the meditation of my heart shall give understanding (Psalm 49:3).

3. The Spirit of Understanding

When you have the Spirit of understanding, the following things will manifest in and through your life. It brings confidence, self-control, and hope to our lives.

- Interpretation of the time and seasons—First Chronicles 12:32 says the *"sons of Issachar who had understanding of the times, to know what Israel ought to do."*

- Interpretation of signs and prophetic pictures and writings—Daniel in the Old Testament had the ability to interpret prophetic signs and writings.

- Interpretation of dreams and visions—Second Chronicles 26:5 says, "[Uzziah] *sought God in the days of Zechariah, who had understanding in the visions of God."* (See also Daniel 5:12.)

- You will not commit sexual sins (see Prov. 6:32).

- Knowledge of God (see 1 John 5:20).

The Spirit of discernment works under this Spirit. The Bible says the eyes of our understanding will be opened or enlightened, it never says the eyes of knowledge. Knowledge is a key that opens doors in the Kingdom and in the natural—understanding is like an eye that enables us to see what we normally would not see.

Now it came to pass, as He sat at the table with them, that He took bread, blessed and broke it, and gave it to them.

*Then their **eyes** were opened and they knew Him; and He vanished from their sight* (Luke 24:30-31).

The Spirit of understanding helps us to understand the Scriptures correctly and gives us the ability to understand the mysteries of Scripture.

Job 32:8 says, *"But there is a spirit in man, and the breath of the Almighty gives him understanding."* When people lack understanding, they err from the truth and get into doctrinal error.

4. The Spirit of Counsel

When you have the Spirit of counsel, the following things will manifest in and through your life. It brings insight, the ability to plan, organizational power, tactics, and the ability to solve interpersonal problems in our lives.

- Plan of how to wage war (see Prov. 11:14; 20:18; 24:6).

- Healing for past emotional wounds and regrets (see Isa. 50:4).

5. The Spirit of Might

When you have the Spirit of might, the following things will manifest in and through your life. It brings power, strength, and victory to our lives.

- Strength for the inner man (see Eph. 3:16-20).

The spirit world responds to you based on the strength of your inner man (also called your new man, or your spirit). What gives strength to your spirit to do the impossible is the Spirit of might.

The explosive power of God will work through you and you will be able to do the impossible in the natural and in the spiritual realm. It usually works in combination with the gift of faith that is mentioned in the New Testament.

Psalm 68:35 says, *"O God, You are more awesome than Your holy places. The God of Israel is He who gives strength and power to His people. Blessed be God!"*

6. The Spirit of Knowledge

> *Talk no more so very proudly; let no arrogance come from your mouth, for the Lord is the God of knowledge; and by Him actions are weighed* (1 Samuel 2:3).

When you have the Spirit of knowledge, the following things will manifest in and through your life. It brings information, imagination, facts, and deliverance from crises into our lives.

- Knowledge is one of the keys of the Kingdom of God (see Luke 11:52).

- Security (see Prov. 1:33; 11:9).

- Increased strength (see Prov. 24:5).

- The earth will be filled with the knowledge of God as the waters cover the seas (see Isa. 11:9). When people lack knowledge, they lack the capacity to know God. Psalm 14:4 says, *"Have all the workers of iniquity no knowledge, who eat up My people as they eat bread, and do not call on the Lord?"*

- Provision for life and godliness (see 2 Pet. 1:3).

- Increased patience and longsuffering (see Col. 1:10-11).

7. The Spirit of the Fear of the Lord

When you have the Spirit of the fear of the Lord, the following things will manifest in and through your life.

- A hunger for true wisdom and knowledge

- You will honor and respect God

- You will put God first in your life

- Obeying God will be the priority in your life

- You will have a good moral foundation and maturity in your life

- Those who have this Spirit will hate evil (see Prov. 8:13)

- Those who have this Spirit will have a long life (see Prov. 10:27)

- Those who have this Spirit will have strong confidence (see Prov. 14:26-27)

- Those who have this Spirit will prosper (see Prov. 22:4)

THE KEY TO OUR BREAKTHROUGH

God's Spirit is the Spirit of wisdom. In the New Testament, Paul often wrote about these Spirits in his Epistles. In Christ are hidden all the treasures of knowledge and wisdom (see Col. 2:3).

When God gives us a promise, He will send a problem, test, challenge, or an obstacle into our life, and the fulfillment of that promise is hidden in that problem. Usually, when we see the problem we do not see beyond it, so we scream and try to run away or ask God to rescue us from it. In truth, your breakthrough is hidden in that problem.

Joseph had a dream that he would become someone great. The first thing that happened toward fulfilling that dream was that his brothers cast him into the pit. How on earth can being thrown into a pit propel you toward fulfilling your dream? But, in fact, that is exactly what he needed to go to the next step. Only God knows the blessings we missed because, when others cast us into our *pit*, we thought that was the end of our dream and we *tried* to kill those who threw us there.

We will be thrown into similar situations in our lives, the most unusual places, which seem to be the opposite of what you dream to be. How can falling into a pit prepare you to become a prime minister of a nation? We might think we need to enroll in the best university to be trained to become a political leader. But God's ways are different than our ways.

Isaiah declares:

"For My thoughts are not your thoughts, nor are your ways My ways," says the Lord. "For as the heavens are higher than the earth, so are My ways higher than your ways, and My thoughts than your thoughts" (Isaiah 55:8-9).

The following equations reveal God's way of fulfilling our dreams and purposes:

- Promise + Problem + Wisdom of God applied + Patience = Breakthrough

- Dream + Test + Wisdom of God applied + Patience = Fulfillment

- Purpose + Battle + Wisdom of God applied + Patience = Abundance

- Need + Faith + Wisdom of God applied + Action + Patience = Miracle

- Salvation + Wilderness + Wisdom of God applied + Patience = Promise Land (Destiny)

David was anointed to be the king of Israel while he was still a shepherd boy. God sent Goliath to challenge the camp of Israel. No one dared to face that challenge because they did not recognize the promotion and financial blessings that were waiting for them, hidden in overcoming Goliath. They ran away from the opportunity because all they could see was the problem that was in front of them. They did not recognize the wisdom of God in sending that challenge to bless them.

Each test we face as a Christian is ordained by God to promote us in the spirit. The reason we get discouraged and afraid is because we do not understand the purpose of the test. The reason we do not understand the purpose of the test is because we lack the wisdom of God.

Wisdom comes from God, along with knowledge and understanding. Blessed is he who finds wisdom and the man who finds understanding. The reason we do not see very many mighty miracles of God these days is because we do not seek the wisdom of God, instead we seek the power of God.

The wisdom of God brings the power of God, and the power of God brings the miracle. Wisdom is the key to the miracle-working power of God. What the Church needs today more than any other time in history is the true wisdom of God.

TRANSITION

We are in a transition from the Church age (age of grace), to the Kingdom age (millennium). At each transition of the different ages, God does not manifest His power as we think, but He manifests His wisdom. As I look at the Church today, everyone is hungering for the power of God. They see all the evil that is taking place around them, the wicked prospering and living shamelessly, and they want to do so much for God, but we have been asking for power—power...always more power.

It takes the wisdom of God to know the time we are in. At the transition from the age of conscience to the age of the law, God revealed His wisdom by giving His laws and commandments to His people Israel. At the transition of the age of the law to the age of grace, again God manifested His wisdom by sending Jesus and having Him die on the cross. Jesus dying on the cross was foolishness to the whole world, but it was the ultimate wisdom of God in manifestation toward humanity.

I believe God is looking for people He can reveal His wisdom to. The only way to solve the problems that surround us today is through the wisdom of God. We ask for the power of God because we want to bring the fire from heaven and burn all the wicked! Well, that is not the way God operates. The terrorism, political problems, the broken families, drugs, the sexual revolution, etc., will all be solved through the wisdom of God. Let us ask God for His wisdom. He says that if we cry out, He will answer us.

> *Yes, if you cry out for discernment, and lift up your voice for understanding, if you seek her as silver, and search for her as for hidden treasures; then you will understand the fear of the Lord, and find the knowledge of God. For the Lord gives wisdom; from His mouth come knowledge and understanding; He stores up sound wisdom for the upright; He is a shield to those who walk uprightly* (Proverbs 2:3-7).

We need to ask God daily to fill us with His seven Spirits. The reason Jesus passed all the tests He faced was because he had these seven Spirits of God operating in His life. *"But of Him you are in Christ Jesus, who became for us wisdom from God—and righteousness and sanctification and redemption"* (1 Cor. 1:30).

May the Lord equip us with His seven Spirits to overcome every test and trial that comes our way in Jesus's name.

Chapter 14

UNDERSTANDING YOUR DESTINY VS. THE AMERICAN DREAM

THE AMERICAN DREAM

Are you really serious about fulfilling your destiny, or do you want to follow the "American Dream"? Let me tell you frankly that if you want to follow the American Dream, you may not fulfill the destiny God has for you. The American Dream is like a virus that is spreading throughout the entire world.

What I mean by the "American Dream" is that we are living in a world where people associate one's success rate according to the amount of money and goods they possess. The American Dream was birthed by a quest for personal achievement. But it has gone to an extreme where people have no regard for life, values, morality, family, or God. All they care about is *how to make a little more* money and self-gratification.

Most people live for one purpose only, and that is to make more money and be considered "successful." They do not care about family, marriage, or the foundations of human life on this earth. If something does not happen immediately, we are all heading for the biggest storm we have ever faced. It is time for preachers to tell the people the real truth.

The motto of the American Dream is "Dream big," "You can do it," and, "If you feel like it, then do it." Everything has to be bigger and better. Well, sometimes that is true, but most of the time, for most people, that may not be the case. Everyone is created for a unique purpose and everyone cannot be on the "top" at the same time.

One of the reasons for all the depression and suicide in the Western world is because of the unreasonable expectations people have about life. It is interesting to notice that poor and rich people commit suicide. When people are trying to do what they are not called to do, the end result will be discouragement and disappointment.

How do you know that you have arrived at the place of your destiny? We have different ideas and concepts when we talk about fulfilling our destiny and dreams. We live in a world where success is rated by how much money we have, how big our house is, and what brand of car and clothes we own. Well, God does not rate a person's success based on their material wealth. That is never a measuring stick to decide if a person's life on this earth was a success or failure.

A DIFFERENT KINGDOM

The Kingdom of God works according to different principles than this world. But, unfortunately, many in the Church are married to the world rather than to Jesus. All they care about is how to make more money, buy the latest fad, and live a comfortable life. The Bible, on the other hand, is full of people who cared more about fulfilling their destiny than their status in this world.

We see in the Bible people like John the Baptist about whom the Bible says, "God sent a man and his name was John" (see John 1:6). And Jesus said about him, "There is no greater person who is born of woman than John the Baptist" (see Matt. 11:11). That means John the Baptist had a destiny—he was a man with a mission. His mission was to introduce Jesus to the world. And when he finally did that, he fulfilled his destiny and was ready to go *home*.

This is what happened: John started his own organization before Jesus began His ministry. He ended up in prison, and people came and told Jesus about it. Jesus did not miraculously deliver John from prison, nor did He send an angel to save him. Why not? It was because Jesus knew that John had already finished his mission on this earth.

What if your whole life's purpose was to touch one life for Jesus on this earth? It would be like the preacher through whom Billy Graham was saved. It was the purpose of that man to preach the gospel so that Billy Graham could come to Jesus. We see another disciple in the book of Acts named Ananias.

What was Ananias's purpose? One day Jesus appeared to him and told him to go and pray for Saul (who would later become Paul), who was in a particular house. Ananias tried to get away from it because he knew about Saul and his former conduct. Nevertheless, Ananias went in obedience and laid his hands on Saul, who received his sight and was baptized and filled with the Holy Spirit. That was Ananias's destiny—to restore Saul back to health and commission him to his preliminary ministry. Can you believe it?

There are so many other things Ananias might have done, but none of them are mentioned in the Bible. Whatever God has written in His book concerning your life is what matters the most. If you have not done what is worthy enough to be mentioned in His book, I would suggest you go back and find where you have missed God. Everything concerning you has already been written in God's book.

This is why the psalmist says, *"Your eyes saw my substance, being yet unformed. And in Your book they all were written, the days fashioned for me, when as yet there were none of them"* (Ps. 139:16).

Jesus said in Hebrews 10:5-7:

Sacrifice and offering You did not desire, but a body You have prepared for Me. In burnt offerings and sacrifices for sin You had no pleasure. Then I said, "Behold, I have come—in the volume of the book it is written of Me—to do Your will, O God."

What would have happened if Jesus opened all the blind eyes, deaf ears, and raised all the dead, but He did not die on the cross? Would His life be considered a success? No. Because the very purpose for which He came to this earth was to die on the cross. That is what I mean by destiny. It is the very intent for which God created your spirit. Do not let your physical body and the temporal things of this world hinder you from discovering and fulfilling the purpose of your spirit.

We live in a world where people only want to do the spectacular and the supernatural. Your whole life's purpose might be to introduce someone to someone else. We see a young girl in the book of Kings, who introduced her master to a prophet so he could be healed.

We do not hear about the people who made the ark for Noah— I am sure there were others involved in the project. Or, we don't hear about the owner of the donkey on which Jesus rode into Jerusalem. These are all people who fulfilled their destiny—you can't be more successful than that!

TOO LATE FOR YOUR DESTINY?

We are all trying to follow the "American Dream"—big house, big car, and big money—when our relationships are in shambles, and our children grow up without really knowing their parents.

I was talking to a very influential government official who told me that he traveled for 30 years for his government and now he is over 60 years old and missed his children growing up. His children are grown, married, and gone, but he has regrets about how much he missed of their childhoods. It is too late now.

God does not want you to feel that way about any area of your life. Do you really believe you have an eternal life after death? When many believers think about eternal life, all they think about is singing and flying around like angels in heaven. That is not at all what we will be doing in heaven or for the rest of eternity when God establishes the new heaven and the new earth.

You decide the quality of your eternal life while you are alive on this earth. The life you lead after death is built by the investment you are making into the Kingdom of God before you die. You cannot change or improve the quality of your life after you die. That is why fulfilling your destiny is very important.

Many are living like the rich man in Luke 16:19, which says, *"There was a rich man who was dressed in purple and fine linen and lived in luxury every day"* (NIV). This rich man's priority was his life on this earth. Jesus did not say he was a sinner; he was simply a rich man who lost the purpose for which God had given him riches. He thought it was for him to buy new clothes and to live in luxury.

> *But Abraham replied, "Son, remember that in your lifetime you received your good things, while Lazarus received bad things, but now he is comforted here and you are in agony"* (Luke 16:25 NIV).

I do not want this to be said to me or to anyone else. I would rather have a better quality of life permanently than live temporarily in luxury down here on this earth. Paul told Timothy to teach that same message to those who were rich on this earth.

> *Command those who are rich in this present world not to be arrogant nor to put their hope in wealth, which is so uncertain, but to put their hope in God, who richly provides us with everything for our enjoyment. Command them to do good, to be rich in good deeds, and to be generous and*

311

willing to share. In this way they will lay up treasure for themselves as a firm foundation for the coming age, so that they may take hold of the life that is truly life (1 Timothy 6:17-19 NIV).

And First Timothy 6:7 says, *"For we brought nothing into this world, and it is certain we can carry nothing out."*

EVERYTHING ALREADY PROVIDED

God has already provided everything you need in order to fulfill your destiny. As you move forward, you will discover everything you need for that season. You may not have enough money to take care of the next 50 years, but I am sure He has provided everything you need for today. So praise Him and thank Him for it, and I know that He is faithful to provide what you need tomorrow. The Bible says the same to us: *"And having food and clothing, with these we shall be content"* (1 Tim. 6:8).

God's purpose for your life is not to dream big, achieve great things, and become a millionaire. He did not call Noah and say, "Dream up the biggest ark you can imagine and build it." No, He gave him specific measurements and instructions, and even the materials to use. When He called Moses it was not, "Be the champion," or, "Be the best you can." He told him to go to Egypt to deliver His people from bondage.

When God called Abraham, He gave him a promise that he would be a blessing to all the nations of the world. When He sent Jesus to this earth, it was not to conquer the world and build the biggest palace on this earth. It was to die on the cross for the sins of the world. Do you see the picture, dear friend?

We are living in a world where people are not happy until they become well known. Ministers are not happy until they have an international TV program. Pastors are not happy until their church becomes a megachurch. Who are we following? Are we following the world, or Christ?

When we stand before Him, we will not get any reward for those things we did. We will only be rewarded for accomplishing the things He created us to do. Paul said, *"But one thing I do, forgetting those things which are behind and reaching forward to those things which are ahead..."* (Phil. 3:13).

Paul was not called to establish orphanages and hospitals. What if he did? Would he get any reward for those things? No, they would be burned with fire and his soul would be saved as though through fire (see 1 Cor. 3:15).

SWIMMING AGAINST THE CURRENT

It is time to swim against the current. Do not follow the world and its examples. Follow the Word of God and the leading of the Holy Spirit. Many people who believe they are led by the Holy Spirit, are not led by the real Holy Spirit. There are so many spirits on this earth. Some of them will sound similar to the Holy Spirit, but they are not the Holy Spirit of God. They are deceiving spirits, dark beings in angelic forms.

Satan appears as an angel of light and has gone into the world to try to deceive the elect of God. I know what I am talking about because I have been there. How many times has someone come to you, saying, "The spirit told me..." but you know that the spirit they are hearing from is not the Holy Spirit?

We are to test all things and hold fast to those things that are good. It also instructs us to test the spirits (see 1 John 4:1). Paul exhorted the believers about the end times, when deceiving spirits and teachers will rise up to deceive many (see 1 Tim. 4:1).

Fulfilling your destiny is to do the will of God for your life, not following a big dream or believing to become a wealthy person. There are so many wealthy people on this earth, but that does not mean they are fulfilling their God-given destinies. It is difficult to find the right people who can help you to fulfill a purpose, because everyone wants to be their own boss.

In India, if someone is in ministry, he is a pastor. Most people do not know there is any other form of ministry that exists. If someone has a spiritual gift, he is an apostle one day or a prophet the next day. There are hundreds of people mentioned in the Bible who were essential in fulfilling the destiny of this earth. Not everyone is a superhero. But everyone is essential and valuable.

There are only a few superheroes in the Bible: men like Moses, David, Gideon, and Samson. There were other people who were essential in fulfilling these people's purposes. Parents are not happy until their children are on the top. No one wants to be second, but that is impossible in the Kingdom of God because if there is no second, there is no first.

> *Two things I request of You (deprive me not before I die): Remove falsehood and lies far from me; give me neither poverty nor riches—feed me with the food allotted to me; lest I be full and deny You, and say, "Who is the Lord?" or lest I be poor and steal, and profane the name of my God* (Proverbs 30:7-9).

Ask the Lord to give you a revelation about your purpose and the works He foreordained for you. Many times, what we feel in our heart is a dream, may not be a dream from God. It is very possible it evolved by hearing, reading about, or seeing the success of other people around us. If we are around people who are "successful," according to the worldly standard, it is normal for us to feel, "If he can do it, I can do it too." But it may not have anything to do with God or your purpose.

Jesus said it is not those who call Him Lord, or those who do *great* things who will enter His Kingdom, but only those who do the will of God. May the Lord help us find what that will is and be found faithful when He comes (see Matt. 7:21-23).

Chapter 15

THE FINAL TEST

THE TEST OF SUCCESS

One thing to keep in mind is that spiritual tests come unexpectedly. Many great men and women fail when they are successful. When we are successful, we often forget the path God brought us through and begin to feel, "Yes, I can do this," or, "My strength made this happen." But Jeremiah warns us:

Let not the wise man glory in his wisdom, let not the mighty man glory in his might, nor let the rich man glory in his riches; but let him who glories glory in this, that he understands and knows Me (Jeremiah 9:23-24).

Many times the tempter comes after we have had a great success or breakthrough in some area of our life. We are more vulnerable to the enemy's temptations when we are successful than at any other time. We will feel like nothing bad will happen to us and that we will never fail. Watch out! The tempter is at the door.

When we are successful, our popularity increases. We should not become people-conscious at that time. We need to keep our eyes on Jesus, who is the author and finisher of our faith. When we become people-conscious, we try to please man rather than pleasing God.

There will be a time in every leader's life when he is at the crossroads of choosing between being popular among people and being pleasing to the Lord. After Jesus fed the 5,000 people, they wanted to make Him their king. Their intention was misguided, however. He was already their king. The Bible says He withdrew from them and went into the wilderness (see John 6:15).

Lord, give us the grace to walk away from the praises of men. They will shout "Hosanna" today and "Crucify" tomorrow. Moses was tested in this area. When the people of Israel rebelled against God, He wanted to destroy all of them and make Moses a great nation. Moses had to restrain God from releasing His anger on the people.

King Saul failed in this test. He could not wait for Samuel to come to offer the sacrifice. He was afraid that he would lose his popularity with the people, so he took things into his own hands and lost his kingship (see 1 Sam. 13:11-14).

THINGS TO WALK AWAY FROM

There are things we need to walk away from temporarily, though it may be our right or opportunity to enjoy them, for a greater achievement later. Below are some of the things we need to walk away from if we want to enjoy everything God has for us. Just because God promised us something does not mean it will manifest in our lifetime. At every major juncture in our life, we will be tested in different areas.

Physical Pleasure

Joseph had the perfect opportunity to commit adultery with his master's wife. A person of character is not the one who does not commit sin because there is no opportunity, but the one who walks away from it based on his inward convictions. It is easy to say, "I will never do that," as long as we are not tested in that area. Were you ever tested in this area and walked away victoriously? That is what matters the most. If Joseph had committed that sin, God would not have promoted him to be the chief minister of Egypt.

Material Blessings

There are blessings that God wants us to enjoy on this earth, but gaining material wealth should not be our ultimate goal in life. Our ultimate goal should be to fulfill God's purpose for our life and be a blessing to as many people as possible. The reason God cannot use many people to the extent He wants is because they are entangled by the material wealth of this world.

Strife and Contention

In life, there will be many opportunities to fight with people, even our own family members. There are also fights that are demonically inspired that we need to walk away from. We should not go to war where there is no spoil; it is a waste of energy and resources. Once you quarrel with someone, the first thing that happens is that you lose the peace in your heart. You will be in an emotionally conflicted state until that relationship is restored and reconciled.

Strife and unforgiveness give room for the devil to come into our life (see 2 Cor. 2:10-11; Eph. 4:26-27).

The Path of the Unrighteous

Psalm 1 begins by telling us not to walk in the path of the unrighteous. There are many innocent people who destroyed their lives because they listened to the counsel of the ungodly and were eventually trapped by the snare of the enemy. The book of Proverbs also starts out the same way.

Merchandising the Anointing

After Jesus fasted for 40 days and 40 nights, He was hungry. The tempter came and whispered in His mind to turn the stones into bread. Jesus had every right to use His power to do that. He was desperately hungry and there was no food available. In the Bible, bread represents our physical needs (and sometimes money).

We should not use God's power with the intention of making money. God is faithful to provide for our needs.

The second temptation came as the devil took Him to the highest mountain and showed Him all the glory of the world and its kingdoms and promised them to Him. Jesus could have received that through the wrong means. He had to walk away from it because that was not His Father's will for Him. We should not use God's power to obtain material wealth or possessions on this earth.

There is also another side to it: in promising people they will receive the anointing if they send us money. There was a person in the book of Acts named Simon who was a sorcerer. When he saw the miracle-working power of God and heard about the Kingdom of God through Philip, he was saved and was baptized in water. Then Peter and John came to pray for the believers to receive the baptism of the Holy Spirit. And whoever they laid their hands on received the Holy Spirit.

When Simon saw this, he offered money to the apostles and asked them to give him the power to do the same thing they were doing. If it was some of today's so-called apostles, they would have told him to come and meet them at the hotel privately and they would lay hands on him and impart the anointing!

> But Peter said to him, "Your money perish with you, because you thought that the gift of God could be purchased with money! You have neither part nor portion in this matter, for your heart is not right in the sight of God. Repent therefore of this your wickedness, and pray God if perhaps the thought of your heart may be forgiven you. For I see that you are poisoned by bitterness and bound by iniquity" (Acts 8:20-23).

How many people have sent money to receive a piece of cloth or any other object because they believed some great preacher had anointed it? Do not be caught by this. The cloth or object they are sending in the mail does not carry any more anointing than the toilet paper you use in your bathroom.

You may ask, "Didn't the handkerchiefs and aprons that were taken from Paul's body heal the sick?" Yes, that is true, but Paul did not send out a mass mailing and ask them to send their best financial offering for a handkerchief so he could rush it to your home before it ran out or lost the anointing! He never did that—if you've done it, repent and turn away from your iniquity as we read in the above scripture.

Anyone who promises you they will send a prayed-over or anointed cloth if you send in your money is doing it to get your money, not to help you, because there isn't any anointing on that cloth. Do not be deceived, dear children.

> *These people must be stopped, because they are upsetting whole families by teaching things they should not teach, which they do to get rich by cheating people* (Titus 1:11 NCV).

Impetuous Actions

Many of the things we regret the most are those things we did without calculating the cost or considering the consequences of our actions. How many of us would say we would not have done what we did if only we had known better? The greater the impact, the greater the importance of the decision we make (and if you are not sure if it is right or wrong, take time to think about it and receive the needed counsel from others). We should not make any permanent decisions if we are not completely sure. One moment of fleshly gratification can sabotage a lifetime of character and promotion.

All the tests I mentioned above are those we need to pass in order to be victorious and successful in our Christian life. There is one final test that we need to go through once we are successful to become everything God intended for us to be. God has no limit and the things He has stored for us have no limit either.

As in the natural, there is a final test before we are promoted to the next grade or level. However, in the spirit, only a few pass this test. It is difficult for us to pass this test because when we are successful, there is a tendency to value more what people think of us than obeying God. There are few who are sold out to do anything and everything God requires them to do, regardless of the cost.

When we are successful, the praise and acclamation of the people blinds us and we become more dependent on our success than on God, who gave us that success. For that very reason, God has set a final test while we are on this earth before we enter into His unconditional blessings.

Everything God gives us is conditional (except His love) until we pass this test. Once we pass this test, every promise and blessing becomes unconditional. We are going to study a few people who went through this test in their life.

The Praise and Glory of Man

When you do something good or become successful, people will attempt to become a part of it. People like to be associated with those who are successful and influential. They do not know the price you paid to reach that place; they only see the fruit of it. It is dangerous to let these people associate with you and allow them into your inner circle. They will be the first ones to turn against you when their needs and expectations are not met. They are like bugs that fly around a lamp only as long as it is lit.

PEOPLE WHO HAVE PASSED THE TEST

Abraham

Abraham was called by God to become the father of many nations, and the father of our faith. He had to pass many tests before God fulfilled that promise. First of all, he had to leave his father's house, country, and relatives. Secondly, he and Sarah could not have children.

God gave them a son in their old age, and when Isaac became a teenager, the word of the Lord came again to Abraham to offer him as a sacrifice. We need to understand that Abraham waited for this son for 100 years. God promised to make him a father of multitudes; and he finally got one son and then God asks him to give him up. That does not sound like God—it must be the devil!

It was indeed God who required Isaac to be sacrificed, not because God needed a human sacrifice, but it was a test from the Lord.

> *Now it came to pass after these things that God tested Abraham, and said to him, "Abraham!"*
>
> *And he said, "Here I am."*
>
> *Then He said, "Take now your son, your only son Isaac, whom you love, and go to the land of Moriah, and offer him there as a burnt offering on one of the mountains of which I shall tell you"* (Genesis 22:1-2).

We read in the Bible that it was a test, but that was not told to Abraham when it was happening. It was real to him. However, he was willing to obey no matter the cost. His love for God was not based on the things he possessed. He loved God more than anything on this earth, including his one and only son.

Abraham passed the test. He took his son to the mountain, laid him on the altar, and was ready to cut his throat. His faith in God was so strong that he believed God could raise his son from the ashes of the sacrifice.

Abraham's obedience was a turning point in the history of the human race, and it was accounted for righteousness to anyone who will believe in Jesus Christ. That includes both you and me. That means that when Abraham believed God and offered his son, we were declared righteous from our sins.

Paul gives us wonderful insight:

He did not waver at the promise of God through unbelief, but was strengthened in faith, giving glory to God, and being fully convinced that what He had promised He was also able to perform. And therefore "it was accounted to him for righteousness."

Now it was not written for his sake alone that it was imputed to him, but also for us. It shall be imputed to us who believe in Him who raised up Jesus our Lord from the dead, who was delivered up because of our offenses, and was raised because of our justification (Romans 4:20-25).

Moses

Moses was another mighty man God used to do extraordinary things. He spoke to God face to face and saw His glory like no other man who ever lived. He saw more miracles than anyone and he was also more humble than all others. There is no doubt that Moses was a chosen vessel of God.

He had to go through many tests in his life. He spent 40 days and nights with God, then came the time for the final test in his life. God told him to command the rock to bring forth water. But Moses gave in to his emotions and reacted rather than obeying the voice of God. He failed the final test and lost the opportunity to enter the Promise Land.

Because he did not glorify God in his body, the devil had a claim on his body when he died. Michael the Archangel had to contend with the devil for the body of Moses (see Jude 9). When we disobey God in our body, giving in to our emotions, there are great repercussions to such actions now and in the life to come.

Paul says we all have to stand before the judgment seat of Christ to receive a reward for everything we did while in our body (see 2 Cor. 5:10).

Jesus

Jesus was tempted in every way we are, yet without sin. Though He was the Son of God, He was not exempt from being tested. The good news is that He passed all the tests. In the Gospels, we see that the devil tempted Him in the wilderness and lost, and then left Him for a more opportune time.

The final test Jesus had to pass was the Garden of Gethsemane—where His will and His Father's will collided head-on. He could have walked away from the cross. He did not deserve it. He had not done anything wrong. It was for us that He went to the cross. It is one thing to be punished for the wrong you did, it is another thing to be punished for someone else's wrong. We may go through challenges for our own benefit, but are we willing to go through trials for someone else's benefit?

Jesus surrendered to His Father's will and endured the cross. He passed the final test. God exalted Him to the highest position that is available in His Kingdom. He put all things under His feet, and every knee shall bow to Him and every tongue shall confess that He is Lord (see Phil. 2:9-11). That is the result of passing our final test. The greatest level of glory we will ever experience will come into our life. But it requires enduring the greatest pain we will ever endure.

David

David was a man anointed three times, to whom God promised the sure mercies, meaning God's faithfulness would never leave him. He promised that his throne would be an everlasting throne. David was a man after God's heart. But still he had to endure a final test before he could have his throne established forever. That was to walk away from everything he ever obtained and be willing to hand it over to someone else. That was the final test David went through in his life.

David had a weakness: women. He brought forth too many sons. Some of them were God-ordained and others were just the result of his fleshly lusts. As king, your son will be the successor of your throne. When you have too many good-looking and ambitious sons, the question is, "Who is going to inherit the throne?"

The princes began to take chance into their own hands because they were not sure which one their father was going to appoint as the next king. They thought that the strongest would be the best and the right person. David kept silent about these things, though he heard of a few of his sons being declared king over the nation even without his knowledge. All that you needed to become king was a group of people (a so-called army and a captain), and a priest to pour some oil on your head. What they did not know was that the anointing of God would not work in your life just because a priest poured oil on your head. Only if the Lord told the priest to pour the oil on your head did it bring the actual anointing.

There were a few oil-dripping, self-proclaimed kings in David's household. They did not like each other, so each of them stayed on a different mountain and proclaimed himself the *real* king of Judah.

The worst challenge David went through in his life came from his son Absalom, who almost killed him and forced him to run for his life. One day David was the mightiest king on this earth, the next day he was fleeing for his life like an ordinary man.

But David did not take revenge on his son Absalom, for he knew that vengeance belongs to the Lord. It was God who had given David the throne in the first place. He protects the throne because, ultimately, it is *His* throne. If God has given you a position, it is His gift to you. He has placed you in that position. If someone comes and pushes you off, let him have it, because no one else can fit in the position God gave you. They can only fake it for a little while, but it will not end well for them.

David left his palace, his concubines, and all that he had. He was willing to lose everything. That was the final test he had to endure. And he passed the test. He gave up everything, every hope of ever sitting on his throne again.

Can you imagine being the CEO of the largest corporation in the world and having someone else cheat you and take your position, leaving you without a dime? How would you react? Could you still love that person?

David did. That is why he passed the test. He did not command that his son Absalom be killed. Instead, he told his soldiers and captains to deal peacefully with him. That is much like Jesus on the cross forgiving those who crucified Him. David did the same: he offered forgiveness to those who persecuted him. There will be times when we have to be willing to walk away from everything we obtained all throughout our life. It is easier said than done. Most will never think about giving up what they have because they invested a lifetime of effort in obtaining it.

There is only one way to gain anything in the Kingdom of God: you must be willing to lose something. Whatever we lose for the sake of the Kingdom, we will gain back, whether it be our life, possessions, etc. Jesus said that if we lose our life for His sake, we will gain it, but if we try to secure it, we will lose it (see Matt. 16:25). And that is the final test we have to overcome.

ABOUT ABRAHAM JOHN

I pray this book is a blessing to you in your walk with the Lord. I encourage you to go through it more than once to receive everything God has for you. I give all the glory, honor, and praise to God Almighty for using me to write this. It ministers to me each time I go through it. God bless you.

If you were blessed by reading this book, we would like to hear from you. If you would like to know more about Pastor Abraham John and his ministry, to order other books by him, or if you would like to invite him to minister at your church or group to receive a prophetic word for the season, please go to www.maximpact.org or call us at (720)-560-4664.

Or write to us at:

Maximum Impact Ministries
P.O. Box 3128
Syracuse, NY 13220 USA

In India:

Maximum Impact Ministries
P.O. Box 6
Kottarakara, Kerala, 691506
India

IN THE RIGHT HANDS, THIS BOOK WILL CHANGE LIVES!

Most of the people who need this message will not be looking for this book. To change their lives, you need to put a copy of this book in their hands.

> *But others (seeds) fell into good ground, and brought forth fruit, some a hundred-fold, some sixty-fold, some thirty-fold* (Matthew 13:8).

Our ministry is constantly seeking methods to find the good ground, the people who need this anointed message to change their lives. Will you help us reach these people?

> *Remember this—a farmer who plants only a few seeds will get a small crop. But the one who plants generously will get a generous crop* (2 Corinthians 9:6).

EXTEND THIS MINISTRY BY SOWING
3 BOOKS, 5 BOOKS, 10 BOOKS, **OR MORE TODAY,**
AND BECOME A LIFE CHANGER!

Thank you,

Don Nori Sr., Founder
Destiny Image
Since 1982